THE RELEVANCE OF THE PROPERTY TEACHING OF POPE PAUL VI

An Ancient Teaching in a New Context

Mark G. Etling

Mellen Research University Press
San Francisco

Library of Congress Cataloging-in-Publication Data

Etling, Mark G.
The relevance of the property teaching of Pope Paul VI : an ancient teaching in a new context / Mark G. Etling.
p. cm.
Includes bibliographical references and index.
ISBN 0-7734-2218-8
1. Property--Religious aspects--Catholic Church. 2. Capitalism--Religious aspects--Catholic Church. I. Title.
HB701.E86 1993
261.8' 5--dc20
93-840
CIP

Editorial Inquiries:

Mellen Research University Press
534 Pacific Avenue
San Francisco
CA 94133

Order Fulfillment:

The Edwin Mellen Press
P.O. Box 450
Lewiston, NY 14092
USA

Printed in the United States of America

DEDICATION

This book is dedicated to my wife Terry. She played an invaluable role in the completion of my dissertation, in two ways. First, her loving support and gentle encouragement helped me through the times when my spirits sagged, when I wondered if I could go on. Second, Terry inspired me by the example of her own life. Over the last ten years she has overcome several formidable obstacles in order to accomplish her academic and professional goals. Terry showed me in her own quiet, determined way that "the strength to run the race to the finish comes from within." I can never thank her enough.

Table of Contents

COMMENDATORY FOREWORD

The wisdom of Paul VI in the Second Vatican Council on freedom (especially religious freedom), on human dignity and equality (expressed in terms of communion), and on historical realism (encouraging the church to face the modern world) continues to have prophetic relevance today, nearly three decades later. He was concerned passionately with human flourishing when confronted with the social concerns in the global community of his time – concerns that have become only more dramatic and exasperated in the ensuing years. As he struggled with the dominant ideologies of communism and capitalism, especially with their political and economic fall-out among under-developed nations, he perceived the classical arguments of the Catholic Natural Law tradition on justice as insufficient for dealing with the gargantuan injustices at hand.

Inspired by the spirit of Vatican II, Paul VI integrated that tradition with the biblical insight of *imago Dei* and an anthropology rooted in historical experience to develop a social teaching that provocatively addressed the international problems contemporary with his papacy. In particular, he articulated a view of property that gave much sharper edge to the traditional Catholic principle of giving priority to its social function over the right to ownership. He understood property as inseparable from the solidarity of the human community, and therefore as dynamically related to world development and especially to international peace.

In this present study the author explores all of these issues from a perspective that is historically attentive and systematically astute. He understands the importance of the rapidly evolving social, economic, and political world that created such international turmoil and worried this pope so anxiously in the 1960s and 1970s. And he coherently traces the nuanced changes in the thought of Paul VI on property throughout his major documents, *Populorum Progressio* (1967), *Octogesima Adveniens* (1971), *De Iustitia in Mundo* (1971), and *Evangelii Nuntiandi* (1975). His analysis of the novelty and the impact of this new teaching on property is an original contribution that provokes challenging questions for students in the fields of social and business ethics. Being the first book length study on this topic, the author appropriately emphasizes the significance of Paul VI at a time when the Catholic Church was attempting, tentatively and courageously, to engage theological discourse in the public arena of the international community.

Dr. Gerard Magill
Saint Louis University
September 1992

COMMENDATORY FOREWORD

The question about stewardship and ownership of property in the Judaeo-Christian tradition is as old as Genesis and as recent as the last national election. God gave the earth, its plants and animals, to all humankind in the persons of Adam and Eve, to cultivate and care for on behalf of the whole world. The goods of the earth were to be a common human inheritance. Yet, implicit in the commandment against stealing and in all the elaborate property laws of the Mosaic covenant is the assumption of personal ownership of some parts of this common inheritance. Furthermore, the idealistic picture of the early years of the Jerusalem community of first Christians as presented in the Acts of the Apostles includes the voluntary sharing of property. "No one claimed private ownership of any possessions, but everything they owned was held in common." (Acts 4:32)

Throughout Christian history there has been a basic tension between this assumed right to private property and some sort of deeper realization that ultimately the goods of the earth belong to God who has endowed all humanity with these goods for the common good of all. Every reform movement, every religious community, every Christian millenarian commune operated out of that assumption and tried to implement that ideal in the structures of everyday life. Classical and medieval culture, in spite of all its cruelties and inequities, demanded that those who had property and wealth didn't somehow absolutely own it all, but rather they administered it for the common good of the community. They, all property owners but more especially the church and its institutions, its bishop and monasteries, had a responsibility to see to the temporal well being of those unpropertied masses entrusted to their care.

What has happened since early modern times, however, has been a breakdown of this system of social relationships. In eighteenth century enlightenment thought personal responsibility and individual rights took on absolute values. The philosophers of the modern age celebrated the liberation of humanity from the antiquated strictures of custom, society and church. The Wealth of Nations, now, according to Adam Smith, depended on the absolutely unrestrained liberties of the individual, and eventually of the business corporation, to pursue private enrichment, untrammeled by any artificial restraint, under the assumption that the invisible hand of economic law would automatically distribute consequent treasure to the good of all. With the French Revolution, not only in France but also gradually elsewhere in Europe, the church was divested of its properties and so lost its economic base for its care of the poor, the sick, and the untutored. Capitalistic industrialization gobbled up the common economic resources of European society with little attention to the needs of unpropertied classes. Industrialization destroyed the guild and corporation systems which ensured much of the equitable distribution of wealth in an earlier age.

It is one of the ironies of history that it was socialist movements, eventually Marxist ones especially, which took up the cause of exploited masses in the pursuit of a common ideal of universal brotherhood and shared wealth, an ideal which owed much to the historic Judaeo-Christian vision of a just society. Unfortunately, these modern social movements were often linked with a militant atheism and a virulent anti-clericalism. Champions of a just society and a fair participation of all humanity in the goods of the earth, could only see the churches as defenders of an antiquated and unjust social order. Conversely, the churches could only see in these often anti-religious social movements an incarnation of all the evils the churches had experienced in the wake of the French Revolution and in the liberal governments of the nineteenth century, evil which included a confiscation of church property, even the dissolution of the papal states.

What has happened in the century from the days of Pope Leo XIII at the end of the nineteenth century through the heady days of Vatican Council II at mid-twentieth century and its aftermath in the teaching of Pope Paul VI has been a gradual sifting out of these issues. Liberal capitalistic democracies gradually came to recognize the values of the traditional Judaeo-Christian concept of the common good, began to recognize the fact that ultimately everyone has a right to a decent life, that people not property are absolutes. Initially the church responded to attacks on late medieval culture by the liberal regimes of the nineteenth century and even to the contrary socialist calls for a radical redistribution of property by a stubborn defense of the right to private property and by a call to paternalistic charity. Only gradually did the church come to realize the anti-Christian dynamics of laissez-faire economic practice and the fundamentally Christian, though unrecognized, aspirations of socialist claims.

It is this gradual reconciliation with and ever more sophisticated critique of the social construction of the modern world which the official teachings of the Catholic church underwent during this past hundred years of so which Dr. Mark Etling outlines in precise detail in the following study. This recovery of ancient values and their application to a modern capital intensive social world by the Catholic church is a process which went on almost unnoticed by outsiders and perhaps even by participants themselves. Consequently, we are much in Dr. Etling's debt for his having disclosed this evolution for us, citing chapter and verse. Part of the reality of the present largely post-modern world is a realization that many of the sacred cows of modern times, like the claims to absolute private property, must now be questioned, for the sake of the happiness of the whole human family and in the name of the deepest claims of the Judaeo-Christian faiths.

Dr. Francis W. Nichols
Saint Louis University
November 1992

AUTHOR'S PREFACE

Research on the official teachings of the popes is a notoriously messy enterprise. Papal documents tend to "say everything" about a subject, making it difficult to extract from them a clear-cut message. The ambiguity of their technical terminology further complicates the issue. The denotation of a term in a nineteenth century encyclical may bear little resemblance to the meaning of the same term in a document of the mid-twentieth century. And at times the meaning of a term evolves from one document to the next within the official teaching of one pope.

In studying the papal social teaching one must also pay special attention to the historical, economic, social, and political contexts in which the documents were written. Context is, of course, an important element in the analysis of any piece of literature. But the researcher of papal documents must be especially mindful of context, because the documents often appear to be timeless statements of universal and unchanging truth. One must be careful not to be fooled by this appearance of disinterested timelessness.

As with all dissertations, this project came to fruition only after a lengthy and bumpy process of formation. The patient and insightful assistance of advisers proved invaluable. The high and low points encountered in the writing of this paper are too numerous to mention in this brief preface, and the reader would no doubt find them tedious. I will point out only the major turning points in the process.

The first task, of course, was to select a topic. In the beginning I knew little more than that I had a personal interest in the social dimension of Christianity, the modern papal social teaching, and Pope Paul VI. I was impressed with Paul VI's leadership of the Second Vatican Council, and with his sincere effort to engage the Church in dialogue with the influential political, economic, and scientific ideas of his time. I had even once had the opportunity to see him in person, at a general audience in 1973, and I recall being struck by his intellectual depth and personal warmth.

As I began to do some general reading I was drawn to the phenomenon of the worldwide economic development effort of the 1960s, and to Paul VI's support of this effort. This confirmed my interest in examining his official teaching on some subject related to the so-called "social question."

At this point I met with my dissertation adviser, Dr. James Pollock, a Jesuit on the faculty of the Department of Theological Studies at Saint Louis University. We discussed the broad direction of my research, and he quickly sensed the need for me to sharpen the focus of my topic, to choose a specific subject within the social teaching of Paul VI.

I consulted several biographies of Giovanni Battista Montini/Pope Paul VI, articles about the Roman Catholic Church in the 1960s and 70s, and the documents which comprise the body of Paul VI's social teaching. I also studied the major documents which make up the century-long modern papal social teaching, beginning with Pope Leo XIII's *Rerum Novarum*.

Of the many subjects in the modern social teaching, the teaching on property emerged as the one which captured my attention. In my initial cursory reading I discovered a fascinating evolution in the papal social teaching on property - in the historical, social, economic, and political context out of which the documents arose; the various applications of traditional Roman Catholic principles on property in light of these changes in context; the theological anthropology which framed the documents; the expansion of the geographical scope of application of the teaching; and even the way the popes defined property itself. In particular, I noticed that the property teaching was greatly enriched by Paul VI. After consultation with Dr. Pollock and the appropriate computer searches, I arrived at my topic - an analysis of the property teaching of Pope Paul VI.

Some refinement of my newly-chosen topic was the next order of business. Given the wide variety of forms of papal communication (everything from encyclicals to addresses delivered at a general audience), I would have to determine which of Paul VI's official pronouncements embodied his position on property with the greatest weight of authority. Even documents which did not bear the signature of the pope, but which clearly were influenced or authorized by him, might qualify for inclusion. Finally, and with Dr. Pollock's agreement, I decided to focus on four documents: the encyclical *Populorum*

Progressio (1967); the pastoral letter *Octogesima Adveniens* (1971); the synodal statement *Iustitia in Mundo* (1971); and the post-synodal statement *Evangelii Nuntiandi* (1975).

These four documents, more than any others, revealed the property teaching of Paul VI in its fullness. They reaffirmed traditional Roman Catholic principles on property (the relationship of private ownership and the social function of property; the definition of property; the geographic range of application of the property teaching), and greatly expanded the implications of these principles in light of prevailing historical circumstances. At the same time they best illustrated the considerable evolution of Paul VI's thinking on the property question between the years 1967-75.

At this point Dr. Pollock alerted me to the significance of the methodological framework of the property teaching - the relationship between the Church's social teaching and its anthropology, its teaching on the human person. Further research confirmed his suggestion. Beginning with Pope John XXIII, Vatican II, and Paul VI, the Church underwent a dramatic shift from a strictly philosophical, natural law anthropology to a more biblically-based theological approach. The starting point of this renewed anthropology was the biblical affirmation that the human person is created in the *imago Dei* (Gen 1:26), and therefore possesses inestimable dignity and fundamental human rights. It highlighted the social dimension of human nature (a reflection of the Trinity of divine persons), and the restoration of the temporal order as God intended it to be at the moment of creation. The influence of this anthropology was evident in Paul VI's emphasis on, and expanded application of, the traditional principle of the social function of property, and his extension of the definition of property.

The next important methodological hurdle was to determine the external structure of the paper. Given that the dissertation would be about the official teaching of Pope Paul VI on the subject of property, what should be stressed in order to adequately cover the topic? Again I had to be aware of the danger of trying to say too much.

This stage of the project required approximately six months' work, and frequent consultation with Dr. Pollock. Finally we agreed that the dissertation would have six chapters. The first (which in this book is titled "Introduction") would briefly introduce the topic. Chapters 2, 3, and 4 (chapters 1, 2, and 3 in this text) would provide needed background information: a survey of the modern papal social teaching from Pope Leo XIII's *Rerum Novarum* in 1891 to the Second Vatican Council's *Gaudium et Spes* in 1965; a biographical sketch of Giovanni Battista Montini prior to his election to the papacy in 1963; and an exposition on three of the Catholic intellectuals who most influenced Paul VI's social teaching. The fifth chapter (this book's fourth) would be the paper's focal point - a comprehensive analysis of the teaching of Paul VI on property. The final chapter would be the conclusion.

The choice of background topics was not simple, and I had to develop a rationale for their inclusion in the paper. The survey of the modern papal social teaching would help to place Paul VI's property teaching in a much-needed historical context. The biographical details of Montini's life would call attention to the life choices, persons and events which illustrated his predisposition to the social dimension of the Gospel, and which helped shape both his general social teaching and property teaching. The introduction to the lives and thought of Jacques Maritain, Louis-Joseph Lebret, O.P., and Pierre Bigo, S.J. would focus on the role they played in the intellectual life of the Catholic Church in the 1950s and 60s, and the confluence of their thought on the social question with that of Paul VI.

One final series of decisions on method were made in the weeks after the unfortunate and sudden death of Dr. Pollock in October 1990. My new adviser, Dr. Gerard Magill, concurred with the methodological decisions made by Dr. Pollock and me regarding the dissertation's topic and external structure. However, he had some misgivings about the internal structure of the chapters. He felt that, without a tight and consistent internal structure within each chapter, the dissertation would lose a certain amount of focus and coherence. He suggested I develop an internal structure that would be basically the same in each chapter, in order to enhance the dissertation's structural integrity.

This task proved to be a tricky one. I found it difficult to develop a structure capable of embracing chapters dealing with a century of papal social teaching, a biographical sketch of Montini, a survey of thinkers who influenced Paul VI, and Paul VI's teaching on property. Several models were proposed, discussed, and refined until a satisfactory internal structure emerged. It consisted of four major headings, with subheadings appropriate to each particular chapter. The first major heading, "Historical setting," would provide a context for the person or document under discussion. The second, "Anthropology," was crucial for a proper understanding of the methodological framework for both the more general social teaching, and the property teaching itself. The third, "Topics related to property," raised issues which surrounded but did not directly address the property question. These issues were necessary for a complete understanding of the property teaching. The final heading, "The property teaching," was, of course, the major focus of the dissertation.

This structure proved to be an extremely useful tool in organizing the dissertation. It was rigid enough to provide a framework for the entire text, yet flexible enough to adapt to the diverse subjects addressed in the various chapters. This phase of the project was painstaking and often frustrating, but ultimately it greatly improved the quality and coherence of the dissertation.

I wish to briefly address one other question in this preface. Given the demise of Marxist Communism in the former Soviet Union and the Eastern European bloc since the late 1980s, some may ask whether Pope Paul VI's teaching on property - particularly its moderate socialism on the issue of the distribution of material goods - remains relevant today. In our time has the Catholic Church's traditional property teaching been discredited, perhaps fatally?

This question, although it falls outside the scope of the dissertation, is well worth considering. My own response is an emphatic "no," for two reasons. To be sure, one might detect an echo of Marxist collectivism in Paul VI's affirmation of the primacy of the just distribution of material goods over the right of private ownership. Nevertheless, there are two crucial differences between Paul VI and Marx on this issue. First, Paul VI's teaching is based on a theological anthropology which exalts the dignity and rights of each human person, while Marxism subjugates the individual to the interests of the state. Second, Paul

VI's property teaching places private ownership and the social use of property in a dynamic tension which subsumes, but does not deny, the right of ownership. Each individual, according to the teaching of the pope, is entitled to own and control as much as is required for the satisfaction of personal and family needs, the fulfillment of personality, and the preservation of peace in society. One may not rightly claim to own anything for purposes other than these. The right of ownership, though derived from and secondary to the more fundamental right of all persons to use the good things created by God, is still affirmed by Paul VI. Perhaps there is wisdom here for economic theorists of all stripes to ponder.

ACKNOWLEDGEMENTS

I am indebted to many friends and colleagues for their generous assistance and support. I want to acknowledge here my special indebtedness to several persons by name. My parents, Howard and Mary Etling, have loved and supported me in whatever I have attempted to do in my life. My wife Terry, and my stepchildren, Jason, Jamie, and Jeff, stuck by me through the many evenings when I sat in front of the computer screen instead of spending time with them. Thanks for understanding.

I am forever grateful to Jim Cochran, the finest teacher I ever had, who sparked the love of learning in my soul. Drs. Belden Lane and Frank Nichols of the Saint Louis University faculty encouraged me when I doubted whether I had the ability to do doctoral work. My dissertation committee - the late Jim Pollock, S.J., Dr. Gerard Magill, Rev. Richard Schebera, S.M.M., and Rev. Frederick McLeod, S.J. - offered many helpful suggestions and criticisms of my dissertation. Many thanks to Ms. Jo Ann Ridgeway for her help in preparing the manuscript for publication. And to Kelley for helping me learn how to use a computer - especially for finding Alt-Z.

INTRODUCTION

An important tenet in the Christian tradition is the belief that the world and all that is in it have been created by God. The material world is considered good in itself, because at the time of creation "God looked at everything he had made, and he found it very good" (Genesis 1:31).

The tradition further maintains that the human person is special in the plan of God's creation. Persons possess immense dignity and worth because they are made in the very image and likeness of God (Genesis 1:27). Human dignity makes each person the subject of rights, including the right to an amount of material goods sufficient to sustain life and fulfill oneself as a person. At the same time, humanity is charged with the responsibility for the well-being of all because persons are created in the image of the Trinity, a society of three divine persons whose love is by nature other-centered.

Material goods, therefore, have been given by God to humanity for two fundamental reasons - the satisfaction of basic needs and the fulfillment of personality; and the establishment of a social order built on love and human solidarity, whose crowning achievement is peace.

Yet Christianity also acknowledges that persons abuse their innate dignity and ignore their social duties, and violate the will of God for the world and for humanity by the sins of self-centeredness and greed. Humanity, therefore, stands in need of a radical reorientation of its relationships to the material world, to itself, and to God, a restoration of these relationships as God intended them at the time of creation. Christians believe this was accomplished in the redemptive life, death, and resurrection of Jesus Christ.

Christians of all ages have attempted to carry on the redemptive mission of Christ - the restoration of that just and peace-filled social order intended by God at the beginning of time. The proper use of material goods has long been understood as an essential aspect of the Christian mission.

The earliest Christians, such as the Jerusalem community described in the Acts of the Apostles, lived a communal life in imitation of Jesus and his disciples. Personal possessions and property were sold, and the proceeds distributed among all the believers on the basis of their need.

In general the theologians of the patristic era condemned private ownership, even though they viewed the material world itself as good. They held that material goods have two purposes: *autarkeia*, which connotes a standard of living consonant with human dignity; and *koinonia*, a mutual relationship of giving and receiving among persons. Property, they said, is ordered to use, not for holding or keeping. Their communal attitude was considered more just and human than the Roman law theory of absolute and exclusive individual ownership. Yet by the time the Christian persecutions ended in the fourth century many Church officials had joined the landholding class, and churches were acquiring far-flung estates.

The monastic movement was in part an effort to preserve the original Christian attitudes of simplicity of life and the sharing of goods. An attitude of detachment from material goods was seen as necessary for the spiritual advancement of the monks, and sharing of possessions among themselves and with the poor was practiced in imitation and preparation for the life of heaven. Monastic reform through the centuries almost always included an attempt to return to these attitudes towards material possessions.

The Church did not stand in the way of the feudal landholding system in which control, but not possession, of fiefdoms was granted by lords in exchange for a vassal's pledge of loyalty. In fact the Church reached the apex of its temporal power during the age of feudalism.

Theologians of the Middle Ages kept alive the original intent of Christianity regarding the ownership and use of property, even though the actual practice of the Church at that time often contradicted it. St. Thomas Aquinas (1225-74) reaffirmed the primacy of the social function of property, which he held to be a natural right, over the right of ownership, which he said was secondary to and derived from property's social function.

One of the outcomes of the Renaissance and the Reformation era was a growing disregard for Catholic thinking concerning matters of science, politics, and economics, and the adoption of a more secular point of view within these fields of study. The philosophies of Thomas Hobbes (1588-1679) and John Locke (1632-1704) were based on an individualism which made ownership of material goods an absolute and inviolable right. Mercantilism and capitalism were legitimated by this view of ownership.

By the nineteenth century the abuses of industrialization in Europe spawned several theories - Karl Marx's (1818-1883) the most notable and influential among them - calling for the abolition of private property and its collectivization for the common good. Marx believed that the greatest share of wealth should accrue to those who contribute their labor to the manufacturing process, rather than those who contribute their capital. Marxism challenged the absolute individualism, and the absolute right of ownership, inherent in nineteenth century liberal capitalism.

In the late nineteenth century Pope Leo XIII (1878-1903) began to make known the views of the Holy See on the social and economic problems of the day. His encyclical *Rerum Novarum* (1891) initiated a tradition which has come to be known as the modern papal social teaching. Each of the "social popes" asserted the traditional teaching of the Church as he understood it, and each applied that teaching in light of the socioeconomic situation of his time.

The major social documents of Pope Paul VI (1963-78) were issued in a rapidly evolving social, economic, and political context over a span of eight years (1967-75). His first social encyclical, *Populorum Progressio* (1967), reflects the optimism of many in the 1960s about the possibilities for worldwide economic and social development and international solidarity. Following on the heels of the Second Vatican Council (1962-65), it was written in the spirit of the *aggiornamento*, which was characterized by the Church's openness to the secular world and willingness to engage in dialogue with it. Four years later the apostolic letter *Octogesima Adveniens* (1971) was issued by Paul VI, and also the document *De Iustitia in Mundo*, or *Justice in the World*, a product by the 1971 Synod of Bishops approved for publication by the pope.

Octogesima Adveniens calls for political activity and local solutions to economic and social problems, while *Justice in the World* urges the practice of justice in temporal society and within the Church.

By 1975, when the apostolic exhortation *Evangelii Nuntiandi* appeared, the world's socioeconomic situation had changed considerably. Optimism about the possibility of economic development in the 1960s had given way to the recognition that the worldwide development effort had largely failed, and often had been abused by both the developed and developing nations. The spiritual dimension of development, which *Populorum Progressio* had understood as a necessary element of fully human fulfillment, had been widely ignored. *Evangelii Nuntiandi* was not even written as an encyclical, the most authoritative form of papal communication. Paul VI's encyclical *Humanae Vitae* (1968) had caused so much dissension within the Church that it was to be his last.

The meaning of the title of this book becomes clearer in light of what has been said so far. In his social teaching Paul VI preserves traditional Christian principles regarding private property - but he expands the application of those principles in light of the circumstances of his time. He reaffirms the most basic principle of the tradition on property - the relationship of the social function of property and the right of ownership - but dramatically expands its application in light of contemporary circumstances. His definition of what constitutes property enlarges the traditional definition in accord with his awareness of the global dimensions of the social teaching. The pope considers the implications of the traditional purposes of property - those personal and social ends to which property is ordered. And he explores the role of the state in promoting and protecting the property right.

The aim of this study is to examine in depth the property teaching of Pope Paul VI as it is found in his four major social documents - *Populorum Progressio* (1967), *Octogesima Adveniens* (1971), *Justice in the World* (1971), and *Evangelii Nuntiandi* (1975). A thorough analysis of these is found in chapter four. But a complete understanding of Paul VI's property teaching will require more than just an examination of his four social documents. The century-old papal social teaching tradition will be considered in chapter one, in order to situate Paul VI's property teaching within that tradition. Included in this overview are the social teachings of Popes Leo XIII (1878-1903), Pius XI (1922-39), Pius XII (1939-58), John XXIII (1958-63), and the Second Vatican Council (1962-65). Chapter two will be a biographical sketch of the life of Giovanni Battista Montini from his birth in 1897 until he became Pope Paul VI in 1963. It will trace the roots of Paul VI's social and property teaching in the life experience, education, and the priestly and episcopal careers of Montini. Finally, Paul VI's interaction with three important members of the Catholic intellectual community - Jacques Maritain (1882-1973), Louis-Joseph Lebret, O.P. (1897-1966), and Pierre Bigo, S.J. (1906-) - will be discussed in chapter three. All four men absorbed the Catholic social teaching tradition, and left their own personal imprint upon it.

Each chapter of this study will contain the same basic internal structure. First, the topic under consideration in the chapter will be situated within its historical setting. Second, a discussion on Christian anthropology will spell out the theology of the human person in which the chapter topic is framed. Third, several topics related to the property teaching will be examined: a critique of capitalism, socialism, and Communism; principles and strategies for the realization of the property teaching - the just social order, economic development, the relationship of the temporal and religious dimensions, and prevailing mood; and the geographic range of application of the property teaching. Fourth, the property teaching itself will be analyzed within the context of each chapter, under four headings: the right of ownership and the social function of property; the definition of property; the purposes of property; and the role of the state in promoting and protecting property rights.

One of the secondary sources cited in the bibliography is a recent work by Matthew Habiger, O.S.B. entitled *Papal Teaching on Private Property: 1891-1981* (Lanham, Maryland: University Press of America, 1990). The subject matter in Habiger's book and in this study bear some similarity. However, Habiger's thesis differs in several significant ways from the focus of this essay. Each chapter, therefore, will include a brief "dialogue" between Habiger's book and this study in order to clearly delineate the differences between them.

This study will argue that Pope Paul VI made an important contribution to the Catholic social teaching on property, one which embraced the ancient principles of the Christian tradition, yet applied those principles in creative ways to the dynamic and evolving world situation of his time. His teaching is both consistent with the tradition and a challenge to the world to which it was addressed.

PAPAL TEACHING ON THE PROPERTY QUESTION FROM POPE LEO XIII TO VATICAN COUNCIL II

I. INTRODUCTION TO CHAPTER

As with much of Pope Paul VI's teaching on questions related to what has come to be known as the "social teaching" or "social doctrine" of the Church, the teaching on the question of property had undergone a centuries-long evolution prior to his papacy. The property teaching, long a minor fixture of the Scholastic tradition, was given renewed attention by the popes beginning with Leo XIII (1878-1903), and continued with Pius XI (1922-39), Pius XII (1939-58), John XXIII (1958-63), Paul VI (1963-78) as well as the Second Vatican Council (1962-65). Paul VI's property teaching, therefore, was new, but only in the sense that he drew new implications from traditional Catholic principles.

This chapter will do more than trace the development of the social teaching from Leo XIII to Vatican Council II so as to understand their property teaching. It will reveal as well the historical settings in which the property teachings were situated. The anthropology of the various documents will be discussed, since this forms the methodological framework for both the general social teaching and the property teaching in particular. A variety of related topics - an evaluation of socioeconomic systems, principles and strategies for the realization of the social teaching, and the geographic range of application of the teaching - will be examined to determine their bearing on the property teaching.

Finally, this chapter will focus on a few key themes which constitute the property teaching itself. These are the relationship of the right of ownership and the social function of property, the definition of property, the purposes of property, and the role of the state in securing and promoting the rights connected with property.

The chapter will also take note of the audiences to whom the various social documents were addressed. While Leo XIII and Pius XI directed their thoughts almost exclusively to the Catholics of Western Europe, Pius XII, John XXIII and the bishops at the Council became progressively more aware of the worldwide scope and implications of their teachings, and they adjusted their words to reach out to the international audience.

The contributions of Popes Pius X (1903-14) and Benedict XV (1914-22) to the property teaching will not be considered in this chapter. This does not mean that they had nothing to say about the issue. Pius X, though quite conservative politically, was not against the advancement of the material status of workers. Yet his approach was more cautious than that of his predecessor Leo XIII, and he stressed the importance of charity in solving social problems as a counterbalance to the social Catholics' stress on justice. Benedict XV's pronouncements likewise indicated his interest in social issues, and a desire for the rich and poor to cooperate for the material betterment of society. Still he felt that the claims of the working class were too extreme, and that the existing economic structure should not be altered in achieving labor reform.[1]

While Popes Pius X and Benedict XV did mention the property issue, their teachings were little more than a restatement of Leo XIII's ideas in *Rerum Novarum* (1891). For this reason their teachings do not constitute a significant enough development of the question to be considered in this study.

The papal social teaching represents the Church's attempt to apply its traditional principles in a dynamic way to some of the pressing social and economic issues of the last one hundred years. In addressing these issues the popes prevented the Church from retreating into a compartmentalized, disincarnate spirituality disembodied from concrete social and economic realities.

A comparison of this chapter with Habiger's *Papal Teaching on Private Property* illustrates the most obvious difference between the two. Habiger's entire book is devoted more or less to what is covered in just one chapter of this study. Where the papal property teaching from Leo XIII to John Paul II is the focus of his entire work, this essay deals with the social and property teaching tradition from Leo XIII to *Gaudium et Spes* in just one chapter, as background to the exposition of the property teaching of Pope Paul VI.

Because of this difference in focus Habiger examines some aspects of the modern papal social and property teachings in greater depth than does this essay. He analyzes several issues related to the property teaching in *Rerum Novarum*, such as the relationship of Leo XIII's teaching to that of St. Thomas Aquinas, the principle of private property in relation to the Fall, and property as it relates to natural law, the law of nations, and positive law.[2] His exposition of *Quadragesimo Anno* details the influence of the so-called "Königswinter circle" of theologians, and discusses at length such themes as the social function of property, the common good, and social justice.[3] In his treatment of Pius XII Habiger examines in great detail the role of natural law and revelation in the formation of principles for the just social order,[4] while this essay does not. Further, Habiger identifies the theme of the just social order as the anthropology of Pius XII,[5] while this study views the dignity of the person as the key to his anthropology. Habiger analyzes only John XXIII's *Mater et Magistra* in his fourth chapter, while this essay deals with the property teaching in *Mater et Magistra* and *Pacem in Terris*. Still, his discussion of topics like the four arguments for property in *Mater et Magistra* is more detailed than the scope of this study allows.[6] Finally Habiger's book includes, in the sixth chapter, the property teaching of John Paul II in *Laborem Exercens*, while this study does not, for obvious reasons.

II. *RERUM NOVARUM* (1891)[7]

A. Historical setting

The socioeconomic and political situation in Western Europe at the time Leo XIII assumed the papacy were marked by two significant characteristics. The first was a fluid and rapidly evolving economic, social, and political order, both in theory and practice. The second was an indifference, and even hostility, to the traditional teaching of the Church on economic matters.

Despite a worldwide depression in the late 1870s, the industrial revolution in Europe was in full force. It was marked by individually-owned, "plutocratic" and often monopolistic companies, and the consequent rapid expansion of an industrial proletariat which, due to lack of organization, often worked for low wages in subhuman working conditions. The industrial revolution in Europe had not yet generated a significant middle class, and the gap in ownership of property between the wealthy and the poor helped to foment social instability.

In reaction to the extreme economic individualism of the prevailing liberal capitalist order, new economic theories were being promoted which focused on the social dimension of property. Pierre-Joseph Proudhon (1809-65) and Henry George (1839-97), for example, called for the abolition of private property and for public sector ownership and control of the means of production.[8] Karl Marx (1818-83) went even further, advocating the overthrow of existing socioeconomic and political systems and the establishment of transitional totalitarian proletarian regimes as steppingstones to a worldwide classless socialist society.

The industrial revolution carried on and accentuated a trend which had prevailed in Europe for almost four centuries - the conscious rejection of the Church's traditional teaching on social and economic issues. Over the centuries the Church had slowly and carefully developed an extensive body of teaching on questions having to do with the ownership and use of private property, the moral uses of money, the role of the state in protecting and fostering the property right, and the proper relation between labor and management. These questions had been of concern to Christians since the very beginnings of the Church.[9]

However, since roughly the sixteenth century the Church's teaching authority in economic matters had been challenged and even ignored with the onset of, among other developments, early capitalism, the mercantile system, the birth of nation-states in Europe, and the Protestant Reformation.[10]

This intellectual schism affected several fields of thought and action - economics, political science, physical science, and morality. The social contract theories of Thomas Hobbes (1588-1679) and John Locke (1632-1704) in the seventeenth century, and the economic theory of Adam Smith (1723-90) in the eighteenth, which maintained that economic systems are self-regulating, represented a complete break with the traditional teachings of the Church.[11] Marx's dialectical materialism in the nineteenth century was overtly hostile to religious thought and practice of any kind.

Several different schools of socioeconomic thought among Catholics competed for Leo XIII's approval. The anti-capitalist school of the Austrian Baron Karl von Vogelsang (1818-90) advocated state confiscation of land with little provocation.[12] French corporatist Cardinal Gaspard Mermillod (1824-92) led the so-called "Fribourg circle" which sponsored annual congresses on the social question from 1884 to 1892.[13] And there was the "middle position" of Wilhelm Emmanuel von Ketteler (1811-77), the bishop of Mainz, who believed that liberal capitalism, though flawed, was capable of reform and improvement. Ketteler advocated, among other things, the formation of "intermediate organizations" for workers in order to protect their rights.[14] Finally, a series of worker pilgrimages to Rome in the 1880s led by the French industrialist Leon Harmel (1829-1915) gave Leo XIII first-hand experience of the economic plight of the working class.

In this context Leo XIII issued *Rerum Novarum* on May 15, 1891. It was the first encyclical, or papal letter addressed to the universal Church,[15] to deal with what has been called the "social question."[16] Rather than retreat from the troublesome economic and social issues that faced Western Europe, Leo XIII chose to boldly assert the thinking of the Church on these issues, particularly regarding the rights of workers.

Rerum Novarum reflected the thought of nineteenth century neo-Thomism in the person of Italian Jesuit Aloysius Taparelli D'Azeglio (1793-1862).[17] It marked the beginning of the papal tradition which has come to be known as the social teaching or social doctrine of the Church.

B. Anthropology

No doubt reflecting the mindset of those who tried to influence him - all of whom were members of the aristocratic ruling class - Leo XIII held to an organic view of society, with overtones of patriarchal authoritarianism.[18] The pope reacted against the prevailing philosophies which called for increasing liberty, equality, and participation by persons in society.[19] Natural inequalities in health, beauty, intelligence, strength, and courage were seen as positive, and even essential for the proper functioning of society. Thus "Leo not only did not promote equality as a virtue or something to be striven for in society, but he stressed the importance of inequality."[20]

C. Topics related to property

1. Economic systems and property

In *Rerum Novarum* Leo XIII chose to steer a difficult course between the anti-capitalist school represented by Vogelsang and the corporatists led by Cardinal Mermillod. The pope adopted much of the social thought of Ketteler, whom he referred to as his "great predecessor."[21] Ketteler viewed capitalism as a flawed but acceptable and perfectible system.

But the encyclical also contains some negative criticisms of capitalism which were surprisingly similar to Marxist doctrine, including the contention that capitalism had enabled a small minority of persons to monopolize the wealth and reduce the masses to poverty. Camp points out that the social Catholics themselves were responsible for this well-meaning but misguided analysis.[22]

Although *Rerum Novarum* examined both socialism and liberal capitalism and found them wanting, its sharpest criticisms were levelled against socialist theories, such as those of Proudhon and Henry George, which called for the abolition of private property. Socialism was faulted on several counts: "it work(ed) on the poor man's envy of the rich, endeavor(ed) to destroy private property" (#3), and undermined the integrity of the family. The encyclical's heavy emphasis on the right of ownership was a reaction to socialism's call for the abolition of private property. *Rerum Novarum* also held that socialism gave the state too much power over the lives of individuals - for example, to appropriate property for public use (#3).

2. Principles and strategies of actualization

Leo XIII's biggest concerns in the encyclical were the rights of the working class and the relations of labor and management. Like Ketteler before him, he saw liberal capitalism as the major cause of the workers' oppression: "Hence by degrees it has come to pass that Working Men have been given over, isolated, defenseless, to the callousness of employers and the greed of unrestrained competition" (#2).[23] The hostility of labor and management he viewed as contrary to the natural law, and the relationship between the two classes should rather be marked by "pleasantness and good order" (#15). Still, he believed that wage-earners should be permitted to organize themselves so that the common good might be promoted, and so that they might secure their natural rights. Among these were the right to form unions on a strictly voluntary basis - here he adopted the idea of Cardinal Tomaso Zigliara (1833-93), writer of the second draft of *Rerum Novarum*[24], the right to strike over unjust working conditions, to a just wage, to rest on the Sabbath, and to private property (##31, 32).

Although several influential Catholic thinkers of Leo XIII's time were corporatists, such as Marquis René de La Tour du Pin (1834-1924), Harmel, and Matteo Liberatore, S.J. (1810-92),[25] *Rerum*

Novarum did not promote the corporatist idea of labor-management associations - organizations within a particular industry composed of both workers and owners. The encyclical maintained that such associations should be strictly voluntary (#36), and only minimally directed by the state.

Rather than focus on the phenomenon of industrial development, *Rerum Novarum* discussed the relationship of the industrialists and the working class. It spelled out the duties of each group relative to the other. Workers were expected to live up to contracts entered into freely, and to do no harm to either the person or the property of their employers. The industrialists were obliged to treat their workers with dignity, and honor their right to a decent living and to family life. The encyclical was more concerned with the distribution of the wealth produced by industry than with increasing production itself.[26]

For many years prior to the papacy of Leo XIII the working class felt abandoned and alienated from the Church. Beginning with *Rerum Novarum*, the popes attempted to assure the workers that the Catholic Church had not forgotten them. The encyclical aimed at improving the condition of laborers by the application of measures reflective of Catholic moral principles.[27] It was assumed, somewhat paternalistically, that adherence to overtly Catholic strategies and programs was the best and only way to help the working class.

There was a decided tone of urgency in *Rerum Novarum*, because the problems it addressed concerning the capitalists and the working class, the rich and poor, were causing social unrest and even violence. For this reason "some remedy must be found, and quickly found, for the misery and wretchedness which press so unjustly at this moment on the large majority of the very poor" (#2).

3. Geographic area of application

Although *Rerum Novarum* claimed to be universal and timeless in its application, it is clear that the problems it addressed, and the solutions it proposed, were meant for the industrialized countries of

Western Europe. Leo XIII had involved himself in the situation of the working class in Europe, and this was reflected throughout the encyclical.

D. The property teaching

The property teaching in *Rerum Novarum* was rooted in the thinking of John Locke. His "labor theory" held that property was the reward of one's industry, and his individualism implied that persons had absolute control over the disposition of their possessions. Locke's thinking was incorporated into the neo-Scholastic tradition by the Jesuit Taperelli D'-Azeglio, and then into the encyclical. Thus the encyclical referred to property ownership as a natural right, in a way that implied absolute discretion over the disposition of property: ". . .every man has by nature the right to possess property as his own" (#5). Thomas Aquinas, however, had called ownership of property a derivative right, a determination of the right of all persons by their nature to use the goods of the earth.[28]

Rerum Novarum defined property almost exclusively in terms of land. Leo XIII's rural, agrarian mindset appears to have been outdated, given the increasing urbanization and growth of the wage-earning class in Europe by the late nineteenth century.

The purposes of property in *Rerum Novarum* reflected the traditional Scholastic teaching. Persons may own property in order to provide for their continued existence: ". . . it is in (a person's) power to exercise his choice not only on things which regard his present welfare, but also on those which will be for his advantage in the time to come" (#5). The advantages of ownership were listed: it was a prerequisite for social peace, and essential for persons in order to perfect the higher qualities of the mind, like education and art.[29] Private ownership protected the worker against the greed of employers, and allowed the worker to better his/her family's standard of living.[30]

The state had a limited role to play in protecting the right to private property, according to *Rerum Novarum.* Consistent with Locke's theory, it held that individuals possessed rights prior to their agreeing to organize themselves into states, and these rights must be respected: "Man is older than the State. And he holds the right of providing for the life of his body prior to the formation of any State" (#6).[31] The state may not abolish property, as the socialists and anti-capitalists like Vogelsang held, but should promote ownership, and "its policy should be to induce as many people as possible to become owners" (#35). Curran adds that Leo XIII's organic view of society placed the state in the role of paternalistic, if benevolent and ethical, protector of its citizens.[32]

E. Conclusion of section

Rerum Novarum is significant primarily because it was the first modern papal document to address the social question. It was issued at a time when the credibility of the Church in the eyes of the poor and the working class was at a low ebb. For this reason its principal focus, the rights of workers in their relation to the wealthy capitalist class, was particularly timely.

Yet the encyclical should not be understood as fundamentally egalitarian in spirit. Leo XIII believed in an organic, hierarchical view of society which viewed inequalities of all kinds as acceptable and natural, and which implied that society should conform to Catholic moral principles in the social order.

Although *Rerum Novarum* advocated the cause of the worker and criticized the abuses of the industrialists, it was tolerant of capitalism and highly critical of socialism.

The encyclical's contribution to the property teaching was its strong endorsement of the right of property ownership, which reversed the traditional Thomistic ordering of the priority of the social function of property and the ownership right. This reversal was a reflection of Leo XIII's aversion to the socialist theories and movements of his time. In the same vein *Rerum Novarum* held that the state should enable as many persons as possible in society to become owners of property.

As a whole *Rerum Novarum* fell short of adequately responding to the challenges of the European situation to which it was so narrowly addressed. Yet despite its shortcomings it represented a crucial first attempt by the papacy and the Church to assume a leadership role in dealing with the pressing economic and social problems of the day. In so doing Leo XIII made a worthy attempt to assert a renewed Catholic thinking, so long disregarded, into the debate over these problems. *Rerum Novarum* remains the cornerstone of the century-long tradition of papal social teaching.

III. *QUADRAGESIMO ANNO* (1931)[33]

A. Historical setting

Pope Pius XI (1922-1939) was faced with a situation which differed in several ways from the European world of the late nineteenth century. The union movement, only in its infancy at the time of Leo XIII, had developed and matured in Europe by the 1920s. One-owner corporations were in the process of giving way to the limited-liability corporation, owned by shareholders but administered by a professional management class.

But overriding all other economic and political concerns was the deep depression which gripped Europe by the late 1920s, and eventually most of the world. The attempt by European governments to rebuild their economies after World War I had given way to the most devastating and longest lasting depression in modern times. Postwar reconstruction had hastened the expansion of democracy in the 1920s, but the depression had the effect of weakening confidence in democracy, and it facilitated the emergence of totalitarian regimes - of the right in Italy, Germany, and Spain, and of the left in the Soviet Union.

Austria and Portugal revived in the 1930s the hierarchically ordered political and social system known as Catholic corporatism. In both these countries, however, corporatist ideals served only as a facade for yet another brand of totalitarianism.[34]

The basic assumptions of classic liberal capitalism - absolute economic individualism and resistance to any form of economic regulation by the state - had given way to increasing state intervention in the economy since at least the turn of the century. With the depression these assumptions proved completely unworkable. In their place the theory of John Maynard Keynes (1883 - 1946) came into prominence. Keynes rejected socialism, but he held that the economic mechanism could be altered by the state to achieve goals consistent with social necessity. He advocated strong state intervention to control individualism, to limit the ownership rights of those who abused it by hoarding their wealth, and to extend the possibility of ownership to those, such as the unemployed, to whom it was being denied or curtailed.[35]

Pius XI issued his major social encyclical, *Quadragesimo Anno*, on May 15, 1931. He took the occasion of the fortieth anniversary of *Rerum Novarum* to restate his basic agreement with the social teaching of Leo XIII, and to revise it in light of changing social circumstances.

B. Anthropology

Pius XI believed in an organic model of society, which accepted inequality among persons as a fact of life, and which called for a hierarchical ordering of society. In this he was in agreement with Leo XIII. Still, the anthropology of *Quadragesimo Anno* insisted on the dignity and rights of the individual, and on the social duties of the human person. Curran notes that the encyclical's criticism of both individualism and socialism was based on this anthropology, which stressed both individual rights and the social duties of the person. He points out as well that the experience of totalitarian regimes led to an emphasis in the encyclical on the defense of the rights, dignity, and freedom of the individual, and on the transcendent character of the human person.[36]

C. Topics related to property

1. Economic systems and property

Quadragesimo Anno examined capitalism to see if the system itself were evil. It levelled several criticisms at the kind of capitalism that had evolved by the 1930s. The concentration of wealth and power in the hands of a few had produced a divorce of capital and labor, and had led to the development of a largely destitute propertyless proletarian class: "This accumulation of power, the characteristic note of the modern economic order, is a natural result of limitless free competition which permits the survival of those only who are the strongest, which often means those who fight most relentlessly, who pay least heed to the dictates of conscience" (#107). Capitalism's exaggerated sense of individualism lessened the spirit of competition: "Free competition is dead; economic dictatorship has taken its place" (#109). Access to credit had also become excessively and dangerously concentrated (#106). The outcome was a situation characterized, in the words of Oswald von Nell-Breuning, S.J. (1890-) who drafted and composed *Quadragesimo Anno*, by ". . . limitless competition without moral restraint."[37] This in turn produced, in the words of the encyclical, a "threefold struggle for domination. First, there is the struggle for dictatorship in the economic sphere itself; then, the fierce battle to acquire control of the state, so that its resources and authority may be abused in the economic struggles; finally, the clash between states themselves" (#108).

Despite these criticisms, capitalism was judged to be susceptible to positive change if "the principles of right reason and Christian social philosophy regarding capital, labor, and their mutual cooperation (were) accepted in theory and reduced to practice" (#110). There should be a recognition of both the individual and social character of labor and capital, so as to avoid the dangers of socialism and individualism. Relations between managers and workers should be governed by social justice, which according to Pius XI rested on the conviction that both the human person's social nature and the divine law required the organization of a society in which all human beings were able to provide for themselves. In particular, wages should be paid justly on the basis of work performed.[38] The state must intervene, within the limits of its competence and authority, to regulate unbridled competition and excessive economic power. "If this is done, the economic system, that most important branch of social life, will necessarily be restored to sanity and right order" (#110).

Quadragesimo Anno's qualified acceptance of capitalism did not extend to the socialist ideologies of the day. Coleman has objected to the description of socialism in the encyclical, calling it "essentialist, ahistorical, and arbitrary," and he suggests that *Quadragesimo Anno* may have been addressed to a small group of religious socialists in Germany and Austria who were urging collaboration between Catholics and socialists.[39]

The encyclical distinguished between two types of socialism which, it claimed, had arisen since the time of Leo XIII. The first was Communistic socialism, which was condemned for its "merciless class warfare and complete abolition of private ownership; and this it does, not in secret or by hidden methods, but openly, frankly, and by every means, even the most violent" (#112). The second, more moderate strains were judged less offensive, especially those that softened the hostility between the classes and showed less negativity toward private property (#114). Under these circumstances "it may well come about that gradually the tenets of mitigated socialism will no longer be different from the program of those who seek to reform human society according to Christian principles" (#114).

However, *Quadragesimo Anno* addressed itself not so much to the various historical manifestations of socialism as to socialist ideologies. No matter how "Christian" the various socialist systems might seem to be in practice, the fatal flaw was in the very idea of socialism itself. That flaw was seen as atheistic materialism - a concern for the efficient production and distribution of material goods to the exclusion of humanity's higher, spiritual goods. This concern for the purely material failed to acknowledge God as the true source of social authority (#119). For this reason the encyclical concluded that "no one can be at the same time a sincere Catholic and a true socialist" (#120).

2. Principles and strategies of actualization

Although he had been somewhat progressive on social issues in the first decade of his pontificate, in *Quadragesimo Anno* Pius XI, concurring with Nell-Breuning as well as Heinrich Pesch, S.J. (1854-1926) and Gustav Gundlach, S.J. (1892-1963),[40] advocated a return to a system much like the conservative, Church-dominated guild system of medieval times. Although he gave qualified support to capitalism, the pope held that a true reform of society could only be achieved by a "massive rebuilding of the social order by the state,"[41] in order to create harmony between the capitalists and the working class, modify the wage system, and ensure social stability, economic security, and peace.

The corporatism envisioned in *Quadragesimo Anno* was the product of Nell-Breuning, who gave credit to the work of Martin Grabmann (1875-1949).[42] It called for the establishment of *ordines* (vocational groups), which were to be based on the diverse functions which persons exercised in society (#82). Order in society would be maintained because a place would be found for each group. When a group's value to society were lost, society as a whole would work to revive it.[43] Corporatism would produce "a unity from an apt arrangement of a multiplicity of parts."[44] This organic model of society was in line with traditional corporatist thinking, and it restated Leo XIII's belief in the hierarchical ordering of society.

Pius XI accepted the fact of industrial development in Western Europe, and his acceptance is reflected in *Quadragesimo Anno*. The encyclical concentrated instead on the character of the employer-employee relationship in the industrialized world. Its advocacy of the establishment of joint employer-worker councils was meant to regulate industrial life.[45]

Cronin notes that *Quadragesimo Anno* promoted the idea of social justice, which he said "involves the embedding of moral ideals in the laws, customs, institutions, and structures of society and this to promote the common good."[46] On the whole Pius XI believed that society should be directed by Catholic moral principles, as had Leo XIII.

Written in the midst of a major worldwide depression, and facing the specter of totalitarianism in Europe, *Quadragesimo Anno* was naturally critical in tone. Its stated intention was to "expose the root of the present social disorder" (#15), and to propose Christian remedies to the crises of the day.

3. Geographic area of application

Some of the major issues addressed in *Quadragesimo Anno*, such as the depression and the union movement, were clearly international in scope. Still, the encyclical dealt with these issues from a strictly Western European perspective.

D. The property teaching

Quadragesimo Anno's treatment of the property issue was given in the context of the encyclical's critique of socioeconomic systems. Pius XI corrected an imbalance in *Rerum Novarum* on the property question, while denying that such an imbalance even existed, by restating the principle of the primacy of the social function of property. Still, *Quadragesimo Anno* defended the right of ownership more than it sought to regulate the use of property (#45).

Nell-Breuning noted in *The Reorganization of Social Economy*, his commentary on *Quadragesimo Anno*, that the German law definition of property as "the unrestricted authority to dispose of an object" should not be modified to say that property includes the right to dispose of an object in any way that is morally permissible.[47] This was because, even though an owner was restricted to morally permissible uses of property, no person should be restricted in his/her pursuit of property: "... it is a grievous error so to weaken the individual character of ownership as actually to destroy it" (#48). Nell-Breuning also maintained that the rules governing the use of "permanent possessions" should be less restrictive than those governing income.[48]

The encyclical went to great lengths to affirm its continuity with *Rerum Novarum* and Thomas Aquinas on the relationship of the ownership and social function of property: "Let it be made clear beyond all doubt that neither Leo XIII, nor those theologians who have taught under the guidance and direction of the Church, have ever denied or called into question the two-fold aspect of ownership, which is individual or social accordingly as it regards individuals or concerns the common good" (#45). In fact, however, Leo XIII, in his desire to disavow the Church of socialism, had declared ownership an ontological right, one which inhered in the person by nature, and had rendered the principle of the social function of property almost invisible (#5).

Nell-Breuning pointed out that "(Pius XI) cautioned against one-sided views," in particular on the property question.[49] Nevertheless, and although the traditional Thomistic relationship between ownership and right use was stated in *Quadragesimo Anno*, the right of ownership seems to have been given the higher priority.

After the publication of *Rerum Novarum* in 1891 theologians had debated the meaning of the "living wage." Some defined it only in terms of the worker, while others believed it should include the needs of the worker's family as well. Cronin points out that this debate came to an end with *Quadragesimo Anno's* assertion that the living wage should be defined in terms of both the worker and his family.[50] In this Pius XI expanded the definition of property beyond *Rerum Novarum*.

Some guidelines for the right use of property were spelled out in *Quadragesimo Anno*, based on the proper purposes of property. Income should first be spent on what is necessary, then on what is useful, and lastly on what is pleasant.[51] The duties concerning the disposal of superfluous income were said to be governed by the Thomistic rules of charity: beneficence, or voluntary, outward acts of charity; and liberality, the use of things, such as money, for good rather than for ill. Beneficence and liberality depended on the good will and intentionality of the giver in his/her relations with individuals, rather than the obligatory duties of justice (#50).[52]

Because there was believed to be a close relationship between property and public order, the state had a necessary, although limited, role to play in governing the use of property. *Quadragesimo Anno* listed the power to levy just taxes (#49) as a legitimate form of state intervention for the promotion of the common good. Yet the state could not hinder in any way an individual's right to own, because - here a direct reference was made to *Rerum Novarum* - possession was seen as "derived from nature (and therefore, ultimately from God); and the state has by no means the right to abolish it, but only to control its use and bring it into harmony with the interests of the public good" (#35).

E. Conclusion of section

The social teaching of Pope Pius XI continued in many ways the principles laid down by Leo XIII. This despite the fact that *Quadragesimo Anno* was issued in the midst of a worldwide economic depression and in the face of an imminent threat of totalitarianism in Europe, a far different historical context than *Rerum Novarum*. *Quadragesimo Anno* reflected both Pius XI's interest in the problems of the modern world as he saw them, and his conservative, even authoritarian suspicion of anything perceived as a radical social movement.[53] Given the kinds of sociopolitical movements which were rising up at the time, with their hostility toward the Church and their attempts to abolish private property, this was hardly surprising.

Pius XI adhered to an organic, hierarchical model of society, as had Leo XIII. This model found concrete expression in *Quadragesimo Anno* in the system known as corporatism, which advocated the formation of labor-management vocational groups. Pius XI also believed the capitalist system to be susceptible of reform, and found socialism to be fundamentally unacceptable. Both popes viewed the socioeconomic order from a strictly European perspective.

Although *Quadragesimo Anno* claimed continuity with *Rerum Novarum* and the traditional Scholastic teaching on the priority of the social function of property, it actually placed greater emphasis on the ownership right. It clarified the definition of the living wage as a form of property, by stating that the living wage should be sufficient to satisfy the needs of the worker and his/her family. The state was assigned the role of protecting public order, in part by not hindering the right of ownership. Disequilibrium in the distribution of material goods was an issue to be addressed strictly on the personal level, and not by the state.

IV. POPE PIUS XII (1939-1958)

A. Historical setting

The pontificate of Pius XII encompassed both the devastation of World War II and the impressive reconstruction and prosperity of the postwar years. In the political sphere this period was marked by the phenomenal growth of the Christian democratic movement in western Europe and the rapid expansion of Marxist regimes in eastern Europe and of Maoist Communism in China. On the economic plane the modified welfare state became the norm in most of western Europe, with governments using tax revenues to provide many social services on a socialized basis. A revolution in the development and application of technology greatly expanded the world's capacity to produce and distribute goods, although there emerged huge regional gaps in levels of production and consumption. The beginning of the end of European colonialism in Asia and Africa led to the birth of scores of new sovereign nations. Yet all too often political colonialism was replaced by a new economic colonialism in which developing nations sold raw materials to industrialized nations at low cost, and then purchased finished goods from those nations at much higher cost.

Significant changes took place in the structure and functioning of the corporation after the war. The shift in corporate structure from single ownership to control by shareholders and management by staff professionals became the norm in the 1950s. Production of many goods and services was increasingly concentrated in the hands of a few large corporations, and as a result these corporations acquired immense economic power. Economist Adolf Berle (1895-1971) noted that in 1954 just 135 American corporations had one-fourth of the manufacturing volume of the world.[54] These large corporations were able to attract huge amounts of capital, and therefore were able to weaken competition in some industries.

Their burgeoning economic power enabled some corporations to expand their operations into several countries, and the name "multinational corporation" was coined to describe them. Some of them became quasi-political institutions which wielded considerable influence in international affairs. Partly because of the multinationals an awareness of the interdependence of the world economy emerged for the first time in history.

A more inclusive concept of property also evolved at this time. Shareholding no longer constituted corporate ownership as it once had, with the emergence of a professional corporate management class. The possession of work skills and talents, and of economic information, came to be seen as forms of property. Berle believed that by the 1950s, "the right to continued employment (was) unquestionably a property right" for the working class.[55] In general, ownership came to be understood more as the possession of power and skills than the control of physical goods. Recall that Leo XIII had understood property almost exclusively as the possession of land, and Pius XI in terms of land and wage income from work.[56]

Pius XII did not use encyclicals to present his social teaching. He communicated it piecemeal in speeches, radio addresses, and letters over the many years of his papacy. The emphases of his teaching evolved over the years to meet the demands of the changing social and economic situation.

B. Anthropology

Pius XII foreshadowed a theme that would become central to the social teaching of Popes John XXIII and Paul VI, in his Christmas radio message of 1942. He said that society must be ordered to the perfection of the human person, and that the dignity and rights of the person must be respected: "The dignity of the human person, then, requires normally as a natural foundation of life the right to the use of the goods of the earth"; and later in the same address: "To this right corresponds the fundamental obligation to grant private ownership of property, if possible, to all." [57] The social teaching of Pius XII was infused throughout with a deep concern for the dignity of the human person. Before and during the war he asserted the need for the preservation of dignity in the face of the threat of totalitarianism. And he cited the demands of human dignity in the context of the economic and technological revolutions of the post-war world. Among those demands was the right of all persons to use the goods of the earth.

C. Topics related to property

1. Economic systems and property

Although Pius XII had corporatist leanings early in his papacy, by the mid-1940s his writings and addresses no longer contained references to corporatism. Instead he began to evaluate the existing socioeconomic systems. He was opposed, for example, to the individualism and overemphasis on personal aggrandizement which characterized free enterprise. Yet he considered it superior overall to socialist and Marxist materialism.

2. Principles and strategies of actualization

As one would expect Pius XII focused on the problems of peace and the reconstruction of a peaceful world order during the war years. His first encyclical, *Summi Pontificatus* (1939), addressed the grave and imminent threat posed by totalitarian regimes in Germany, Italy, and the Soviet Union.[58] Under the authorship of the neo-Thomist Gustav Gundlach, the encyclical exhorted states in traditional Thomistic terms to promote the national common good (#54).

In general Pius XII envisioned the just society as "an organically united society where the service of the common good would be the basic motivation of all the different groupings of which it would be composed." [59]

He laid down five conditions for order in social life in a radio message on December 24, 1942: the dignity and rights of the human person; the unity of social life; the dignity and prerogatives of work; the reconstruction of the juridical order; and the Christian conception of the state.[60] That vision was developed further in a letter to the French Social Week in 1946.[61]

Pius XII did not directly address the concept of economic development, as would John XXIII and Paul VI after him. He referred only indirectly to the subject, in such a way that his acceptance of the need for industrial development, at least in the Western world, was a necessity. For example, he assumed that the rebuilding of the industrial complex was an essential aspect of the reconstruction of Europe after World War II. As Pius XI had done before him, Pius XII preferred to address the issue of the relationship of labor and management in the industrial effort.

His statements on the social teaching reflected Pius XII's belief in the primacy of the Church and of its moral principles in social and economic life. In his view the temporal and religious spheres were engaged in a battle for the minds and hearts of humanity: "The fundamental theme of his principal speeches was the confrontation of contemporary civilization and culture with the Catholic outlook on life."[62]

3. Geographic area of application

In his later years Pius XII raised the issue, for the first time in the history of the papal social teaching, of the "underdeveloped" nations - those which had not yet achieved a level of industrial production and economic sophistication to enable them to provide a sufficient amount of material goods for their people.[63] Pius XII thus acknowledged for the first time the international scope of the social teaching and the property question. The international scope would be strongly emphasized in the teachings of John XXIII and Paul VI.

D. The property teaching

In his Pentecost radio message of 1941 the pope placed the right of all persons to use property prior to the right of ownership, echoing the traditional Thomistic ordering. Pius XII also pointed out the need for a just distribution of goods within nations.[64] During the darkest days of the war Pius XII noted, in his Christmas radio address of 1941, that one of the premises for the creation of a renewed world order was overcoming the "disequilibrium of the world economy," so that all nations could "secure for their children an appropriate standard of life."[65] He called for a more equitable sharing of the world's resources as part of this new world order.

When referring to property in his various statements on the social teaching Pius XII normally used the general terms "goods of the earth." However, he specified this term, and expanded the scope of the definition of property by including the means of production among the goods classified as private property.[66]

In general Pius XII viewed the right of property ownership as the foundation of a just social order, and held that property gave external expression to human liberty and allowed persons to provide for their personal needs.[67] The acquisition of property also served as an incentive to the worker to work, to thrift, and to sobriety.[68]

Pius XII agreed with Leo XIII and Pius XI that the state had a limited role to play in the regulation of property. Each was concerned about the demand of socialist regimes for the abolition of property. Therefore Pius XII sought to limit governments to only the regulation of the use of property. He held that it was not permissible for public authority to abolish the right of persons to own material goods.[69]

E. Conclusion of section

The Second World War, and the corporate and technological revolutions which followed it, produced for the first time in history the awareness of the global scope of the economy and the interdependence of the world community. Pius XII grasped these insights, and they are reflected in his social teaching.

Pius XII attempted to preserve the dignity of the human person in the face of world war and worldwide postwar economic expansion. Still, he was opposed to excessive individualism, particularly as embodied in capitalism.

A better balance was struck by Pius XII between the right of ownership and the social function of property than by his predecessors. He taught that while the right of ownership helped to promote order in society, the social function implied the necessity for a more just distribution of goods.

The social teaching of Pope Pius XII did not deviate in any significant way from the principles established by Leo XIII and Pius XI. His teaching, however, served as an important bridge between the narrow, cautious outlook of his predecessors and the more dynamic and expansive views of his successors, John XXIII and Paul VI.

V. *MATER ET MAGISTRA* (1961) AND *PACEM IN TERRIS* (1963)[70]

A. Historical setting

By the late 1950s the global scope and complexity of the world's socioeconomic problems and challenges were facts which the Church could no longer overlook if its social teaching were to have credibility and validity for the Church and the world. General economic prosperity prevailed in many parts of the world. Revolutions in technology and communications were just as earth-shaking, though quieter, than those which brought an end to the colonial domination of Asia and Africa by European countries. For the first time in history the world economy was truly interdependent, and no country could claim economic self-sufficiency.

Yet the material benefits of this prosperity were neither produced nor shared by all peoples in equal measure. A tremendous and ever-widening gap existed between the "developed" nations of Europe and North America and the "underdeveloped" countries in Asia, Africa, and Latin America. Although vastly more goods were being produced than ever before, their distribution and consumption were anything but equitable. Property in many forms - land, material goods, wage income, knowledge, technical and managerial skill, and economic power - came to be concentrated increasingly in the developed nations.

Corporations were largely responsible for this considerable economic output, and the trends which had begun early in the 1950s - the growth of multinational corporations, the expansion of the managerial class, the increase in corporate political power - continued apace as the decade came to a close.

The definition of property underwent further theoretical and practical refinement during the 1950s. Economists such as Berle noted that ownership was coming to be understood and measured not just in terms of the tangible - land, wage income - but increasingly in terms of the intangible - skill, information, power.[71]

Pope John XXIII (1958-1963) initiated what was known as the *aggiornamento* in the Church. This period was characterized by the acknowledgement of the autonomy of the secular world. The Church understood that it was just one voice among many in the shaping of world events. A willingness to enter into dialogue with persons and movements of all kinds, even though they might disagree with the Church's point of view, was central to the *aggiornamento.*

The *aggiornamento* also produced a new outlook and methodology in the social teaching. Although he maintained a fundamentally Thomistic natural law perspective, John XXIII was the first pope to incorporate into his social teaching the findings of the social sciences, and to place his teaching in the context of the prevailing social, economic, political, and historical situation - the "signs of the times." Rather than state his teaching as if it were timeless and unchangeable, as had been done by the previous social popes, John XXIII acknowledged that his social teaching was a development, at times even a redirection of the teaching of his predecessors.

B. Anthropology

John XXIII's anthropology was best understood in his notion of the "whole man" (*Mater et Magistra,* ##2, 3; *Pacem in Terris,* #57). He accepted the concept, rooted in Sacred Scripture, of the human person as a unity of body, mind, soul, and spirit. This implied that each person was entitled to have his/her material and spiritual needs satisfied, including the need for work and property, so that the "whole man" might be fulfilled.

John XXIII's personalist anthropology highlighted the dignity, the social duties, and the rights and liberties of the person, and held that the economy must be ordered to the fulfillment of the person. His anthropology reflected a reversal of the attitudes of Leo XIII and Pius XI, who believed that a hierarchically ordered society was needed to grant material benefits to a basically uneducated multitude. He developed fully the anthropology of Pius XII, who initiated the call for greater participation and active involvement of persons in the securing of their rights.[72]

C. Topics related to property

1. Economic systems and property

John XXIII embraced neither socialism nor capitalism, the two operative socioeconomic models in Europe, North America, and the Soviet Union. In fact he criticized any economic system that gave top priority to maximum production and sacrificed every consideration of justice to this narrow objective.

Cronin points out that John XXIII endorsed the type of responsible capitalism practiced in the United States. Still, the pope did not consider it to be the same as the "unlimited right of property as interpreted by the proponents of individualism."[73]

Despite its liberal tone, *Mater et Magistra* should not be construed as an endorsement of socialism. For example, in its brief treatment of economic systems the encyclical called for a just wage so that workers can accrue savings and acquire property. In light of this, John XXIII expressed surprise that some, including socialists, would "reject the natural role of private ownership" (#112).

In *Pacem in Terris* John XXIII was careful to distinguish between Communist theories, which he said were false and unchanging, and Communist movements, which were subject to change over time. He concluded that these movements, "insofar as they conform to the dictates of right reason and are interpreters of the lawful aspirations of the human person, contain elements that are positive and deserving of approval" (#159). The pope's intention, consistent with the *aggiornamento*, was to open avenues of dialogue with Communist regimes in eastern Europe.

2. Principles and strategies of actualization

John XXIII introduced some new themes to the social teaching. First among these was "socialization."

The term, not to be confused with socialism, was used to acknowledge the explosion of social contacts and relationships brought about by the communications and technological revolutions of the 1950s. In *Mater et Magistra* socialization was defined as the collection of "those mutual relationships, daily on the increase, which have introduced into the lives and activities of man, a close network of social bonds, generally respected by public and private law" (#59). As Calvez noted: "Every man, as it were, has become a crossroads of social relations that are constantly expanding both numerically and extensively."[74] *Mater et Magistra* called socialization "one of the characteristic marks of our time" (#59).

John XXIII's concept of socialization challenged the assumption of unrestrained individualism in Western economic ideology and activity. Socialization had been brought about by the forces of industrialization, urbanization, unionism, and advances in technology and communications. These changes had helped to shape a far more interdependent world with a sense of its shared destiny and common challenges.

The idea of socialization accounted in part for John XXIII's views on property, which de-emphasized the individual right to own and laid greater stress on the social function of property.

Calvez makes the claim that John XXIII's greatest contribution to the social teaching was on the subject of work, and certainly he had much of importance to say about work.[75] John XXIII's theology of work emphasized the positive value of work as a participation in the divine work of creation, rather than as punishment for sin. The progress of workers over the previous several decades was seen by the pope as "an indication of progress on the part of humanity" (*Mater et Magistra*, #107). He said that work had primacy over tangible property because work is "of the person" - it is integral to, or part of the very nature of the person. Property, on the other hand, is "for the person" - it contributes to the well-being and fulfillment of the person, but in a mediated fashion.[76]

As had the previous social popes, John XXIII restated many of the traditional rights of workers: the just wage (*Mater et Magistra*, ##68, 71; *Pacem in Terris*, ##20, 64); profit-sharing (*Mater et Magistra*, #77); worker participation in the business enterprise (*Mater et Magistra*, #97); the right to unionize (*Mater et Magistra*, #100).

John XXIII related the theme of development to his concept of socialization. He acknowledged a legitimate pluralism of models of development, and noted that whatever model a society pursued, it must serve and enhance humanity and not enslave it. He believed that economic systems exist for persons, and not vice versa.

John XXIII was aware of the widely divergent rates of development around the world, and he believed that world peace would be threatened if the imbalance between the developed and developing nations were not addressed and corrected. Development implied a sharing in the wealth produced, and in the sacrifices necessary for development. The seriousness of the imbalances between the rich and poor countries led John XXIII to call for massive increases in international aid.

Although development was an important theme for John XXIII, it would receive more comprehensive treatment in the teaching of Paul VI, particularly in *Populorum Progressio*.

Recognizing the rightful autonomy of the secular world, John XXIII attempted to strike a careful balance between the temporal and religious spheres of activity. On the one hand he was careful to point out that it was improper for believers to "become quite remiss in their specific Christian contributions" in the exercise of their temporal activities. At the same time he admonished Christians not to "abandon the activities of this world in order to strive for Christian perfection" (*Mater et Magistra*, #256).

John XXIII's social teaching was infused throughout with a sense of optimism - about the benefits of technological progress (*Mater et Magistra*, #47), the prospects for worldwide development (*Pacem in Terris*, #130), and about the possibility of a worldwide community of persons (*Mater et Magistra*, #130). His optimism would carry over into Vatican Council II in *Gaudium et Spes*, and Paul VI in *Populorum Progressio*.

3. Geographic area of application

John XXIII touched on two themes which previously had not received serious attention in the papal social teaching - the recognition of the international scope of the social problem, and the acknowledgement of the interdependence of the human family worldwide. In *Pacem in Terris* he extolled the need for the "establishment of . . . a world community of peoples . . . urgently demanded today by the requirements of the universal common good" (#7). And in *Mater et Magistra* he indicated that the growing interdependence of the world's people was appropriate, due to the increasing socialization of humanity (#200).

D. The property teaching

John XXIII's teaching on private property was considered controversial enough to have held up the issuance of *Mater et Magistra* for two months in 1961.[77] On the whole, however, his property teaching did not significantly diverge from previous papal teaching.

The framework for John XXIII's property teaching was the Thomistic natural rights argument, as interpreted by Mgr. Pietro Pavan (1903-).[78]

The pope upheld the permanent validity of the right of private ownership (*Mater et Magistra*, #109, *Pacem in Terris*, #21), and balanced the right of ownership with the right of all persons to use the good things of the earth (*Pacem in Terris*, ##21, 22).

John XXIII expanded the list of concrete manifestations of property to include professional qualification, information, and economic power (*Mater et Magistra*, ##92, 106). The development of insurance and social security programs in many countries meant that property in land and wages need "no longer be considered as the unique or even the principal means of a person's material security."[79]

Reflecting the Church's lingering wariness of the dangers of socialism, and consistent with his personalist anthropology, John XXIII viewed property as a concrete manifestation of human freedom, and as a guarantee of the priority of persons in relation to society. He held that the provision for private property was one of the necessary conditions of a free political regime.[80]

John XXIII believed that the state should have broader powers to intervene in the economic sphere than had his predecessors. The state could actively promote the right of ownership, and its power to intervene "in a wide variety of economic affairs" was asserted for the promotion of the common good (*Mater et Magistra*, #55). State intervention should "not only avoid restricting the freedom of private citizens, but should also increase it" (*Mater et Magistra*, #55). A wider distribution of property was needed to enhance personal freedom and promote social peace (*Mater et Magistra*, ##74, 115, 120).

E. Conclusion of section

Pope John XXIII recognized that by the late 1950s the world had become interdependent in terms of economic and social life. The *aggiornamento*, in which the Church acknowledged the autonomy of the secular world and attempted to reach out in dialogue with the world, embodied the spirit of John XXIII's papacy. His social teaching reflected that global awareness and the spirit of *aggiornamento*.

Pius XII's emphasis on human dignity in society was expanded by John XXIII into an anthropology of the "whole man." His anthropology stressed the unity of the person as a temporal and spiritual being, and the dignity, rights, liberties, and social duties which prescinded from human nature.

Unlike his predecessors, John XXIII was somewhat open to socialism, although he stopped short of an outright endorsement. Consistent with the *aggiornamento*, he found a way to open avenues of dialogue with the Communist world. He distinguished between Communist theories, which he considered to be false, and Communist movements, which might contain some elements of truth and value.

The theme of socialization was introduced into the social teaching by John XXIII to serve two purposes. It symbolized the explosion of relationships which characterized the modern world, and it was intended to counterbalance the excessive individualism of the capitalist system.

John XXIII was optimistic about the possibilities for worldwide economic development to create a greater equilibrium in the world economy. This important theme would be developed more fully by Paul VI.

For the most part the property teaching of John XXIII was entirely traditional. He emphasized the social function of property, while continuing to affirm the validity of the right of ownership. The definition of property was broadened to include professional qualification, information, and economic power. Because of the importance of property for human and economic and political freedom, states were called upon to use their power to ensure a wider distribution of property both within their own borders and among all nations.

The property teaching of John XXIII was significant in that it introduced some new themes into the teaching - the international range of its application, an anthropology firmly tied to human dignity and rights, the phenomenon he called socialization, an openness to socialist and Communist movements, an expanded definition of property, a spirit of optimism about the prospects of human progress. These themes would be taken up and expanded by Pope Paul VI.

VI. *GAUDIUM ET SPES* - THE PASTORAL CONSTITUTION ON THE CHURCH IN THE MODERN WORLD (1965)[81]

A. Historical setting

As progressive as John XXIII's property teaching had been, it still left considerable room for further development.[82] That task was taken up by Pope Paul VI and by the bishops assembled at the Second Vatican Council.

Vatican II carried on several trends in the social teaching that had been initiated by John XXIII which, taken together, characterized his *aggiornamento.* The Church acknowledged its place as one voice among many in shaping the values of individuals, groups, and nations. The valuable contributions of the social sciences were incorporated by the Council into the analysis of social problems. Rather than issue timeless, universal pronouncements to a world that was presumed to be listening, the Council attempted a genuine dialogue with the modern world, and to recognize the autonomy and legitimacy of the "secular" fields of knowledge in the formation of the social teaching.

Gaudium et Spes, the Pastoral Constitution on the Church in the Modern World, was an *aggiornamento* document,[83] and in many ways it reflected the social teaching of John XXIII. Many of its major themes - the international scope of the social question, economic development, the worldwide distribution of goods - were contained also in *Mater et Magistra* and *Pacem in Terris.*[84]

But *Gaudium et Spes* bore the imprint of Paul VI as well. Not only did Paul VI influence *Mater et Magistra*, but he was very influential in the formation of Schema XIII, which provided the conceptual framework for

Gaudium et Spes. Louis-Joseph Lebret, O.P. (1897-1966), whose thinking would be the inspiration behind *Populorum Progressio*, was named an expert to the Council for Schema XIII by Paul VI.[85]

B. Anthropology

While previous social documents had been cast almost exclusively in a philosophical framework of scholastic and natural law thinking, *Gaudium et Spes* was written from the point of view of a clearly articulated Christian anthropology which preserved the natural law, but which also employed a wealth of biblical and theological language and images. It preferred to read and discern the "signs of the times," which are susceptible to change over time, than to make a claim of timelessness which would be impossible to support. As a result *Gaudium et Spes* was more descriptive than prescriptive.[86]

Part I, Chapter 1 of the document was devoted to Christian anthropology. Taking Sacred Scripture as its starting point, the document viewed the human person as a creature of God (Genesis 1:27), an incarnate unity of body and soul. This meant that the person has a spiritual dimension, an openness to the transcendent in the here and now. The body/soul dualism often found in traditional Catholic natural law theology was not present in *Gaudium et Spes*.[87]

The creation of the human person in *imago Dei*, and his/her call to communion with God, were the source of human dignity (##12-22). Riga commented on this point: "It is man who is the measure of all things and for whom all things were created."[88]

Human dignity gave each person the vocation to master and control the earth. The dignity of the person thus served as the premise for the discussion of social and cultural issues.[89] In general terms, this meant that the ultimate aim of every society was the promotion of the human person

(#25). Economic activity in particular must be person-centered. As Riga wrote: "Economic activity must respect the dignity of man as well as promote it."[90]

The dignity of the person had another important implication: it meant that each person was the subject of universal and inviolable rights (#26). A lengthy list of these rights was spelled out: food, clothing, shelter, vocation and family, education, employment, good reputation, respect, appropriate information, the freedom to act according to one's conscience, privacy, religious freedom. All of these rights were intended to help persons lead "a life more truly human" (#26).

But even with his/her great dignity, the person suffered an interior division within his/her being, and this led persons to sin (#13). Riga pointed out that *Gaudium et Spes* used the Augustinian notion of alienation to describe the reality of sin: "Man who disobeys God is alienated from the very source of his being; consequently, the cosmos and the constructs of man rebel against him" in personal and social disorder.[91]

The anthropology of *Gaudium et Spes* then moved beyond the consideration of the individual, and noted that the person was also social by nature: "By his innermost nature man is a social being" who must relate to others in order to find him/herself (#12). His/her social nature meant that each person had certain duties for the promotion of the common good of society.

C. Topics related to property

1. Economic systems and property

The Council fathers restated the Church's longstanding objections to both unbridled capitalism and totalitarian socialism, insofar as each deprived persons of the freedom to participate in their own economic well-being and that of society as a whole (#65). *Gaudium et Spes* asserted that the Church did not promote any one political or social system - rather, it promoted the human person (##75-76).

Riga points out that *Gaudium et Spes*, continuing a theme of John XXIII, called for economic democracy as part of its recognition of the dignity and the social nature of the human person.[92] *Gaudium et Spes* advocated equality and participation in the economic sphere to match the equality and participation achieved in much of the world in political life. Concretely, this meant that persons had a right to "active participation" in economic life (#65). Significantly, the phrase *actuosa participatio* in *Gaudium et Spes* was also used in the Constitution on the Sacred Liturgy to describe the kind of participation to be promoted among the congregation in the celebration of the Eucharistic liturgy.[93]

The document asserted that economic democracy was needed to remedy the lack of participation by workers in capitalist countries. Capitalism had tended to make human dignity and work a mere commodity. Riga noted that:

> insofar as the direction of an enterprise is concerned, the worker is a perpetual minor, a number that can be dismissed or hired according to the 'need,' determined solely by market demand. His muscle and professional skills are needed, but his opinion and consent are never requested. He is an automaton who is turned on and off. This view of a man violates all canons of social justice.[94]

Since workers and capitalists were co-producers of goods, workers were entitled to a fair share of profit and participation. There was, in other words, a need for a greater diffusion of ownership among all who participate in the production of goods. This meant that workers had a right to more than just the traditionally recognized measures of participation and compensation, and that they were entitled to such things as profit-sharing, cooperatives, and stock ownership.[95] The kind of economic democracy called for in *Gaudium et Spes* implied that the mere multiplication of goods or material benefits, while useful and needed, did not in itself contribute to the enhancement of human freedom and dignity.[96]

2. Principles and strategies of actualization

In *Gaudium et Spes* socialization was understood as "a type of global and universal interaction of persons and things," a "complicated intertwining of many and varied relationships in the economic, social, and technological fields" on an international scale. Socialization acknowledged the growing interdependence of the world community, and it aimed at personalizing the global situation by promoting human dignity.[97] John XXIII had developed the concept of socialization at length in *Mater et Magistra* (##59-68).

With the world becoming progressively more interdependent, persons could no longer pretend to live in isolation from one another (#23). Socialization, then, necessarily involved the promotion of the common good, "the sum of those conditions of social life which allow social groups and their individual members relatively thorough and ready access to their own fulfillment" (#26). By the 1960s the scope of the common good had become universal, with an increasingly complex set of mutual rights and duties (#26). Human dignity meant, among other things, that all persons in society had a right to an amount of goods and services sufficient for human dignity. The universal common good compelled each person to "consider his every neighbor without exception as another self" (#27) who possessed equal dignity and rights. Each person was called to have a sense of responsibility for all others - and a moderate amount of material possessions was seen as a precondition for the development of this sense of responsibility (#31).

The first fact noted in *Gaudium et Spes* about economic life was the tremendous social inequalities it had created. For example, even with the great strides that had been made since World War II in economic development, the FAO reported in the mid-1960s that 35 million people were dying each year of hunger.[98] All too often, the document continued, the very wealthy and the destitute lived side by side: "Luxury and misery rub shoulders" (#63). Still, economic development activity had the potential to minimize and eliminate those gaps (#63).

One implication of the anthropology of *Gaudium et Spes* was that involvement in temporal matters, including economic activity, was not considered inherently sinful. Rather, it was seen as a participation in the ongoing work of divine creation.

In its very first sentence *Gaudium et Spes* conveyed the spirit of the *aggiornamento*: "The joys and hopes, the griefs and anxieties of the men of this age, especially those who are poor or in any way afflicted, these too are the joys and hopes, the griefs and anxieties of the followers of Christ" (#1). This spirit prevailed throughout the entire document.

3. Geographic area of application

Gaudium et Spes clearly reflected the Church's cognizance of the international scope of the questions and problems which it addressed: "The destiny of the human community has become all of a piece . . ." (#5). The Council fathers addressed many issues in the document on the basis of their worldwide significance.

D. The property teaching

The social question, and the property issue in particular, were taken up in Part II, Chapter 3. As Riga pointed out, this chapter was probably the least original of all in *Gaudium et Spes*, in that it summarized and restated the principles of the social teaching from Leo XIII to John XXIII. Its power derived from its application of the traditional teaching to the new problems and challenges posed by the modern world.[99]

The property question was dealt with in nos. 69-71. Number 69 restated in terms clearer than any previous papal social document the ancient teaching of the Church on the priority of the social function of property over the right of ownership. It stated that God created the earth and the things of the earth for the whole person, and for all people. Citing the traditional Thomistic treatment of property, it taught that one's property should never be considered one's own absolutely, but also as common in that others should be able to benefit from it. Material goods should always be considered common property, even when they were the lawful possessions of an individual.[100] Private ownership was considered a basic right of the person (#71), but ownership was viewed as a relative, not an absolute right.

Each person had the right to an amount of material goods sufficient for oneself and one's family. In this regard the worldwide imbalance in the distribution of goods was seen as an offense against human dignity and a threat to world peace. Economic imbalances could be overcome only by a "genuine sharing of goods" by individuals and by governments (#69). *Gaudium et Spes* noted that persons have the obligation to provide relief for the poor not merely out of their excess wealth but from their substance. The right of the extremely poor person to take what he/she needed from the riches of others was restated.

In no. 71 the definition of property was discussed. The forms of property included not just material goods, but intangibles such as professional skills. This definition of property by the Council, an important aspect of its call for economic democracy, reflected the fact that by 1961 70% of Western workers derived their livelihood from the use of professional skill.[101]

Gaudium et Spes cited the four traditional benefits of ownership as listed by Thomas Aquinas: an expression of personality; the opportunity for social and economic service; an incentive to responsible work; a condition of civil liberties.[102] Without the right of property the dignity of the person is diminished, and the person "is reduced to economic and personal slavery." [103] Still, private property could be the occasion of greed and serious abuses. For this reason the social function of property must always be given priority.

Gaudium et Spes addressed the issue of the expropriation of land (#71) in the context of the abuses of property. It noted that in some parts of the world huge tracts of land remained uncultivated while many people lived in dire poverty. Human dignity and the social function of property demanded that this land be redistributed by the state, as long as the owner received just compensation.

E. Conclusion of section.

Although *Gaudium et Spes* was a conciliar document rather than a papal encyclical, it bore the imprint of John XXIII and Paul VI, the popes who presided over the Council. Perhaps it would be most accurate to say that *Gaudium et Spes* was a product of the *aggiornamento.*

One of the highlights of the document was its anthropology rooted in divine revelation. The human person derived his/her dignity from the fact of being created in the very image of God. This, in turn, gave persons rights and social duties based on their dignity.

Several topics related to the property teaching were addressed as well. Greater democracy in the economic realm was called for, to match the level of political democracy attained in the modern world. Humanity was charged to promote the universal common good to achieve the complete fulfillment of all. The overall mood of the encyclical was one of identification with the joys and sorrows of the human family.

Gaudium et Spes was noteworthy not because it broke new ground on the issue of property. At best it can be said that its emphasis on certain traditional points - the priority of the social function of property over the right of ownership, the obligation to help the poor for reasons of justice and charity, the right of the destitute to take from the rich in their extreme need - restated and updated longstanding principles of Church teaching. Its power derived from its application of these traditional principles in the context of the world economy of the 1960s.

VII. CHAPTER CONCLUSION

The aim of this chapter has been to offer an overview of the modern social teaching from Pope Leo XIII to the Second Vatican Council. At several points the teaching underwent a quite dramatic evolution because of changing historical circumstances. Some principles of the teaching appeared in the documents of more than one of the popes, but their meaning changed as new implications were drawn from them. Only a few aspects of the teaching remained basically the same in the social documents of all the social popes.

The historical setting in which the social documents were issued, for example, changed drastically between 1891 and 1965. *Rerum Novarum* appeared in the midst of labor turmoil and growing hostility to the Church. The worldwide depression of the 1930s and the rise of totalitarianism in Europe framed the teaching of *Quadragesimo Anno*. Pius XII's teaching responded to the Second World War and the rapid but uneven economic expansion which followed the war. *Mater et Magistra* and *Pacem in Terris*, the social encyclicals of John XXIII, reflected the Church's new awareness of the interdependence of the modern world, and the willingness of the Church to dialogue with it. Vatican II's *Gaudium et Spes* fostered the spirit of *aggiornamento* initiated by John XXIII.

The anthropology of the social documents underwent equally sweeping changes. Both Leo XIII and Pius XI assumed that society was inherently unequal, and that a certain hierarchical ordering of society was natural and normal. Pius XII turned that assumption upside down by focusing on the dignity of the individual and the rights of the person in society. This basic insight was developed into a biblically based anthropology by John XXIII and the Council.

One of the most consistent features of the modern social teaching was its critique of socioeconomic systems. Capitalism was viewed by all as a less than perfect but reformable system. A negative assessment of socialism prevailed until John XXIII. Similarly, Communism was rejected by all the social popes, although John XXIII attempted to open the door to dialogue with Communist movements.

The range of application of the social teaching expanded rapidly over the years. Leo XIII and Pius XI addressed their encyclicals to a strictly Western European audience. But a seminal awareness of the global scope of the social teaching emerged in Pius XII, and was fully acknowledged by John XXIII and the Council.

The general trend within the property teaching itself was that traditional principles were repeated, but with changing emphases and applications. *Rerum Novarum*, in an effort to discredit the prevailing socialist theories and movements of its time, highlighted the ownership right and the authority of the state to ensure that as many persons as possible could become owners of property, which was defined solely in terms of land. Pius XI sought to restore the traditional balance between the right of ownership and the social function of property, and he expanded the definition of property to include the family wage. Still, his antisocialist sentiments led him in *Quadragesimo Anno* to stress the right of ownership, and his understanding of the role of the state reflected his belief in corporatism. The property teaching of Pius XII placed greater emphasis on the social function of property and the power of the state to regulate its use, in response to the political threats against property during World War II, and the economic threats posed by both capitalism and socialism in the postwar world.

A more dynamic and expansive property teaching was initiated by John XXIII in *Mater et Magistra* and *Pacem in Terris*. These encyclicals placed the social function of property within the context of the international economy for the first time. The definition of property was enlarged to include intangible possessions such as information and economic power. Nations were called upon to ensure a wider distribution of property within nations and regions. In *Gaudium et Spes* the priority of the social function was consistent with the document's biblical anthropology, which emphasized human dignity and rights. The issue of expropriation was also introduced as a corrective to the abuses of property in some parts of the world.

Clearly the property teaching evolved between 1891 and 1965 to meet changing economic, social, and political circumstances. Paul VI accepted and passed down in his social documents the essential aspects of the teaching he inherited from his predecessors. He was always careful to conserve the fundamentals of the tradition. But he also helped to shape the evolving property teaching by expanding the application of some of its fundamental principles in his own unique and creative way. This chapter has helped set the stage for the analysis of Paul VI's property teaching by introducing the reader to the modern social teaching background from which it sprang.

Paul VI learned and interacted with the social teaching tradition, but his views were also shaped by other forces - his life experience, and the intellectual climate of his day. These provide the focus of the next two chapters of this study.

NOTES - CHAPTER ONE

1 Richard L. Camp, "The Rights and Duties of Labor and Capital," in *Readings in Moral Theology No. 5*, eds. Charles E. Curran and Richard A. McCormick, S.J. (New York: Paulist Press, 1986), 42-48.

2 Matthew Habiger, O.S.B., *Papal Teaching on Private Property: 1891-1981* (Lanham, Maryland: University Press of America, 1990), 22-28, 28-32, 37-45.

3 Habiger, 67-71, 80-82, 94-103, 103-26.

4 Habiger, 165-71.

5 Habiger, 152-59.

6 Habiger, 210-14.

7 Pope Leo XIII, "Rerum Novarum" (May 15, 1891), *Acta Sanctae Sedis 23* (1890-91), 641-70. English text in *The Social Teachings of the Church*, ed. Anne Freemantle (New York: Mentor-Omega, 1963).

8 Pierre-Joseph Proudhon (1809-1965) was a French socialist and political writer. He claimed, in *What is Property?* (1840) (Benjamin R. Tucker, trans., Princeton, Massachusetts: B.R. Tucker, 1876), that property and capital are the power to exploit the labor of others, to claim the results of labor without having made an equivalent contribution. His noted saying "Property is theft" is a paradoxical statement of this general principle. Proudhon rejected the prevailing moderate French socialism of his day, and his theory of property is substantially the same as that of Marx and most of the later socialists. *The Encyclopedia of Philosophy*, vol. 6 (New York: Macmillan, 1967), 507-9.

Henry George (1839-1897), American author and economist, is best known for his concept of the "Single Tax," which he proposed in *Our Land Policy, 1871* (Garden City, New York: Doubleday, Doran, & Co., 1930) and refined in the well-known *Progress and Poverty*, 1879 (New York: Robert Schalkenbach Foundation, 1954). He held that the land of a country belonged to all the people of that country. Private ownership of land had no more foundation in reason or morality than private ownership of air or sunlight. Nevertheless, he said, land should be divided in private parcels among those who would pay the highest price (called "rent") for the use of each parcel. Since rent was always more than sufficient to defray all necessary expenses of government, those expenses should be met by levying a "single tax" on ground rent. All other taxes should be abolished. This would lead to a situation of absolute free trade, since nothing produced would be taxed at all. The right of private property would be absolute, for the owner of land could not be divested of it. See "Single Tax," in *New Catholic Encyclopedia*, vol. 13 (New York: McGraw-Hill, 1967), 251-52.

9 The moral use and ownership of property has been a living question in the Church since its earliest days. In the Acts of the Apostles the Jerusalem Church was conscious of fulfilling the material needs of all its members, and some property was held in common to provide for the poor. Several of the Fathers of the Church wrote on the subject from a variety of viewpoints, from Clement of Alexandria's (c. 150-c. 215) distaste of excessive wealth in the midst of poverty, Basil's rather radical socialism and condemnation of the rich, Ambrose's (339-97) orthodox emphasis on the primacy of use of property over the right of ownership, John Chrysostom's (c. 347-407) stress on the right use of property for the sake of *koinonia*, and Augustine's (354-430) position that all created goods are to be used as a means to God. See Charles Avila, *Ownership: Early Christian Thinking* (Maryknoll, New York: Orbis, 1983). The monastic movement in the West preserved the tradition of common ownership and use of goods, and proscribed an austere lifestyle. These practices were undertaken in imitation of the Lord, and in anticipation of life in the Kingdom of God. See Jean Leclerq, *The Love of Learning and the Desire for God* (New York: Fordham University Press, 1961).

In the Middle Ages the mendicant orders, and lay groups like the Brethren of the Common Life, lived a life of poverty and sharing in imitation of the Lord. They often reacted to the more established monastic orders which had largely abandoned their original ideal of simplicity of life.

10 This does not mean that Catholic authors were silent on the subject of property. The humanist Thomas More (1478-1535), for example, described an ideal land where private property did not exist, in *Utopia (1516)* (Everyman's Library, New York: Dutton, 1919). During the Catholic Reformation the Jesuits predicated a natural rights theory of property, in the tradition of Thomas Aquinas. Luis de Molina, S.J. (1535-1600), in his *De Iustitia De Jure (1593-1600)* (Antwerp: Ioannem Kerrbergium, 1615), wrote that property was common according to the natural law only in the sense that the natural law did not proscribe how it should be divided; thus the right of property was seen as a natural right. The property theory of Francisco Suarez, S.J. (1548-1617), was also faithful to Aquinas, but was coupled with a theory of contract which held that each state was created by popular agreement and its form was determined by the terms of this agreement. Therefore the right of property was prior to the state, because it existed as part of nature and not by social agreement. See Richard Schlatter, *Private Property: The History of an Idea* (London: George Allen and Unwin Ltd, 1951).

11 See Thomas Hobbes, *Leviathon (or Matter, Form, and Power of a Commonwealth, Ecclesiastical and Civil)*, (1659) (*Great Books of the Western World*, vol. 23, Encyclopedia Britannica, in collaboration with the University of Chicago, Robert Maynard Hutchins founders' ed., Chicago: W. Benton, 1952); John Locke, *Treatise on Civil Government and a Letter Concerning*

Toleration (1690) (Charles A. Sherman, ed., New York: D. Appleton Century, 1937); and Adam Smith, *The Wealth of Nations (1776)* (New York: Random House, 1937). See also Casimir Czajkowski, *The Theory of Private Property in John Locke's Political Philosophy* (Ann Arbor, Michigan: Edwards Brothers, 1941).

12 Vogelsang, an Austrian, advocated a return to the medieval socioeconomic order of Christendom. He believed that the social misuse of property, or even its nonuse (as in the case of absentee landlords) was reason enough for expropriation. See John Coleman, S.J., "Development of Church Social Teaching," in *Readings in Moral Theology No. 5*, 169-87.

13 Also known as the "Union of Fribourg," a series of international Catholic social conferences called by Cardinal Mermillod at his residence in the city of Fribourg, Switzerland, between 1884 and 1892. The "circle" advocated a living wage, among other ideas. See Camp, *Readings in Moral Theology No. 5*, 32-50.

14 Coleman, 177-78.

15 Although there have been formal papal letters written for the universal Church from the earliest days of the Christian era, since about 1740 the term "encyclical" has referred to a papal letter, as distinct from other forms of papal communication, which is pastoral in nature, and thus pertains to doctrinal or moral matters, and written for the universal Church. Modern encyclicals have a rather stylized form, and in their preparation the pope may depend upon individuals or groups of scholars, as well as his own thoughts. They are generally considered an exercise of the pope's ordinary magisterium, and therefore not infallible. See the *New Catholic Encyclopedia*, vol. 5.

16 The "social question" refers to that set of issues, such as the rights of workers, the just wage, and the property issue, which deal with socioeconomic realities as they have evolved over the last century.

17 The teachings of Aloysius Taperelli D'Azeglio, S.J. (1793-1862), an Italian sociologist and neo-Thomist, and long-time rector of the Roman College of the Society of Jesus, are considered by some to be the precursor of the modern Catholic social movement in its theoretical side. See, for example, Edward Cahill, S.J., "The Catholic Social Movement: Historical Aspects," in *Readings in Moral Theology No. 5*, 3-31. He influenced Leo XIII, especially in his Thomistic restatement of the theory of the property right, and in his equal criticism of socialism and liberal capitalism. At the same time, one senses the paternalism of all those who most influenced Leo XIII's thinking - in this case, Taperelli's position that civil government originates in an extension

of paternal power through the patriarchal head of groups of families. See *Dictionnaire de Thèologie Catholique*, vol. 15.1 (Paris: Librairie Letouzey et An, 1946).

18 Richard L. Camp, *The Papal Ideology of Social Reform*, (Leiden: Brill, 1968), 30.

19 Such as liberal democracy and Marxist Communism. See Charles Curran, "The Changing Anthropological Bases of Catholic Social Ethics," in *Readings in Moral Theology No. 5*, 188-218.

20 Curran, 190.

21 *The Social Teachings of Wilhelm Emmanuel von Ketteler* (Washington, D.C.: University Press of America, 1981), xi.

22 Camp, *Readings in Moral Theology No. 5*, 40-41.

23 Throughout this paper improperly used gender-specific words which appear in the texts of papal documents and other books will be retained, but only in order to be faithful to the original texts.

The numbers with the symbol "#" before them refer to the numbering system found in the Church documents themselves, and will be used throughout this paper.

24 Joseph N. Moody, "Leo XIII and the Social Crisis," in *Leo XIII and the Modern World* (New York: Sheed and Ward, 1961).

25 Marquis René de la Tour du Pin (1834-1924) was, along with Count Albert de Mun, one of the founders of the Catholic social movement in France. He, along with de Mun and others, issued an "Appeal to Men of Good Will" in 1871, which advocated the formation of Catholic Workingmen's Clubs in France, which were to be under the patronage of the wealthy classes. See Cahill in *Readings in Moral Theology No. 5*, 11-13.

Leon Harmel (1829-1915), a French industrialist, formed company unions in France, and led workers in a series of pilgrimages to Rome in the 1880s. See Coleman in *Readings in Moral Theology No. 5*, 179-180.

Matteo Liberatore, S.J. (1810-1892), who composed the first draft of *Rerum Novarum*, believed in "mixed unions" made up of employers and workers who would join together under the guidance of the Church. See Moody, 76.

26 Camp, *Readings in Moral Theology No. 5*, 37-41.

27 Camp, *Readings in Moral Theology No. 5*, 32.

28 Aquinas' treatment of the property question is found in the *Summa Theologica*, II, II, question 66, St. Thomas Aquinas: *Summa Theologiae*, English translation edited by Thomas Gilby, O.P. (New York: McGraw-Hill, 1963). Thomas said in this regard that "man ought to possess external things, not as his own, but as common, so that, to wit, he is ready to communicate them to others in their need."

29 Renato Cirillo, "Capitalism, Private Property, and Freedom," *Review of Social Economy 24* (September 1966), 161.

30 Charles Curran, *Directions in Catholic Social Ethics* (Notre Dame, Indiana: University of Notre Dame Press, 1985), 23.

31 According to Taperelli, who accepted the thinking of Locke on this point, individuals exist prior to the state, and the state is a creation of consenting individuals. Therefore persons do not surrender their innate rights, including the right to own property, when the state is created.

32 Curran, *Directions in Catholic Social Ethics*, 10.

33 Pope Pius XI, "Quadragesimo Anno," (May 15, 1931), in *Acta Apostolicae Sedis 23* (1931), 177-228. English text in *Twelve Encyclicals of Pius XI* (London: Catholic Theological Society, 1943).

34 Camp, *Readings in Moral Theology No. 5*, 37.

35 Sr. Mary Thomasine Cusack, O.P., *The Significance of a Changing Concept of Ownership in Social and Economic Planning*, dissertation (Washington, D.C.: Catholic University Press, 1940), 82.

36 Curran, *Readings in Moral Theology No. 5*, 193-94.

37 Oswald von Nell-Breuning, S.J., *Reorganization of Social Economy* (Milwaukee: Bruce, 1936), 274.

38 See Nell-Breuning, 277. Pius XI understood social justice as the institutionalization of basic economic and political rights for all, through legislation and other government activity. In this respect it represents an important departure from Leo XIII, who advocated a hierarchical social order in which rights would be secured through reliance on the good will of the ruling class. See David Hollenbach, S.J., *Claims in Conflict* (New York: Paulist Press, 1979), 54-55.

39 Coleman, 183-184.

40 Heinrich Pesch (1854-1926), German Jesuit and self-taught economist, wrote the five-volume *Lehrbuch der national Ökonomie* (Freiberg im Breisgau: Herder and Co., 1913-24) as an attempt to construct an integrated economic theory based on Aristotelian-Thomistic philosophy. His social philosophy, known as solidarism, rejected both socialism and individualism, and found in

the nature of society and the human person a principle of order for the economy. He viewed the economy as an organic and moral unity of many autonomous economic units bound together by the desire to achieve the common good. In this system the state assumes the positive role of directing, supervising, stimulating, and restraining the many economic units as the common good demands. See the *New Catholic Encyclopedia*, vol. 11.

Gustav Gundlach (1892-1963) was also a German Jesuit, neo-Thomist, and economist. His major work is the two-volume *Die Ordnung der menschlichen Gesellschaft* (Cologne: Bachem, 1964). He wrote some of the communications of both Pius XI and Pius XII.

41 Camp, *Papal Ideology*, 159.

42 Martin Grabmann (1875-1949), a theologian, specialized in the history of scholasticism. His principal interests were the works of Thomas Aquinas and the development of scholasticism, Thomism, Aristotelianism, and German mysticism. See *New Catholic Encyclopedia*, vol. 5.

43 Nell-Breuning, 218-19.

44 Nell-Breuning, 225.

45 John F.Cronin, S.S., "Forty Years Later: Reflections," in *Readings in Moral Theology No. 5*, 71.

46 Cronin, 74.

47 Nell-Breuning, 105-6. Nell-Breuning cites the German legal definition of property found in *BGB* (Civil Code), paragraph 903.

48 Nell-Breuning, 114.

49 Nell-Breuning, 97.

50 Cronin, 70.

51 Nell-Breuning, 114.

52 Nell-Breuning, 114. See also William J. McDonald, *The Social Value of Property According to St. Thomas Aquinas* (Washington, D.C.: Catholic University of America Press, 1939), 47-48.

53 Camp, *Papal Ideology*, 51.

54 Adolf A. Berle, *The Twentieth Century Capitalist Revolution* (New York: Harcourt, Brace, and World, 1954), 39.

55 Berle, 95.

56 Cronin, 74.

57 Freemantle, 156.

58 Pius XII, Pope, "Summi Pontificatus" (October 20, 1939), *Acta Apostolicae Sedis 31* (October 28, 1939), 413-53. English text in *The Pope Speaks: The Words of Pius XII* (New York: Harcourt, Brace and Company, 1940).

59 Donal Dorr, *Option for the Poor: A Hundred Years of Vatican Social Teaching* (Maryknoll, New York: Orbis, 1983), 80.

60 Pope Pius XII, "Radio Message of December 24, 1942," in Paul-Émile Bolté, *Les Droits de L'Homme et la Papauté Contemporaine* (Montreal: Fides, 1975), 32.

61 Freemantle, 89.

62 *New Catholic Encyclopedia*, vol. 11, 417.

63 Pope Pius XII, "Evangelii Praecones," *Acta Apostolicae Sedis 43* (1951), 497-528. English text in *Selected Documents of His Holiness Pope Pius XII - 1939-1958* (Washington, D.C.: National Catholic Welfare Conference, 1959).

64 "La Solennita della Pentecoste" (June 1, 1941), ##200-201, in Donal Dorr, *Option for the Poor* (Maryknoll, New York: Orbis, 1983), 83.

65 Anne Freemantle, ed., *The Papal Encyclicals in Their Historical Context* (New York: Mentor, 1956), 137.

66 Pope Pius XII, "Discourse of December 24, 1942," in *Acta Apostolicae Sedis 35* (1943), 17.

67 Jean-Yves Calvez, S.J., and Jacques Perrin, S.J., *The Church and Social Justice* (Chicago: Henry Regnery Co., 1961), 193.

68 Nazareno Padellaro, *Portrait of Pius XII*, trans. Michael Derrich (New York: E.P. Dutton, 1957), 214.

69 Pope Pius XII, "Discourse of December 24, 1942," 17.

70 Pope John XXIII, "Mater et Magistra," (May 15, 1961), in *Acta Apostolicae Sedis 53* (1961), 401-64. English text in *The Gospel of Peace and Justice*, Joseph Gremillion, presenter (Maryknoll, New York: Orbis, 1976), 143-200. "Pacem in Terris" (April 11, 1963), in *Acta Apostolicae Sedis 55* (1963), 257-304. English text in *The Gospel of Peace and Justice*, 201-41.

71 Adolf A. Berle, *Power Without Property* (New York: Harcourt, Brace, and World, 1959), 11.

72 Curran, 189-94.

73 John F. Cronin, S.S., *The Social Teaching of Pope John XXIII* (Milwaukee: Bruce, 1963), 15.

74 Jean-Yves Calvez, S.J., *The Social Thought of John XXIII* (Chicago: Regnery, 1964), 4.

75 Calvez, 33.

76 Calvez, 24.

77 Cronin, *The Social Teaching of Pope John XXIII*, 37-38.

78 Pavan (1903-), elevated to the rank of cardinal in 1985, was a professor at the University of Lateran and an expert in theology at the Second Vatican Council. He has written on, among other subjects, the role of the laity after Vatican II and on religious liberty. He was involved in the writing of *Mater et Magistra*.

79 Calvez, 16.

80 Calvez, 23-24.

81 "Gaudium et Spes" (December 8, 1965), in *Acta Apostolicae Sedis 58* (1966), 1025-1115. English text in *The Documents of Vatican II*, Walter M. Abbott, ed. (New York: America Press, 1966), 199-308.

82 Donald Campion, S.J., "The World-Wide Response," in *Challenge of Mater et Magistra*, ed. Joseph N. Moody (New York: Herder and Herder, 1963), 169.

83 Richard Horchler, "The Church's 'Yes' and 'No' to the World," in *Eyes on the Modern World* (New York: P.J. Kennedy, 1965), 19.

84 Donald Quinn, "Man's Social Relationships to a Changing World," in *Eyes on the Modern World*, 75-76.

85 François Mally, O.P., *Le Père Lebret: L'Economie Au Service des Hommes* (Paris: Les Éditions du Cerf, 1968), 247.

86 Peter J. Riga, *The Church Made Relevant* (Notre Dame, Indiana: Fides Publishers, 1967), 15.

87 Gregory Baum, O.S.A., "Commentary," in *Pastoral Constitution on the Church in the Modern World 2* (New York: Paulist Press, 1967), 12.

88 Riga, 40.

89 Riga, 39.

90 Riga, 231.

91 Riga, 44.

92 Riga, 232.

93 Donald Campion, S.J., "Commentary," in *Pastoral Constitution on the Church in the Modern World*, 55.

94 Riga, 233.

95 Riga, 246.

[96] Riga, 234-35.

[97] Riga, 22.

[98] Riga, 249.

[99] Riga, 229.

[100] Riga, 56.

[101] Riga, 252.

[102] Roger Charles and Drosten Maclaren, *The Social Teaching of Vatican II: Its Origin and Development* (San Francisco: Ignatius, 1982), 308.

[103] Riga, 261.

A BIOGRAPHICAL SKETCH OF GIOVANNI BATTISTA MONTINI FROM 1897-1963

I. INTRODUCTION TO CHAPTER

It is helpful at this point to take a look at the life and thought of Paul VI prior to his assuming the papacy in 1963. His upbringing, life experience, education, and career in the Church reveal a predisposition and willingness to deal with social issues which he would incorporate into his papacy. And his social pronouncements as pope, including his teaching on property, were rooted in and influenced not just by the papal social teaching tradition, but also by the colleagues he worked with and befriended as a priest and bishop, and by a number of important events in his life.

This chapter will not attempt a detailed biography of Montini. Several are available to the reader.[1] Rather it will highlight those aspects of his life up until 1963 which seem likely to have informed and influenced the direction of his social teaching as pope. Selections from his writings and speeches as a bureaucrat and bishop will be also be analyzed to detect the outlines of what would be his papal social teaching and property teaching.

This chapter is subdivided into four main parts. The first is strictly biographical, and will call attention to significant persons and events in the life of Montini. A topical exposition of Montini's thoughts on Christian anthropology, topics related to the property teaching, and the property teaching itself are contained in the second, third, and fourth parts.

II. BIOGRAPHICAL SKETCH OF MONTINI

A. Historical setting

1. Montini's early years

Giovanni Battista Montini was born September 26, 1897 in the village of Concesio, in the northern Italian province of Brescia. His father Giorgio was a journalist whose newspaper, *Il Cittadino*, attempted to implement *Rerum Novarum*, and a politician who had earned a law degree but never practiced law. Giorgio Montini was deeply involved in the Catholic lay movement, and was among the founders of the first Catholic trade unions.[2] Clancy makes the claim that Giorgio Montini profoundly influenced his son: "(Giovanni's) gifts as an organizer, his involvement in social questions, his commitment to all the aspects of modern life - these were to come from his father, as in his home he received the most modern of educations, free from the narrowness and provincial flavor which characterized so many homes in those years before the First World War." [3] His mother, Giuditta Alghisi Montini, was also an activist, and she was known for her generosity to the poor.[4]

Montini was a sickly child and teenager; he was educated at home and attended the diocesan seminary only when his health permitted. Still he was an excellent, hard-working student who took an interest in theology, philosophy, literature, and canon law. His work for the Vatican, however, would prevent him from earning a degree until the 1940s.[5]

Although he failed the physical exam for military service, in World War I Montini worked in civilian assistance programs for the wounded.[6]

After his ordination to the priesthood in 1920 Montini continued his studies at the Gregorian University in Rome. During this time he volunteered to do priestly work among the migrant workers on the outskirts of the city and the poor in the Trastevere, and he worked with the St. Vincent de Paul Society in the Porta Metronia.[7] Jean Guitton notes that even as a young priest Montini had a deep interest in matters both within and outside the Church: "Young Montini, although a seminarian, although a priest, knew he was an Italian citizen and through Italy was associated with the world of nations."[8]

2. Career in the Vatican

In 1925 Montini was assigned to the office of Extraordinary Ecclesiastical Affairs in the Papal Secretariat of State. The Secretary of State at the time was the formidable Cardinal Pietro Gasparri (1852-1934), who would hold the position from 1914 to 1929, first under Pope Benedict XV during World War I, and then under Pius XI. Montini's immediate superior in the Office of Extraordinary Ecclesiastical Affairs was Mgr. Eugenio Pacelli, the future Pope Pius XII. The two would remain collaborators until Montini was appointed Archbishop of Milan in 1954 by Pius XII.

At this time Montini also served as spiritual advisor to the Roman branch of the Italian Federation of Catholic University Students (FUCI). Montini made a habit of taking his students to some of the worst slums in and around Rome and ministering to the poor there. Some of the student leaders of FUCI in the 1920s would eventually become members of the Christian Democratic party and leaders of Italy after World War II.[9]

The students of FUCI were viewed with suspicion and hostility by the Fascist government, and there were frequent clashes. One of the most violent took place at Macerata in central Italy in 1926. A group of Catholic students, with Montini leading them, were ambushed and attacked by a group of Fascists, and several students required medical care.[10]

In the 1920s Montini also helped organize a Catholic publishing house. He did this because, according to Gonzalez and Perez, he was interested in "giving Catholic thought a modern bent, a new cultural framework, a broader diffusion, a coherent and progressive application."[11] Montini also translated Jacques Maritain's *The Three Reformers* for the Catholic students - an indication of his dedication to the intellectual life, and an early sign of his great personal regard for Maritain and his thought.[12]

Upon the retirement of Gasparri in 1929, Pacelli was named Secretary of State, and Montini was named his assistant. The two worked very closely during the 1930s; Pallenberg describes Montini as Pacelli's "right-hand man."[13]

When Pacelli was elected to succeed Pius XI in 1939, Montini and Mgr. Domenico Tardini (1888-1961) were appointed assistants to the new Secretary of State, Cardinal Luigi Maglione (1877-1944). During this time the Church had to deal with totalitarian regimes in several countries - Fascism in Italy, Nazism in Germany, and Communism in the Soviet Union. Although the Vatican, and Pius XII in particular, were critical of Fascism and Nazism, these regimes were tolerated because they were anti-Communist.

With the outbreak of World War II Montini was charged with the dual roles of diplomat and coordinator of refugee services and relief work for the Vatican. The relief and refugee efforts were gargantuan - by the end of the war 885 people worked for Montini, and they handled almost 10 million requests for help. Millions of meals were served to the hungry (1.8 million in 1944 alone), and some 15,000 homeless persons were sheltered in the papal villa at Castel Gandolfo at one time or another.[14] Silvio Negro, a writer and friend of Montini, commented that "the entire government of the universal Church during the difficult years of World War II, went through the hands of Montini."[15]

In 1943 the Vatican Secretariat of State intervened to keep Rome an open city free from military installations. This effort was largely successful, although Pius XII and Montini twice personally ministered to victims of Allied bombings of San Lorenzo, a suburb of Rome.[16]

Montini established personal ties with the French neo-Thomist Jacques Maritain in 1944 through the *Renouveau Catholique* movement in France. A year later Maritain was named French ambassador to the Vatican. Barrett stated that "the two men met on many areas of thought, common to both of them, and they spent much time together."[17] Also in 1944 Montini arranged for Mgr. Angelo Roncalli to be named papal nuncio to France. Roncalli greatly respected his superior Montini, and the two would become close collaborators upon Roncalli's election to the papacy in 1958.[18]

After the war Montini remained deeply involved in social issues. Although he was not named Secretary of State following the death of Cardinal Maglione in 1944 because Pius XII decided to lead this department himself, he worked even more closely with the pope over the next ten years. As head of the Ordinary Affairs section of the Secretariat of State he helped organize the Pontifical Work of Assistance for the poor, and the Association of Christian Workers (ACLI).

During this period Montini took a series of stands on controversial social and political issues which were regarded with suspicion in Rome. He was a strong early supporter of the priest-worker movement in France, in which priests lived outside of church rectories and worked at jobs not traditionally considered priestly work. His reputation suffered when the movement was discredited.[19]

Even more controversial was his position regarding the "turn to the left" in European politics. It was generally believed that Montini had persuaded Pius XII to give the Church's active support to the liberals of the Christian Democrat parties in Europe, which supported concrete programs for social reform.[20] Montini supported the Christian Democrats of Alcide de Gaspari in the Italian election campaign of 1948. But in 1954 the Christian Democrats, whose ranks included Marxists, lost some local elections. That same year Montini was appointed by Pius XII, his colleague of many years, to be Archbishop of Milan, perhaps at the suggestion of the so-called conservative "pentagon" within the Curia.[21]

3. Archbishop of Milan

Milan was a modern industrial city facing the problems of urbanization, class tension, and a large population in poverty. The new archbishop made it clear from the very beginning that under his leadership the Church would confront these social problems head-on. On the day of his arrival in Milan he had 1,200 of the city's poor as his guests for dinner. In the sermon at his installation Mass he said: "Wherever there is suffering or injustice or legitimate aspiration for social improvement there will be the frank and solid defense of a pastor and father." [22] He celebrated his first Christmas Mass in a wood and tin shanty rather than in the splendor of the Duomo, the cathedral of Milan.

Archbishop Montini paid particular attention to the workers of Milan, many of whom were only nominally Catholic, by encouraging them to pursue their rights and to return to the Church. Knowing full well that there were many Communists among the working class of the city, he reached out in a genuine effort at dialogue with all the workers. In the first week after his consecration he visited the most heavily Communist area of the diocese, the factory at Sesto San Giovanni, known as "little Leningrad." After overcoming the silent hostility of the workers as he entered the factory, Montini addressed them at length. He assured them that the Church was not blindly allied with the capitalists, and said that he hoped his ministry would enable him "to dissipate the misunderstanding which some individuals want to create between the Church and the working class." [23] Clancy noted Montini's "directness, his identification with the workers, his obvious affection for them, his sharply articulated social messages, his tireless pursuit of his people." [24] Montini's concern for the working class was twofold - he wanted their rights to be secured, and he wanted them to return to the faith.

Montini paid a price for his notoriety as the "Archbishop of the Workers," however, as the right wing resented his outreach to the left. Their hostility peaked when, in January 1956, his residence was bombed by members of the neo-Fascist party.[25]

The death of Pius XII in 1958 brought the College of Cardinals together to elect a successor. Montini was considered a candidate even though he was not a cardinal, having declined Pius XII's offer of cardinal in 1953. Still, the election of Cardinal Angelo Roncalli was considered a victory for the "Montinians," who were progressive, reform-minded, defenders of the workers, and liberal in Italian politics.[26]

Pope John XXIII's surprise announcement early in 1959 of his intention to convene a second Vatican Council received a mixed reaction from the Catholic hierarchy, but Montini was one of its early and avid supporters. There are at least two reasons for this. Gonzalez and Perez suggested that John XXIII may have consulted with his former superior Montini before calling the Council.[27] And since John XXIII and Montini knew each other well, Montini very likely felt assured that the Council would move in a direction that he himself could support, especially in the social field.

Montini exercised a powerful influence over the preparations for the Council. Many bishops consulted with him in Milan either on their way to or from Rome.[28] He was the only bishop invited by John XXIII to live in the Vatican during the Council, which gave him easy access to the Pope.[29] Murphy stated that "John relied heavily on Montini for advice and counsel in setting up Vatican II." [30]

The first session of the Council also reflected the influence of Montini. He reportedly helped prepare John XXIII's remarkable opening address to the Council in October 1962.[31] During the course of the first session he maintained contacts with bishops from all over the world. His "Letter from the Council" to the people of Milan in December 1962 suggested some procedural revisions for the Council which were accepted by John XXIII.[32] Although he addressed the full body only twice during the first session, his second intervention, delivered near the end of the session on the subject of the Church, was considered crucial to the Council's deliberations.[33] Gonzalez and Perez stated that "when (Montini) spoke or wrote, the Council Fathers perhaps had the impression that they were listening to 'an official voice' providing something of an authentic summary of the work that had been accomplished."[34]

The two social encyclicals of John XXIII - *Mater et Magistra* (May 1961) and *Pacem in Terris* (April 1963) broke new ground in the anthropology and content of the social teaching. *Mater et Magistra* seems especially to have been influenced by Montini, because so many of its themes - land reform, legitimacy of unions, the duties of rich countries to help the underdeveloped countries, the right of the state to intervene in economic matters - had already been addressed by Montini in similar fashion.[35] *Pacem in Terris* likewise contained themes which were common to both men.[36]

Cardinal Montini was quickly elected pope in the conclave that met in 1963 after the death of John XXIII. As he had done when he became Archbishop of Milan, Pope Paul VI immediately made known his intention to deal with social issues. In his address at his papal coronation he said: "(The Church) aspires to justice, to a progress that is not merely the precarious suspension of hostilities among nations or among social classes, but that would permit at least an openness and a collaboration among men and peoples in a spirit of reciprocal confidence."[37] And in his first televised address to the world: "The certain order of love for others, a test of love for God, demands of all men a more equal solution of social problems, demands aid and care for underdeveloped countries in which the living standard is often not worthy of human dignity."[38]

One of Paul VI's first official acts was to declare that the Second Vatican Council would continue. This was hardly surprising, given his involvement in the Council under John XXIII. He preserved the fundamental direction of the Council as established by his predecessor, and he continued to be a strong guiding force in its deliberations, particularly in the formulation of the pastoral constitution *Gaudium et Spes.*

B. Anthropology

Montini's philosophy of human nature, revealed in fragmentary form in his writings and speeches, was positive throughout. He believed that a principal source of the great dignity of the human person is Christological - that human dignity flows from the redemptive birth, life, death and resurrection of Jesus. "The universality of the Redemption . . . is among the greatest truths ever announced to humanity. It is at the heart of the modern world's search for unity, for equality among all peoples, brotherhood among men."[39] But Montini's anthropology was intensely humanistic as well. In his conversations with Jean Guitton in *The Pope Speaks*, for example, he told of his attitude "which makes a whole world" of each person he encountered.[40]

C. Topics related to property

1. Economic systems and property

In the 1950s Montini faced a complex and paradoxical economic situation in Italy. Capitalism had brought material prosperity to many - yet it had also alienated a large segment of the working class. Italian Communism was gaining increasingly broad support among the working class because of its promise to better their lives. Yet it threatened totalitarian measures to fulfill that promise.

Montini steered a difficult middle course, neither condemning nor unconditionally condoning either system. He supported capitalism's freedom of initiative, and contrasted it to the excessive state control of Communism: "If the so-called liberal conception is based on serious erroneous principles, no less erroneous and dangerous is the notion which attributes to the state (the power of) a complete levelling of the economic world, for the added reason that it would lead to the crushing and death of fundamental human rights." "The economic world is primarily the creation of the free will of men; it pertains to the state, therefore, to create the conditions which enable private initiative to expand within the limits of the moral order and the common good."[41]

But Montini did not hesitate to criticize the abuses of capitalism. In his speech to the factory workers at Sesto San Giovanni he refuted the notion that the Church was an uncritical supporter of capitalism: "Religion is not an ally of capitalism, which is an oppressor of the people. The first ones to cut adrift from religion were not the laboring men, but the great bosses and the great economists of the last century, who dreamed of founding a progress and a civilization without God and without Christ."[42] He rejected the notion that the economic autonomy of capitalism included autonomy from morality. And he decried the idea that the material prosperity produced by capitalism leads persons to true happiness.[43]

Montini adopted a similar middle position on Communism. He was negative about the limitations to freedom imposed by Communism, yet he believed in its advocacy of the workers.

Montini continually warned of the dangers inherent in Communist ideology. At various times he referred to Communism as "slavery,"[44] a "mirage,"[45] and even a "menace."[46] He believed that Communism exchanged the promise of material prosperity and equality for the surrender of personal freedom: "(Communists) crush their adversaries. Where they prevail, liberty is gone. If they won, we would all be crushed."[47]

Montini also strongly disagreed with Communism's call for class struggle. He felt that the Church rather than the Communists should take the leading role in promoting the rights of workers. On many occasions he pledged to personally serve as an advocate for the working class, as on the feast of Epiphany in 1955: "It will be my care to cooperate so that instead of a field of battle, labor will become a terrain of sincere and peaceful human encounters of the classes to increase the common good and to give wherever there is suffering or injustice or legitimate aspiration for social improvement, the frank and solid defense of a pastor and a father."[48]

2. Principles and strategies of actualization

In expressing his wonderment at the achievements of social and economic activity, Montini gave credit to both labor and management, and he was a persistent advocate of peaceful relations between the two. Yet he felt a special affinity for the working class, especially during his days in Milan. The "Archbishop of the Workers" consistently made it clear that the Church stood shoulder to shoulder with workers in their struggle for justice. In 1958 he addressed the Eighth National Week of Pastoral Renewal in these words: "Nor must we ever submit in silence to calumnious assertions that because the Church has condemned Communist atheism, as was her duty, she is an enemy of the working classes and supports a regime whose laws and social organization aim to prevent the bettering of these classes."[49] He believed that the Church should take the initiative in reaching out to the working class, to attract them back to the Church and away from Communism. "The world of labor waits to see if our social action is merely deceptive propaganda or is, instead, an actual force towards its redemption. Certainly, the force is actual. But it must become efficacious . . . able above all to dissipate the enormous misunderstanding between labor and religion."[50]

Milan was the chief industrial city in Italy when Montini came there as archbishop in 1954. He accepted industrialization as a necessary aspect of Italy's economic development. Yet he was concerned about its effects on the worker. The Church, he believed, should not be too closely allied with capitalism because it had all too frequently abused the working class. At the same time the "Archbishop of the Workers" reached out in dialogue and action to the Communist workers, in his desire to bring them back to the faith. Montini viewed the atheism of Communist ideology as an affront to the human dignity of the worker.

Montini believed that, while the temporal and spiritual spheres have their own proper autonomy, there is a relationship of interdependence between the two. Society functions most effectively, he said, when each sphere operates fully according to its identity: "Thus the christian mission is neither a simple statement of a few principles which the philosophical evolution of human thought can make its own, nor is it a vague spiritualism designed either to intoxicate our emotions or narcotize our suffering." [51]

At the same time Montini lamented the growing pre-eminence of the temporal order, and the prevailing attitude that the material world is sufficient for the fulfillment of persons. In his pastoral letter to the Archdiocese of Milan in 1957 he spoke to this issue:

> "Thus the act of producing things has triumphed: industry and commerce have surrounded modern man with such an abundance of sophisticated material riches that he is constantly tempted to give way to the intoxicating illusion that he is happy, and to believe that the whole circle of objective reality - his world, and of subjective satisfaction - his spirit, can be summed up in this wonderful, heady temporal experience. And so man has barred his own way out of his vast materialistic cage. He has forgotten and denied his God." [52]

Montini believed in the primacy of the religious dimension of Christianity over any other, including action to improve the temporal order.

Montini addressed the issue of the relationship of economics and religion on several occasions, and the thrust of his argument was always the same. Economics, he said, is an autonomous and necessary part of life, with its own laws and methods. Yet it must never be divorced from the demands of the moral and spiritual life: "A subtler formula of the same kind is, 'The economy is autonomous and sovereign; it cannot be subject to moral scruples; we must make a free economy.' By 'free' they mean an economy determined solely by the intrinsic laws of self-advantage and the play of the market. These people do not consider that the economy is also a human factor and should obey human laws."[53] In his book *The Christian in the Material World* he added that "religion is indispensable in the life of man even in the domain of economics."[54]

The world's poor were a constant concern of Montini, and his pastoral zeal for the poor was matched by his words. In his Christmas day sermon of 1957 he stated simply and directly: "These are (Christ's) favored ones: the needy, the suffering, the persecuted."[55] And at the very beginning of his papacy he expressed his personal attitude toward the poor: "I embrace with a father's love all those who suffer: those who are ill, those who are poor, those who are in prison, those who are in exile, those who are refugees."[56]

While he spoke of the necessity of meeting the basic material needs of all, Montini also cited the need for poverty of spirit. He believed that material deprivation was not good in itself, but that it could find meaning as a reflection of Christian poverty of spirit.[57] Poverty of spirit, expressed through simplicity of life, was a necessary part of the Christian life. This evangelical poverty amounted to a "denial of the primacy of the economic and of the capacity of temporal goods to satisfy the heart of man."[58]

Montini projected a positive attitude toward the rapidly evolving world around him. He believed that Christians were in a position to assume roles of leadership in that world: ". . . our Catholic formation should predispose us to understand and foster the significant currents of modern civilization and progress."[59] Rather than escape from or remain outside the cultural mainstream, Christians should have a love for "our own age, our own civilization, our own technology, our art, our sports - our entire world."[60]

A theme which would become prominent in his social teaching as pope was Montini's stress on the urgency of the social question. In

The Christian in the Material World he noted the urgency of the Church's teaching on material goods.[61] And Clancy detected a note of urgency about the problems of the world's poor in two of Paul VI's earliest messages as pope.[62]

3. Geographic area of application

There are points of emphasis in his social teaching as pope which found an earlier echo in the writings of Montini. One was his awareness of the international scope of the social question: "For today we have all become citizens of the world, and our neighbor may be someone far from us geographically."[63] And in a letter to Bishop Gonzalez Menendez-Reigada of Cordova during the 14th Spanish Social Week: "The topic of your deliberations, housing problems, could not be more opportune. It is not a local problem nor even a national one: you are dealing with a universal problem of manifest gravity . . ."[64]

D. The property teaching

In *The Christian in the Material World* Montini affirmed the Thomistic distinction concerning property: that every person has the right to some property, and that all property must have a relationship to its public use.[65] On more than one occasion he pointed out that the Christian's attitude toward temporal goods ought to be "optimistic; friendly, not hostile; admiring and sympathetic, not scandalized or alarmed."[66]

Although he usually addressed the related issue of the distribution of goods only on the personal level, he explicitly called for a more just distribution of goods on a worldwide scale on more than one occasion. For example, writing on behalf of Pope Pius XII to the 26th Italian Catholic Social Week in September 1953, Montini said, concerning the problem of overpopulation, that the demands of social justice obliged the wealthy nations to assist those which were not.[67]

There is no reason to doubt that Montini accepted the definition of property as it had evolved since *Rerum Novarum*. In particular he advocated a just wage for the workers of Milan, so that they could acquire a sufficient amount of material goods to satisfy their own needs and those of their families.

Montini did not consider material possessions to be good in and of themselves: "It is the use we make of (material goods) which determines them as good or bad." [68] Nor did he believe in the sufficiency of merely material progress: "Temporal goods can certainly help the full development of man, but they do not constitute the ideal of human perfection nor the essence of social progress." [69]

Yet Montini also seems to have been somewhat skeptical of property, seeing in it a potential source of many problems. On one occasion he said that ownership necessitated a "mine" and a "yours" which created division, imbalance, and distance between persons.[70] He believed that material goods are a temptation because they foster "a fatal illusion: that the goods of this world are the ultimate and supreme purpose of human activity, that they are its paradise, its happiness." [71] The Church, he said, had constantly warned of the "moral and social dangers of selfish wealth." [72]

To avoid these dangers, Montini believed that the possession of material goods should be seen as an "opportunity of service, to be made use of in accordance with the brotherly love that knows that it is better to give than to receive." [73]

Montini believed the primary role of the state in securing economic rights was to institutionalize them in law. For example, in upholding the right to property he wrote: ". . . it is indispensable that the legal prescriptions which define and protect the property of economic goods, their production and their distribution, be rigorously observed." [74] And on another occasion, while writing on the subject of housing: "One way to contribute to the desired solution of this problem would be to draft tax laws more favorable to urban ownership, designed to protect the legitimate rights of property owners, a protection which would surely be reflected in positive favor of construction." [75]

III. CHAPTER CONCLUSION

Giovanni Battista Montini's upbringing, life experience, education, and career in the Church gave him a well-rounded perspective of the world of the twentieth century, and of the Church's place in that world. Here was a man at home in two worlds, the religious and the secular.

On the one hand he was steeped in the traditions of the Roman Catholic Church. Montini was born into a deeply religious family. He entered the seminary as a young man, and his theological education there was entirely traditional. Early in his priestly career, after serving as chaplain of a Catholic student organization, he became a part of the Vatican bureaucracy and remained in it for almost thirty years. After being elevated to the episcopacy and assigned as ordinary of Milan, he was eventually elected pope.

On the other hand Montini came in contact throughout his life with persons, events, and forces which helped to shape the political, economic, and social dynamics of the twentieth century. His parents were social and political activists, and viewed their activism as a necessary dimension of their Catholic faith. As the young chaplain of FUCI he influenced many of the future Christian Democrat leaders of Italy. Confrontations with a hostile Fascist party gave him first-hand experience of authoritarian political regimes and their propensity for repression and violence. In his position at the Vatican Secretariat of State he was exposed to many of the persons who would shape international events before, during, and after the Second World War. During the war he directed the Church's refugee effort, and more than once personally ministered to victims of the war. He served as Archbishop of Milan, a cosmopolitan city where political and class conflicts engaged him much of the time. And he became pope during the era of *aggiornamento*, a time of interior renewal within the Church and of dialogue with the world outside it.

Montini's sense of religious tradition and of modernity are reflected as well in his speechings and writings as a Vatican bureaucrat and bishop. Several key themes would reappear in his social teaching as pope, and would affect the direction of his teaching on property.

His Christian anthropology would become the methodological framework for Montini's social teaching as pope. He had a Christological and yet humanistic vision of the human person, one which exalted the dignity of each individual. This positive anthropology was reflected in his words about the world's poor. Often he spoke of the need to identify with the brother or sister in poverty, and to adopt a lifestyle of material and spiritual poverty.

The sense of tradition and of modernity in Montini were also reflected in his critique of capitalism and Communism. He supported those aspects of these ideologies - capitalism's emphasis on personal freedom and initiative, and Communism's identification with the working class - which were consistent with the Christian vision of the person and society, and which were most appropriate and timely for modern society. At the same time he criticized capitalism's oppression of the working class, and Communism's denials of personal freedom.

Montini was especially sensitive to the plight of workers during his tenure in Milan. His concerns were twofold - he wanted to secure the rights of the working class, and he hoped to bring them back into the Church.

Montini's speeches and writings manifested his obvious openness to modernity and his grasp of the international range of the world's economic and social problems. He accepted and tried to understand the complex and rapidly changing world, and he examined the world with an open yet critical mind. The Church, he believed, should not be aloof from the world, but active and involved in it, always seeking to challenge and transform it.

Yet while he believed that Christians must engage in social, economic, and political activity, he also maintained that these kinds of activity by themselves were insufficient to bring about genuine personal fulfillment and social progress. He held that the realm of the spirit must be pre-eminent in personal and social life. This theme would re-emerge most forcefully in *Evangelii Nuntiandi*, his last major social document.

Many of Montini's thoughts on the property question would later be incorporated into his property teaching as pope. He concurred with the traditional Thomistic teaching on the primacy of the social function of property, and he focused on the right of all persons to share in the good things of the world. In particular he called attention to the contemporary problem of the maldistribution of goods worldwide. His attitude toward material possessions combined an optimism founded on the belief that the material world was created by God, with a skepticism based on the potential of property for evil and self-centeredness. The state's role, he said, was to promote social justice by institutionalizing property rights within the law.

Habiger devotes one chapter of his book to the property teaching of Paul VI, and just one page of that chapter to the life and career of Montini.[76] This study has devoted an entire chapter to Montini's background, in order to understand in depth this crucial component of the historical background of his papal property teaching.

This essay is in total agreement with Habiger's contention that Paul VI was eminently qualified to address the social question. However, the only supporting evidence Habiger cites concerning Montini's qualifications is that he was archbishop of Milan, and that he toured the United States and Africa prior to his becoming pope.[77] The present chapter of this study has been devoted in its entirety to the life, education, bureaucratic and episcopal careers, and the speeches and writings of Montini on the social question. One would expect this to be the case, given that the principal focus of this study is the property teaching of Paul VI, while Habiger deals with the papal property teaching from Leo XIII to John Paul II.

Just as there were significant persons and events which affected Giovanni Battista Montini, there were intellectuals with whom he interacted and who helped to shape his property teaching. Their thoughts on the social teaching tradition, their influence on the man who would become Pope Paul VI, and his influence on them will be considered in the next chapter.

NOTES - CHAPTER TWO

1 There are several popular biographies of Pope Paul VI available in English. Among them are William E. Barrett, *Shepherd of Mankind* (Garden City, New York: Doubleday, 1964); John Clancy, *Apostle for Our Time* (New York: Kennedy and Sons, 1963); J. L. Gonzalez and T. Perez, *Paul VI* (Boston: St. Paul, 1964); Corrado Pallenberg, *Pope Paul VI* (New York: Putnam's Sons, 1968); James Walsh, S.J., *The Mind of Paul VI* (Milwaukee: Bruce, 1964). Also see Francis X. Murphy, "A Brief Biography of Paul VI," in *Paul VI: Critical Appraisals*, ed. James F. Andrews (New York: Bruce, 1972). Another helpful, if not entirely biographical source is Jean Guitton, *The Pope Speaks* (New York: Meredith Press, 1968).

2 Pallenberg, 14-17.

3 Clancy, 7.

4 Clancy, 8.

5 Pallenberg, 27.

6 Murphy, 136.

7 Barrett, 79-81.

8 Guitton, 34.

9 Among them were Aldo Moro, Giovanni Gronchi, Mario Scelba, Giulio Andreotti, Paolo Taviani, and Giuseppe Spataro. In Gonzalez and Perez, 150.

10 Pallenberg, 35.

11 Gonzalez and Perez, 160.

12 Murphy, 138.

13 Pallenberg, 41.

14 Pallenberg, 53-54.

15 Gonzalez and Perez, 165.

16 Pallenberg, 65-66.

17 Barrett, 206-7.

18 Pallenberg, 82.

19 Clancy, 73.

20 Clancy, 95 (footnote).

21 The members of the "pentagon" were Cardinals Pizzardo and Micara, and Mgrs. Tardini, Ottaviani, and Ruffini. In Murphy, 140.

22 Clancy, 104.

23 Gonzalez and Perez, 186.

24 Clancy, 104.

25 Pallenberg, 99.

26 Pallenberg, 111.

27 Gonzalez and Perez, 224.

28 Gonzalez and Perez, 261.

29 Gonzalez and Perez, 260.

30 Murphy, 141.

31 Clancy, 149 (footnote).

32 Gonzalez and Perez, 274-77.

33 Gonzalez and Perez, 272.

34 Gonzalez and Perez, 279.

35 Pallenberg, 121.

36 Pallenberg, 121.

37 Clancy, 202.

38 Clancy, 211.

39 Walsh, 4.

40 Guitton, 19.

41 "Letter to the Italian Social Week," in *Catholic Mind 51* (January 1953), 55.

42 Gonzalez and Perez, 204.

43 Walsh, 83.

44 Walsh, 139.

45 Francis Bruce, "The Archbishop of the Workers," *The Sign 34* (May 1955), 15.

46 In *Catholic Mind 52* (September 1954), 560.

47 Archbishop Giovanni Battista Montini, "The Christian and the New Society," *Jubilee 4* (March 1957), 4.

48 Bruce, 15.

49 Walsh, 47.

50 Montini, "The Christian and the New Society," 32.

51 Cardinal Giovanni Battista Montini, *The Church* (Baltimore: Helicon, 1964), 32.

52 Walsh, 83.

53 Walsh, 103.

54 Cardinal Giovanni Battista Montini, *The Christian in the Material World*, Rev. Michael M. McManus, trans. (Baltimore: Helicon, 1964), 33.

55 Walsh, 5.

56 From a sermon delivered at the Cathedral of Frascati (September 1, 1963), in *Dialogues by Paul VI*, translated and arranged by John Clancy (New York: Trident, 1965), 6.

57 Walsh, 195.

58 Montini, *The Christian in the Material World*, 29.

59 Walsh, 49.

60 Montini, *The Church*, 46.

61 Montini, *The Christian in the Material World*, 63.

62 Clancy, *Apostle for Our Time*, 216-217.

63 Montini, *The Christian in the Material World*, 64.

64 Archbishop Giovanni Battista Montini, "Letter to the 14th Spanish Social Week," *Catholic Mind 53* (April 1955), 253.

65 Montini, *The Christian in the Material World*, 49.

66 Walsh, 192.

67 Bishop Giovanni Battista Montini, "Letter to the 26th Italian Social Week", *Catholic Documents 13* (November 1953), 36.

68 Montini, *The Christian in the Material World*, 34.

69 Montini, *The Christian in the Material World*, 22-23.

70 Clancy, *Dialogues by Paul VI*, 49.

71 Clancy, *Dialogues by Paul VI*, 43.

72 Clancy, *Apostle for Our Time*, 103.

73 Walsh, 150.

74 Montini, *The Christian in the Material World*, 50-51.

75 Archbishop Giovanni Battista Montini, "Housing Problems," in *Catholic Mind 53* (April 1955), 254.

76 Matthew Habiger, O.S.B., *Papal Teaching on Private Property: 1891-1981* (Lanham, Maryland: University Press of America, 1990), 246.

77 Habiger, 246.

INTELLECTUAL INFLUENCES ON POPE PAUL VI'S SOCIAL TEACHING

I. INTRODUCTION TO CHAPTER

Each of the papal social encyclicals examined in this paper has been a product, in part, of the intellectual climate of its time. Thinkers representing a variety of schools of thought have sought to influence the direction of the social teaching, and there have been both contradictions and complementarity in their positions.

Pope Leo XIII was courted by the anti-capitalists whose spokesperson was Baron von Vogelsang, the so-called "Fribourg circle" of Cardinal Mermillod, the paternalistic reformers such as La Tour du Pin and Harmel, and the "social Catholics" who were disciples of Bishop von Ketteler. *Quadragesimo Anno* reflected the corporatist and strongly anti-socialist views of Nell-Breuning, Pesch, and Gundlach, but Pius XI also attended to the views of German and Austrian socialists, members of the German Center Party, and Fascists in Italy and Spain. The early pronouncements of Pius XII were heavily influenced by the German Jesuit Gundlach.

In the years after World War II the intellectual climate within and outside the Church changed in several significant respects. The traditional neo-Thomism of the first half of the 1900s, a product of the Church's reaction to the modernist controversy at the turn of the century, was challenged and tempered by the emerging existentialist, personalist, and process philosophies. After Pius XII issued the encyclical *Divino Afflante Spiritu* in 1943, which gave

Catholic scholars the freedom to apply the methods of modern literary criticism to the Scriptures,[1] Catholic theology regained a more scriptural orientation. Sociology and psychology came to be respected as legitimate disciplines by Rome, while other fields of study, such as history and economics, were incorporated into theological methodology. The social sciences exerted considerable influence on the methodology and content of papal social teaching beginning with Pope John XXIII.[2]

This was the intellectual climate to which Mgr. Giovanni Montini was exposed, as a bureaucrat with a scholarly bent in the late 1940s, and as archbishop of Milan after 1954. Montini did more than passively observe this rapidly evolving and challenging new intellectual situation. He embraced it, immersed himself in it, and became an active participant in it. His social teaching as pope would reflect both the traditional orientation of his formal education and the progressive intellectual developments of the postwar years.

This chapter will focus on three of the thinkers who most influenced the direction of Montini's thought on subjects related to the social teaching in general, and the property teaching in particular - Jacques Maritain (1882-1973), Louis J. Lebret, O.P. (1897-1966), and Pierre Bigo, S.J. (1906-). Montini was exposed to Maritain as early as 1932, when he translated the book *Three Reformers*. In 1945 Maritain was named French ambassador to the Vatican, and Barrett wrote that over the three years Maritain served as ambassador "the two men met on many areas of thought, common to both of them, and they spent much time together." [3] The Dominican Lebret and the Jesuit Bigo, both from France, represent the interdisciplinary thinking adopted by a growing number of Catholic intellectuals in the 1950s. Their influence on the thinking of Paul VI was acknowledged by Coleman when he mentioned their contribution to the authorship of *Populorum Progressio*. Bigo himself has stated that the work of Lebret was the inspiration for *Populorum Progressio*.[4]

Certainly there were other prominent theologians and intellectuals to whom Montini paid close attention. This chapter will focus on Maritain, Lebret, and Bigo for two reasons. First, Montini greatly respected their thinking. This has already been noted and will be documented further in the chapter. The second has to do with their respective disciplines. Besides being theologians, each was a specialist in another field. Maritain was a philosopher, Lebret an economist, and Bigo a political analyst. Together they represent much of the spectrum of critical fields which helped to shape the social teaching of Paul VI.

This chapter will briefly summarize the lives of Maritain, Lebret, and Bigo, and then synopsize their thought in topical fashion. It will discuss their views on Christian anthropology, which determined to a large extent the shape of their property teaching. Their evaluations of capitalism, socialism, and Communism were important since the ownership and distribution of property were understood and effectuated differently in each of these systems. Each had a different understanding of the principles and strategies needed to build the just society, and thoughts about the range of application of their ideas.

The thinking of Maritain, Lebret, and Bigo on the property question is, of course, central to the purpose of this chapter. Included in this discussion will be their notions of the relationship between the right of ownership and the social function of property, the definition of property, the purposes of property, and the role of the state in relation to property.

A methodological note is in order. It has to do with the meaning of "influence" in the context of this chapter. Specifically, what does it mean to say that Maritain, Lebret, and Bigo "influenced" Montini-Paul VI? Is it possible that a concept in Lebret, for example, can be found preserved intact in one of Paul VI's social encyclicals? Perhaps. But such a discovery, or even such a claim, is problematic. The research simply does not exist to validate the claim that Montini read or discussed an idea of Lebret, absorbed and accepted that idea in its entirety, and then incorporated it, without modification, into one of his social documents. The nature of research into papal pronouncements necessitates a more modest claim - that a certain parallelism exists between certain ideas as they appear in Maritain, Lebret, or Bigo and as they are found in the social teaching of Paul VI.

The question of influence, of course, extends in both directions. Not only did Maritain, Lebret, and Bigo influence the thought of Montini on the social question and the property teaching - he influenced them as well. The relationship among these men is best described as interactive.

II. JACQUES MARITAIN (1882-1973)

A. Historical setting

1. Early years and conversions

Jacques Maritain was born in Paris in 1882, the son of Paul Maritain and Genevieve Favre-Maritain. Although his father had little influence on Jacques, his mother's was profound. She had inherited from her father, a French statesman, a strong sense of liberty and of the spiritual possibilities of humanity, and these she passed down to her son.[5]

In his youth Maritain considered himself an unbeliever. But in 1906 he converted to Catholicism under the influence of Leon Bloy (1846-1917) and Henri Bergson (1859-1941). Bloy was a minor Catholic author whose self-professed aim was to purify Christianity of its excessive moralism and base it more on a direct knowledge of God.[6] The philosopher Bergson inspired generations of French intellectuals by offering a way beyond relativism and materialism to a new synthesis of faith and science.[7] Maritain gave up his atheism primarily as a result of Bergson.

A second, intellectual conversion occurred after 1908 when, at the suggestion of his spiritual adviser, Maritain read the *Summa Theologiae* of St. Thomas Aquinas. As Amato wrote: "Here Maritain discovered his career and vocation: 'Woe to me if I don't thomisticize.'"[8] For the rest of his life he revered Aquinas and attempted to apply Thomistic philosophy to contemporary art, politics, and education. He began his teaching career in 1919 as a professor of philosophy at the Institut Catholique de Paris, where he remained until 1933.

2. Social activist and Catholic intellectual

His indirect connection with the *Action Française* movement in 1926 put Maritain in the middle of a controversy with Rome. *Action*

Française, founded in the last years of the nineteenth century, advocated the restoration of the monarchy in France, even though its members were not part of the conservative aristocracy.[9] In the summer of 1926 the Archbishop of Bordeaux published a letter exhorting young people not to get involved in *Action Française*, and Pope Pius XI wrote in support of the archbishop. Maritain was a friend of many in the movement and, although he was never formally connected with *Action Française*, its members had praised his philosophy and his books. When *Action Française* was condemned later in 1926, Maritain wrote a book entitled *Primacy of the Spiritual (or The Things That Are Not Caesar's)* which inspired many both in and outside the movement.[10] Maritain's reputation among the intellectual community in France grew as a result, and his thoughts about a series of human and temporal problems thereafter were given serious consideration.

His dignified outspokenness during the Spanish Civil War in the mid-1930s earned Maritain sharp criticism, especially from Catholics. He rejected Francisco Franco's claim of a holy war, and he refused to believe that the war was a battle of pure good (Catholics and patriots) against pure evil (Communists). His goal, he said, was to promote civil peace between Catholics on both sides.[11]

Maritain befriended Emmanuel Mounier (1905-50), the editor of the periodical *Esprit*, in the 1930s.[12] The two men both promoted and debated social issues. At times Maritain had to intervene to keep *Esprit* from being condemned by Rome for its leftist orientation.

Feeling the need to clarify his vision of the ideal socio-temporal order, Maritain published *True Humanism* in 1936. The book spells out Maritain's idea of the "new Christendom," a society marked by pluralism, civil toleration, an economy freed from capitalist excess, a recognition of the rights of the human person, and a personalist democracy based on the achievement of brotherhood/sisterhood among all people.[13] Maritain's uncompromising and articulate

Thomism earned him many distinguished allies in the fields of theology and philosophy.[14]

Maritain was in New York at the time of the Nazi takeover of France in the summer of 1940. Because he had been an outspoken critic of Nazism for several years, he was forced to remain in New York for the duration of the war. Still, he was a secret supporter of the French resistance movement.[15]

At the conclusion of the war in 1945 Maritain was invited by President Charles de Gaulle to serve as French ambassador to the Vatican, and he held that post until 1948. Also in 1945 Bishop Angelo Roncalli, the future Pope John XXIII, was appointed apostolic delegate to France. The two men worked together on a variety of vexing social and ecclesiastical problems, such as state subsidies to private schools, the rebuilding of churches, the status of the province of Alsace, and the removal of bishops who had collaborated with the Nazis during the war.[16]

During his tenure as ambassador to the Holy See Maritain also befriended Mgr. Giovanni Montini. The two men communicated often during this time, and dined together regularly. Kernan wrote that they were "on especially intimate terms," and noted that when Montini was named Archbishop of Milan in 1954 he "undertook to put into practice much of Jacques Maritain's social philosophy as he devoted himself to the workers and the poor of that great industrial city."[17]

Upon the completion of his three-year term as ambassador Maritain resumed his career as a teacher and lecturer. He taught at Princeton from 1948-1952, and lectured at several other schools, among them Notre Dame and Chicago University.

3. Final years

In 1961, a year after the death of his wife Raissa, Maritain returned to Toulouse to live in retirement with the Little Brothers of Jesus, a Dominican monastic order. In 1969 he entered the order.

Maritain's influence on Montini continued even after the latter became pope. Paul VI would express on many occasions his indebtedness to "my teacher, Jacques Maritain." [18] At the closing session of the Second Vatican Council Paul VI, after the Council's message to intellectuals was delivered, placed the text in the hands of Maritain.[19] Doering noted that Paul VI used Maritain's social and political thought as the foundation for his social encyclicals,[20] and Maritain was cited in *Populorum Progressio.*

At the age of 84 Maritain published his last book, *Peasant of the Garonne* (1967), in which he criticized the Second Vatican Council. While consistent with his philosophy and theology, *The Peasant* was more strident in tone than his other works. He attacked the existentialists, the phenomenologists, the Freudians, the extreme ecumenists, and the Teilhardians, labelling them "neomodernists" for abandoning the primacy of the spiritual and adapting too easily to the modern world and its ways.[21] While insisting that Vatican II had been a call to the temporal mission, he believed that the spiritual dimension should remain paramount, and guide the Church's work in the world.

Jacques Maritain died in Toulouse in 1973, at the age of 91. Paul VI spoke publicly about Maritain upon his death in 1973, and sent his personal secretary to attend Maritain's funeral.[22]

B. Anthropology

Maritain represented an important bridge between the strict natural law framework of the papal social teaching prior to Pope John XXIII and the scriptural, human rights orientation of John XXIII and Paul VI. He was a Thomist, yet his philosophy and theology reflected a biblically-based consciousness of the dignity of the human person and the rights which stem from that dignity. That consciousness emerged in the Church after World War II, in part because of Maritain.

As early as the 1930s Maritain was calling for what he termed a new, "integral" humanism which would "essentially tend to render man more truly human and to make his original greatness manifest by causing him to participate in all that can enrich him in nature and in history."[23] Integral humanism was based on the conviction of the absolute dignity of the human person, which derived from his/her "direct relationship with the Absolute."[24] At the same time integral humanism was inseparable from temporal civilization and culture. With its dual emphases on personal dignity and social participation, integral humanism implied a complementarity and a tension between the personal and the social. The absolute dignity of the person as a creature of God was seen as both the source of personal rights, which it is society's duty to secure, and the source of each person's duty to contribute to the well-being of society. Integral humanism thus transcended both absolute individualism, which too easily overlooked the common good, and an excessive regard for the state, as embodied in totalitarian systems. Integral humanism upheld a positive and balanced relationship between the individual and the common good.

As a Thomist Maritain adhered to the natural law, which he defined as the "order or disposition according to which the human will must act in order to attune itself to the necessary ends of the human being."[25] Consistent with his natural law perspective, Maritain held that the rights of the person flowed from human nature. Because of this he believed that human rights are anterior to civil society - that is, rights existed prior to the creation of societies, because they inhered in human nature. Societies had an obligation to secure the rights of each person, but never the power to grant or establish them.

Natural law philosophy asserted a second essential aspect of human nature - the social dimension. Maritain concurred with the natural law tradition when he said that "man is a social creature by nature, not a monad."[26] He rejected the Enlightenment notion of absolute individualism, and believed that each person by nature had a relationship to society. That relationship involved the promotion of the common good, "the good of each individual and of society as a whole,"[27] and "the betterment of the conditions of human life itself."[28] This meant that the individual had certain obligations as a member of society. Maritain preserved the traditional natural law balance between individual rights and social obligations, which he believed the Enlightenment had obscured.[29]

C. Topics related to property

1. Economic systems and property

Maritain did not reject capitalism outright as a system of production and distribution of material goods, but he was highly critical of it in several ways. He said that capitalism is bound to antihumanist aims: productivity, technology, and money.[30] In particular he found fault with capitalism for reducing the poor person to an instrument of production, and the rich person to merely a consumer.[31] Its inherent materialism did not allow sufficient space for the spiritual in everyday life. For this reason Maritain did not tie his vision of the "new Christendom" to capitalism.[32]

Maritain briefly discussed socialism in his book *True Humanism.* Socialism, he believed, raised a much-needed voice of protest "against evils which cry to heaven" in liberal capitalism. It worked to secure the rights of the working class, and for a better life for the poor.[33]

"Yet the deception (socialism) has caused among men is for all that only the more bitter." This was, he said, because socialism as a theory was based on errors of metaphysics and social philosophy. Its metaphysical flaw was its disregard of the spiritual dimension of the human person. And its social philosophy lacked a sense of the balance between the individual and the common good which Maritain viewed as essential to society. What was required, he concluded, was a radical reconstruction of socialist humanism which would transform it along the lines of his integral humanism.[34]

Maritain was often criticized for his acknowledgement of certain positive aspects of Communism. The liquidation of the profit system and the restoration of the dignity of work were cited as its major accomplishments, and he empathized with its advocacy of the working class.[35] But he also believed that Communism fundamentally distorted Christian values. He criticized its dialectical materialism, which he believed was absolute, its basic contempt for the human person, and its atheism, which he said caused Communism to reject God in the name of the social collectivity.[36] As a result Communism viewed itself as a "secularized Kingdom of God," and was therefore incompatible with the Christian view of society.[37]

2. Principles and strategies of actualization

Maritain believed that the Kingdom of God must be prepared "in the midst of the pains of earthly history." [38] Christians, he said, were required to " work here on earth for a realization in social and temporal terms of the truths of the Gospel." [39]

His term for this visible, historical, societal manifestation of the Kingdom of God was the "new Christendom." This would be, in the words of O'Donnell, "a democratic Christian society which will begin to realize the gains to be obtained in a society governed by justice, caring about human rights and boldly engaged in creating a great commonwealth of peoples." [40] It would be an image of the kind of world Maritain believed intelligent and good persons would like to see made out of the world. It would be based on understanding and love, the grace of God, and the wise exercise of freedom and authority. It would be both communal - ordered to the common good - and personalist - seeking the spiritual good of individuals.[41] It would be led by a "civic fraternity," "the most evolved politically and the most devoted part of the Christian laity." [42]

Maritain proposed the idea of the "new Christendom" as an historical, and not an absolute, ideal. It would strive for social forms consonant with the common good here and now. O'Donnell rightly observed that Maritain cannot be accused of either utopianism or of attempting to resurrect the medieval world of Christendom.[43]

The major characteristic of Maritain's "new Christendom" was pluralism in all aspects of life in society, including the economy. His acceptance of the fact of industrialization was reflected in his advocacy of co-partnership rather than salaries in the sphere of industrial economy. At the same time he called for the maintenance of rural, family-type farms and businesses.[44]

Maritain detailed his position on the relationship of the temporal and religious spheres in *True Humanism.* There he defined Christian humanism as "a theocentric humanism, rooted in what is radical in man: integral humanism, the humanism of the Incarnation." Christian humanism was marked by three characteristics: it involved "self-consciousness according to the Gospels;" it held for the primacy of transcendental values; its goal was to bring about the transformation of society, leading to a "socio-temporal realization of the Gospels."[45]

Maritain's last book, *Peasant of the Garonne*, was noteworthy in part because of its uncharacteristically negative tone. In general he spoke of the need for a hope-filled outlook, one which transcended mere optimism or pessimism.[46]

3. Geographic area of application

By the end of World War II Maritain was calling for the establishment of a "supra-national community" which would be founded on respect for human dignity and the rights of the person.[47] Although he was a proponent of world government, Maritain did not envision a superstate, but rather a federation that would respect the integrity of individual nations.[48] In his later writings Maritain saw the "new Christendom" as an international society.[49]

D. The property question

Maritain believed that the right to private ownership was rooted in the natural law. This meant that ownership was grounded in human nature, in what constituted human personhood.[50] Therefore Maritain considered ownership to be among the fundamental, or natural rights of the person.[51] He also believed, however, that ownership should be widespread, and not concentrated in the hands of just a few as so often happened under liberal capitalism.[52] Material possessions should be ordered to the common good, so that the social function of property would be realized.

In *True Humanism* Maritain discussed two economic concepts which he considered to be forms of property. He viewed the co-proprietorship of the means of production by labor and management as a "form of possession of more human significance." And he understood work as "a form of personal possession, the possession no longer of a thing in space, but of a form of activity in time, the possession of a 'trust' or worker's title, which assures a man that his employment is rightly his." [53]

Maritain sought to purify and ennoble the right to ownership by ordering it to the common good.[54] He placed primary emphasis on the *usus communis*, or right to common use of property, and he advocated a certain collectivization of ownership, so that persons may own "as many things as possible for nothing." [55] And he proposed a policy of ownership intended to insure that "the use of goods individually appropriated must itself serve the common good of all." [56]

Maritain said that the state, because it existed to help make life more human, had a necessary but limited role to play in promoting ownership. Its system of laws should be structured for the purpose of "helping persons acquire material and spiritual goods." [57]

E. Conclusion of section

Jacques Maritain and Giovanni Battista Montini were contemporaries, and in their lifetimes they witnessed, and at times participated in the same dramatic events which have shaped the course of much of the twentieth century. Both were committed to political and social issues, as well as to the Church. Yet Maritain pursued the intellectual life, while Montini worked within the Catholic Church's bureaucracy and hierarchy.

The Christian anthropology of Paul VI, which stressed the dignity, rights, and social duties of the person, was similar to Maritain's "integral humanism" concept. Integral humanism focused on the fulfillment of the whole person through the achievement of rights and duties.

Maritain acknowledged some of the positive elements of socialism and Communism. This represented a major change from the positions of Leo XIII, Pius XI and Pius XII. Paul VI's assessment of these systems was comparable to Maritain's.

According to Maritain the just social order should be embodied in the "new Christendom," a pluralistic, democratic, Church-dominated society. This position was somewhat like, yet more progressive than the corporatism of the early social popes. But by the mid-twentieth century the "new Christendom" concept was an anachronism, and it was never incorporated into the social teaching of Paul VI.

On the property issue Maritain was consistent with the traditional teachings of Aquinas and the social popes up to Pius XII. Still, his emphasis on the ordering of property for the common good was timely, and appeared in the property teaching of John XXIII and Paul VI.

Maritain was deeply committed to the Scholastic tradition, and he analyzed modern economic, social, and political issues in light of that tradition. His major shortcoming may have been that he overestimated the influence of the Catholic Church in the modern world. While he agreed with the general thrust of Maritain's social thinking, Paul VI's social teaching differed in one important respect: it recognized the autonomy of the secular world, and the need for the Church to dialogue with that world rather than try to dominate it.

III. LOUIS J. LEBRET, O.P. (1897-1966)

A. Historical setting

Louis-Joseph Lebret was born in 1897 into a family of sailors who were closely connected to the somewhat agricultural, somewhat maritime peasants of the Minihic-sur-Rance coastal region of France. His exposure to the farmers and sailors of the region prepared him, as he said, to be a "citizen of the world." [58]

His first vocation, not surprisingly, was to the navy. He was preparing for study at the Ecole Navale when he enlisted in the navy in 1915. After a tour of duty on a battleship in World War I, he took up his studies at the Ecole Navale, and graduated in 1917. Lebret was an instructor at the Ecole Navale until 1923, when he left the navy to enter the Order of Preachers.[59]

A trip to St. Malo on the coast of Brittany in 1929 marked the beginning of the activity which was to characterize Fr. Lebret's life. He joined with the fishermen there in dealing with the multiple crises of the industrialization of the fisheries, the internationalization of the fishing industry, and the effects of the Great Depression, and he worked successfully for legislative reform of the sea fisheries in France.[60] His investigations of the fisheries and the fish trade continued, first along the French coast, then throughout Europe and in the Mediterranean basin.

His experience with the fisheries taught Lebret that the economy had to be rethought and rebuilt on more human terms, that the economy should be in the service of humanity.[61] He defined the human economy as "a discipline of thought and action, at once a science and an art, enabling a specific and more or less homogeneous population to pass from a less human to a more human phase, at the fastest rate and at the least cost, considering the inter-related development of all peoples."[62]

Lebret's shift in interest to the problems of world economic development was complete by the early 1940s, when he helped found a study center and a periodical of the same name, *Economie et Humanisme*.[63] Cosmao noted that many of the ideas put forth by the center in the 1940s, particularly those having to do with urbanization and land use, came to fruition in the 1960s.[64]

Lebret's focus sharpened even more after 1947, when he was invited to give a series of lectures on human economy in Brazil. He discovered on this trip the severe problems of the underdeveloped world, and he began to travel extensively through what would come to be known as the Third World to seek solutions to this many-sided crisis.[65] The study of underdevelopment, which he termed "the problem of the century," would absorb him for the rest of his life.[66]

Although his study always began at the local level Lebret was, in the words of Cosmao, "pre-eminently a man for synthesis and world vision."[67] He came to believe that the United Nations and its agencies should be the locus of decision making for international development. The Vatican, recognizing his talent and vision, made him its representative at several international conferences, including the U.N. Conference on Trade and Development in Geneva in 1964, where he delivered an important address on the need for a more equitable distribution of the world's goods.[68]

Pope Paul VI called on Lebret to play a role in the formation of the social teaching. He was named an expert to the Second Vatican Council in 1965, where he worked passionately on the Pastoral Constitution on the Church in the Modern World, *Gaudium et Spes*. At the same time, Cosmao noted that "Pope Paul VI asked him to prepare the draft of an encyclical on the development of nations (which would be *Populorum Progressio*), a work the results of which he never saw, though his philosophy pervades it completely, and the Pope himself presented the encyclical as a 'tribute to his memory.'"[69] Lebret was working for the creation of what would be the Pontifical Commission 'Justice and Peace' at the time of his death in July 1966.[70]

B. Anthropology

Adopting the biblical perspective of "man as the pinnacle of creation," Lebret asserted the need to "assure all men a life worthy of man."[71] By this he meant that each person should have those rights and needs secured which are the preconditions for the attainment of material, social, and spiritual fulfillment.

C. Topics related to property

1. Economic systems and property

Lebret was critical but not condemnatory of capitalism. He praised it for the freedom it gives to the entrepreneur, for the benefits derived from competition and productivity, and for its overall contribution to development, at least in its industrial phase.[72]

Yet for all its strengths, Lebret believed that capitalism was powerless as a means of effective world development. He cited several reasons for this in his book *The Last Revolution.* First, he said capitalism tended toward the profitable rather than toward what is necessary for true development to take place. It focused on blind growth rather than on planned development. Capitalism tried to inhibit industrialization in the underdeveloped nations in order to ensure the dominance of the Western economies. This economic imperialism, he said, had created a dialectical relationship between the developed and developing countries, and had given Communism an opportunity to expand in the developing world. Further, he said that capitalism had led to a serious militarization of the world by making arms readily available to developing nations, when it should be seeking instead the universal common good through humanitarian aid.[73] If capitalism were to survive, he concluded in *Pour Une Civilisation Solidaire*, "it must open itself to the needs of a worldwide solidarity."[74]

Although he criticized various aspects of socialism, Lebret did not reject it outright, as so many Catholic thinkers - and the papal social teaching prior to John XXIII - had done. He criticized what he called socialism's idealism and lack of practicality.[75] But he agreed with socialism's call for a greater *d'organisation collective* in the methods of production and ownership.[76]

The evaluation of Communism on the part of some segments of the Catholic intellectual community and hierarchy changed dramatically in the years after World War II. Some thinkers, including Lebret, began to note the positive aspects of Communist ideology, even while continuing to criticize its materialism and atheism. A distinction came to be made between Communism as an ideology, which on the whole could not be found acceptable in the light of Catholic principles, and Communist movements involving real people in their struggles for economic justice.

It is noteworthy that Lebret's evaluation of Marxism did not include a listing of its "errors," a commonplace in previous Catholic scholarship. In *Human Ascent*, Lebret saw Marxism as a kind of humanism, in that it represents an attempt at the liberation of peoples.[77] He also noted the appeal of its "cry for justice" for the oppressed.[78]

At the bottom line, however, Lebret considered Marxism an "illusory solution" because its humanism was atheistic and materialistic.[79] He said it was incapable of producing the kind of development and society which Christianity envisioned because it overlooked the human and spiritual dimensions of persons. For this reason he concluded that Marxism was ultimately unsatisfactory because it diminished humanity.[80]

2. Principles and strategies of actualization

Having observed and studied the international economic situation for many years, Lebret decried the unequal distribution of goods worldwide, declaring that "humanity is torn apart by a poorly controlled love of goods, that a small number have too much, while the multitude have not enough."[81] His qualified acceptance of socialism was based in part on his conviction that the excessive concentration of wealth in the hands of a few was a negative outcome of purely private ownership.[82] This imbalance had already led to the economic exploitation of many, and could lead eventually to war: "Only a balance in the distribution of material (and spiritual) goods, only a balance between needs and resources will assure world peace by cooperation in justice."[83]

Lebret said that a more just distribution of material goods worldwide was a crucial component in the development effort, and a necessary step toward world peace: "A civilization of betterment, based on the equitable distribution of possessions, is the only one which should be encouraged."[84] "Only a balance in the distribution of material (and spiritual) goods, only a balance between needs and resources will assure world peace by cooperation in justice." [85]

Lebret also believed that every person should have "his share of the necessary food, material goods, light, warmth, tenderness, culture, and truth." [86] He said all people were entitled to their rightful share of the goods of the earth because their human dignity made them worthy of it, and because their fundamental rights entitled them to it. Those who have many possessions, he said, should overcome the avarice which had led to the unjust distribution of goods in the first place.[87]

This theme, which would become a cornerstone of Paul VI's social teaching in *Populorum Progressio*, was treated at great length by Lebret. He said that development, if it were to be authentic and lasting, must be human - that is, it must take persons in their actual existence into account more than purely economic measures of progress. The human measures of development - the securing of human rights, the preservation and enhancement of human dignity, the creation of truly unified communities of people, the securing of the common good of all - must be accounted for just as much, if not more than profits, trade balance, gross national product, and the like.[88] Lebret recognized a hierarchy of values which placed the human person, a human and spiritual being, in a superior position to those measures of advancement which were merely instrumental to a more human life.

Lebret said the Church should take a leadership role in the work of development, so that development can be truly human and integral; that is, affecting every dimension of the person.[89] He believed that the wealthy nations of the West should offer financial and technical assistance to the developing nations, and he suggested that money be diverted from the escalating arms race to help the poor.[90] *Populorum Progressio* would make just such a call for a diversion of funds from the arms race to establish a world fund to assist the poor nations.

In the book *Human Ascent* Lebret noted the need for a Christ-centered approach to the work of development.[91] He wrote that if the work of development were not rooted in the person of Christ it would remain chained to the strictly material, and would not find its complete fulfillment in the realm of the spirit. The dignity of the human person must be tied to the dignity of the God-man if it were to attain its proper orientation.

According to Lebret Christianity was a major factor in the creation of a just and lasting civilization. He maintained that "the search for God ought not in any case contradict or compromise the Christian's task as a man." Likewise he acknowledged the autonomy of the secular world, and the need for "all men of true good will," whether Christian or not, to contribute to the betterment of society.[92]

Lebret wrote often of the extreme urgency of the world's socioeconomic problems, and of the urgent need to find solutions to those problems.[93] This sense of urgency would become a recurrent emphasis in the social teaching of Paul VI after *Populorum Progressio*.

3. Geographic area of application

Lebret consistently called for *solidarité universelle* as a necessary social, economic, and spiritual precondition for development and peace.[94] He believed that the interdependence of the world community was a fact that should no longer be overlooked by the Church or by humanity.[95] Issues that previously had been evaluated by the Church from a strictly Eurocentric or Western perspective, such as property ownership, the distribution of goods, and the rights of workers, must be viewed globally. Humanity could no longer afford to linger in a kind of socioeconomic myopia - a "conversion to the worldwide view" was needed.[96]

Lebret was sensitive to the international scope of the economic order at a time when global consciousness was just emerging in the Church. As an economist he was acutely aware of the growing interdependence of the world economy, and as a Catholic theologian he viewed global interdependence in relation to the dignity and solidarity of the human race.

D. The property question

Aquinas' distinction between ownership and the social function of property achieved a newfound timeliness in Lebret. Consistent with Aquinas, he stated that the use of material goods constituted a *droit naturel fondamental*, which enabled persons to reach their *destine humaine*. Material goods, he maintained, are "ordered to the use of man and all men."[97] Property ownership, while assuming a subordinate position for Lebret, was still viewed in a fundamentally positive light.

Consistent with his global perspective on the social teaching, Lebret included goods connected with the international economy among the forms of property. In *Human Ascent* he said that raw materials, sources of energy, and finished products, which should have been the "common patrimony" of all, were overly concentrated in the hands of a few, leading to economic exploitation and the threat of war.[98]

Property ownership was seen by Lebret as a means of securing liberty, responsibility, and security, and of safeguarding personal freedom.[99] At the same time, he believed that "amassing material goods does not make men happy; authentic happiness is in giving them."[100]

Lebret was critical of what he called the "new colonialism" in which the industrialized countries of the West exploited the developing and underdeveloped nations. Capitalism was partly to blame for the "economic imperialism" which resulted. To remedy this injustice Lebret called upon all nations to adopt two strategies. First, the nations of the West should provide aid to the Third World for economic development rather than to pursue their own strategic interests. Second, all the nations of the world should engage in planning for worldwide economic development.

E. Conclusion of section

Lebret is an example of the type of Catholic intellectual who came to prominence in the Church in the 1950s. His seminary education was framed in traditional Thomistic philosophy and theology, yet he also gained expertise in the secular field of economics. His multidisciplinary training enabled him to identify some of the tendencies in international economics and to interpret them in the light of traditional Christian principles.

But Lebret was a man of action as well as an intellectual. He was personally involved in many social and economic problems, from the fisheries of France to Third World development. This combination of action and reflection, which Lebret shared with Paul VI, may have been the source of the attraction between the two.

His concern for the rights and needs of the world's poor was behind Lebret's call for the creation of "a life worthy of man." The anthropology of Paul VI was similar in its demand for human dignity.

Similarly, the criterion for Lebret's evaluation of socioeconomic systems was their ability to be "at the service of man." His critique of capitalism was more negative than that of the social popes before Paul VI, in that he saw economic imperialism and the increasing militarization of the world as byproducts of capitalism. He was somewhat positive about socialism's potential to humanize the economy, and he distinguished, as did the social teaching of John XXIII, between Communist ideologies and movements.

A principal focus of Lebret's work was the need for economic development to create a more just distribution of goods worldwide - as long as economic development was measured first by human standards. Lebret advocated such specific strategies as the diversion of money from the arms race for the development effort. His optimistic attitude about the potential benefits of international economic development, and his call for a world fund for development, were incorporated into *Populorum Progressio*.

The treatment of the property question by Lebret was reflected in some ways in the property teaching of Paul VI. Both men emphasized the priority of the social function of property. Lebret's additions of raw materials and finished products to the definition of property were included in *Populorum Progressio*. Likewise *Populorum Progressio's* call for international economic aid and worldwide economic planning were probably inspired by Lebret.

IV. PIERRE BIGO, S.J. (1906 -)

A. Historical setting

Pierre Bigo was born in Lille in the north of France in 1906. He entered the Society of Jesus in 1924, where he was educated in literature and philosophy, and he earned the degree of Docteur en Droit, Licensié en Lettres.

In 1932 he was assigned to *Action Populaire*, a Jesuit social action center which had been founded in 1903. Bigo himself refers to this assignment as his "first option for the poor."[101] At this time he took up the study of the social sciences, and earned a Diplome de l'École des Sciences politiques.

After completing his studies in theology, Bigo was ordained to the priesthood in 1938. For the next two years he served in World War II, with the rank of corporal.

After teaching for several years at the Institut Catholique de Paris, Bigo went to work as a manual laborer in 1950-51 in order to, in his own words, "become acquainted with a world of which I had been ignorant."[102] He then returned to *Action Populaire*, and he served as its director from 1952-60.

Bigo was sent to Latin America in 1965 to continue his work in the social ministry by teaching, giving conferences and retreats, and writing. He helped to found the Institute of Doctrine and Social Studies (Ilades) in Santiago, Chile in 1965, and the Brazilian Institute for Development (Ibrades) in Rio de Janiero in 1968. From 1974-78 he inaugurated the

Social Section of CELAM, the episcopal conference of Latin America. He has worked in similar capacities in Africa as well. Bigo was named an expert by the Holy See to the CELAM conferences at Medellin in 1968 and at Puebla in 1979, and contributed to the documents produced at these two historic meetings.[103]

As of this writing Bigo continues to teach and write in Santiago, Chile.[104]

Bigo has written extensively on development and the economic and social problems of the Third World, and his specialty is the analysis of Marxism. In his first book, *Marxisme et Humanisme* (1953), which was an interpretation of Marx's *Capital*, Bigo maintained that Marx studied the modes of human existence and alienation more than he analyzed the mechanisms of the economy. *La Doctrine Sociale de L'Eglise* (1965) was a wide-ranging study of economic and social issues in light of Church teaching, and was used in the preparation of *Populorum Progressio.*[105] In *L'Eglise et la Révolution du tier monde* (1974) Bigo discussed the accomplishments and deficiencies of the economic and social revolutions caused by capitalism and Marxism, and called for a "third revolution" characterized by worldwide solidarity. Bigo is also the author of *Foi chréttiene et engagement social* (1981), and a collaborator in *Débat dans l'Eglise, Théologie de la liberation* (1990).

B. Anthropology

Bigo's analysis of the prevailing social, economic, and political order is permeated by his concern for the human person. Bigo views the person as more than just a temporal being - he/she is a subject of rights, a moral being, a being with a spiritual origin and destiny. And the person is more than just an individual monad - he/she is a social being, and the rights to which he/she is entitled are due also to all others.

Bigo's theologically based humanism likewise colors his analysis of socioeconomic systems. He maintains that the primary criterion by which systems are to be evaluated is their effect on the human person. Any system, whether it be capitalist, socialist, or Communist, which treats persons with anything less than the dignity that is their due, or any system which fails to allow persons the opportunity to attain truly human existence, is considered to be flawed. Bigo is critical of socialism, for example, because it seems to treat persons as only temporal beings.[106] And he questions whether Marxism is a system in which "man exists for production or where production exists for man." [107] His emphasis on the individual overshadows, but does not do away with, his stress on the obligation of each person to promote the common good. He believes that the person and society have an interdependent relationship - the person needs society in order to attain human existence, and societies cannot exist independently of the persons who comprise them.

Bigo is careful to point out that the human person is more than merely a bundle of material needs and wants. In *La Doctrine Sociale de L'Eglise*, for example, he discusses his anthropology in the context of the relationship between civilization and evangelization. Civilization "reveals man as a subject," a possessor of dignity in one's own right, and not a passive victim of the prevailing socioeconomic system. As such the person is a "subject of rights," who should recognize all others as subjects of rights. At the same time, the human person is social by nature - a "being for society," and because of this he/she is necessarily a moral being.[108]

C. Topics related to property

1. Economic systems and property

Bigo's evaluation of capitalism takes note of both its "dynamism and defect." [109] He said that while the early liberal capitalism of Adam Smith, Necker, Ricardo, and Malthus affirmed the value of liberty in economic matters, the neo-liberalism of the twentieth century is flawed because it pretends that the mechanisms of the market are sufficient to assure the regulation of production and exchange. The individualism of liberal capitalism, which is its fundamental tenet, is opposed to Christian thinking because it is absolute rather than egalitarian. At its worst liberalism is, according to Bigo, "Darwinian, anti-democratic, and it resembles state collectivism." [110]

Bigo is not so negative about the more moderate form of capitalism that has evolved in the twentieth century. He said that it is "miraculous" in its international scope and complexity, and for its impressive ability to organize markets. It allows for great economic development, private initiative and the acquisition of private property. Yet its "hell" lay in the fact that it is a materialism which destroys the harmony of social life. This is because it favors capital over workers, and profit accrues more to the producer of goods and services than to the worker. This gives the producer, the capitalist, the unfair advantage of dictating economic relations by force and not by rights. This is what has created the historical inequities of capitalism, and what for Bigo constitutes its dilemma - it allows for great development, and also for great injustices.[111]

Bigo discusses the concept called "socialization" by John XXIII in *Mater et Magistra* as an economic alternative to capitalism, because socialization recognizes the interdependence of production and distribution. Its strength is that it calls for the redistribution of property on the basis of work and need rather than capital. In this, Bigo maintains, socialization represents a "necessary and beneficial evolution toward the greater mastery and control over the collective realities of life." But socialization can also be a menace to the human person. The individual can get lost in the collective, and his/her needs can be overlooked.[112]

Bigo's assessment of the various forms of socialism is, as one might expect, far more positive than in the social teaching from Leo XIII to Pius XII. He recognizes in the essential tenets of socialism - that the human person is social by nature, and the emphasis it places on the value of work - the potential for good in society. But its "collective sovereignty" can be dangerous, and must be modified by the right of property, in order to preserve a healthy balance between the individual and society. Also, socialism treats the human person as only a temporal being, and Bigo questions whether it recognizes the truest, spiritual dimensions of the person.[113]

Bigo has written extensively on the subject of Marxist Communism.[114] Rather than condemn Communism outright, Bigo examines both its strengths and weaknesses.

For example, Part Two of *Marxisme et Humanisme* is entitled "The Value of Marx." Bigo said that Marxism's contributions to economic theory are its belief in the demise of capital, money, and private property, and "the birth of a collective civilization of work" which leads to "the promotion of the masses into a universal solidarity."[115] Marxist analysis correctly claims that capitalism leads to a "fetishism of commodities" resulting from its total lack of control over the law of supply and demand.[116]

Yet Bigo also detects an ambivalence in Marxism between its humanism, which he said bears the character of a religious belief, and its atheistic materialism.[117] Its great error is that it exposes humanity to new forms of slavery - to the state and to the collectivity - because it fails to situate humanity in relation to God.[118]

In *The Church and Third World Revolution* (1977) Bigo, in an extensive analysis of the Marxist model in the Third World, lists both its values and deficiencies. Its values: except for the bureaucratic elite, the standard of living is the same for all; education is a high priority; medical care is free; almost all people have simple, decent housing; there is no prostitution, low crime, and no drugs or pornography; farming and manual labor are honored, and everyone works. According to Bigo Third World Marxist movements embody these positive values, which are compatible with Christian social teaching.

On the other hand, Marxist movements have several deficiencies: they abolish civil and political freedoms; workers are unmotivated by the collectivist ideology; there is no freedom of religion, and faith is stifled. This final criticism is especially crucial in light of Christianity and the papal social teaching, since both see the fulfillment of development in the spiritual dimension.[119]

2. Principles and strategies of actualization

Rerum Novarum held that justice played a rather limited role in socioeconomic affairs - the regulation of the relations between workers and management. The alleviation of poverty and misery, which involved a more equal distribution of property and material goods, was understood to be the work of charity. Bigo, while noting the traditional Thomistic relationship between justice and charity, advocates a greatly expanded role for justice, calling it "the virtue proper to social economy."[120]

Although Bigo recognizes the importance of industrialization in the development efforts of the poor countries of the world, he is critical of some of its effects on their people. All too often it leads to economic exploitation, leaving the peoples of the developing world "marginalized," or lacking the material, social, and political necessities required for human dignity. This, in turn, places them in a relationship of dependence on the industrialized nations. Industrialization and development have also contributed to a loss of cultural identity among Third World people.[121]

Bigo was one of many thinkers in the Church in the 1950s and 60s who rejected the notion that the Church should dominate temporal society.[122] He believes that civil society and religious society are independent of each other. At the same time he holds that the Christian faith has a legitimate and necessary role to play in civil society - it must help to bring about the "consecration of the world," a phrase originally used by Pope Pius XII.[123]

Bigo criticizes several positions on the relationship of faith and culture which he finds to be erroneous. "Laicism," which holds that economics is a strict science, denies that secular life is connected with Christianity. The "progressive" doctrine, which makes the secular world autonomous from religion and is a part of the Communist revolution, is more radical in that it attempts to completely dissociate secular life from religion. In this, he maintains, it has become a "substitution for faith." But he also finds the "integrist" position wanting, because it advocates the formation of a Catholic state. This position wrongly seeks the pre-eminence of religion in the political world. Bigo advocates what he calls the "practical attitude" which sees the religious person operating within the temporal world.[124]

Two distinct attitudes surface in the writings of Bigo. One is a sense of cautious optimism about the possibilities of economic development and human solidarity in the modern world. At the same time, there is an awareness that the benefits of economic and social progress are never easily obtained, that they are brought about only as a result of conflict and struggle.

3. Geographic area of application

In all his writings Bigo recognized the global dimensions of the social question. His analysis of the problems of the existing social order, and his recommendations to remedy them, are presented from an international perspective. One of his basic convictions, as he explained in *The Church and Third World Revolution*, was that "life is one, and the world is one."[125]

D. The property question

For Bigo the crucial contemporary question regarding property is its social function. This requires a reconciliation of the long-standing Thomistic emphasis on the right to dispose of property with the contemporary demands of social justice.[126] Concretely this demand should assume two forms - "socialization," which would divide and redistribute property on the basis of work and need; and "nationalization," which is the appropriation of property by the state for the common good.[127]

Bigo notes that in the eighteenth century ownership was considered an absolute right by several economic theorists. He believes these theories were defective because the absolute right of ownership necessarily implies the exclusion of others, especially those in need.[128]

In the nineteenth century the Marxist theory of property radically opposed this economic individualism. Marx maintained that property stood as an obstacle to the liberation of humanity. He called for the abolition of property, because it allows the wealthy to dominate other people.[129] Bigo agrees with Marx that property has historically been a source of oppression. Still - and here Bigo concurs with the position of Popes Pius XII and John XXIII - the misuse of property is not a sufficient reason to abolish altogether the right of property.[130] A proper understanding of ownership includes its social use, which necessitates a wide diffusion of property.[131]

Bigo attempts to preserve the balance between the individual and social dimensions of property. As a result he defines property as "the stable, exclusive, and transmissible power to inherit, manage, and dispose of material goods according to their common destination (orientation), in order to assure a decent life for oneself and one's own, and to provide for the necessities of others."[132]

Bigo accepts Aquinas' distinction between the power to *procurandi* (obtain, procure) and the power to *dispensandi* (dispose of) property. He also agrees with Aquinas' assertion that property is a responsibility rather than a right.[133] Aquinas had reasoned that property is a condition that, in its use, is not destructive of community, but rather is necessary in society to bring about a measure of care, order, and peace.[134] Bigo thus argues that in the Christian tradition the expression "private property" is not recognized, since the power to dispose of property is not absolute, but conditioned by the needs of the community.

Bigo's position on the role of the state upholds both the dignity and rights of the individual and the overall good of society. Consistent with the Thomistic teaching, and with papal social teaching prior to John XXIII, he holds that the person is anterior to the state - that is, the dignity and rights of the individual do not depend on the virtue or the good will of any particular political system. At the same time, the common good is superior to the particular good, and it is the function of the state to provide for the common good. Thus there exists a relationship of interdependence between the person and the state. The individual cannot attain truly human existence without the state. Yet society cannot exist independent of individual persons.[135]

E. Conclusion of section

Like Lebret, Pierre Bigo is a man of the Church who is familiar with, and has been deeply involved in the secular world. His work with *Action Populaire*, his service in World War II, his year of self-imposed manual labor, and his work in Third World countries all demonstrate his commitment to temporal affairs. And like Lebret, Bigo has this characteristic in common with Paul VI.

Bigo's anthropology, like those of Maritain, Lebret and Paul VI, stresses the importance of the human person as a subject of rights and also as a social and moral being. His extensive evaluation of socioeconomic systems is based on their effect on persons.

The critique of economic systems, especially Communism, is a principal focus of Bigo's work. His assessment of capitalism is mixed - it allows economic development to occur, but it is seriously flawed because of its materialism. Bigo proposes socialization as an alternative to capitalism, because socialization promotes the interdependence of production and distribution. Socialism also receives a mixed review. While socialism promotes the social nature of the person and the value of work, its emphasis on the collectivization of property needs to be modified by the right of private property. In the same way Communism was evaluated according to its strengths and weaknesses. Bigo praised Communism for its advocacy of the demise of capital, money, and private property; its creation of a collective civilization of work; and its call for universal solidarity. Its weaknesses are its materialism and its reduction of the person to the role of a slave of the state and of the collectivity.

His views on the relationship of the religious and the secular reflect Bigo's own life experience. The two realms are seen as independent but not entirely autonomous. He believes that religious persons should be competent and willing to work in the temporal world.

Bigo's position on the property question places greater importance on the ability of property to promote the common good than the property teaching of Paul VI. The legitimacy of the socialization and nationalization of property are applications of Bigo's emphasis on the social function of property. He holds that the right of ownership is always conditioned by social needs. And he believes that the role of the state regarding property is to provide for the common good.

Although Bigo accepts the traditional principles of the property teaching, his application of those principles in the context of the contemporary economy is both creative and progressive.

V. CHAPTER CONCLUSION

This analysis of three thinkers who reacted with and helped shape the social teaching of Montini reveals a convergence, a confluence of thought on several important issues. The differences among the three in most cases are more of emphasis than of fact.

Although Maritain, Lebret, Bigo and Montini had basically different backgrounds, the four were contemporaries, and each was committed to the social agenda of the Church in his own way. Maritain was committed to the intellectual life. Lebret and Bigo devoted their lives to economic development and to social and economic analysis. Montini's life was spent in service to the Church as a bureaucrat and member of the hierarchy.

Each proposed a Christian anthropology which focused on the dignity and rights of the human person. Maritain's integral humanism was based on human dignity and realized through participation in society. But where Maritain based the notion of integral humanism on Thomistic theology, Paul VI founded his anthropology on the biblical teaching of the human person as a creature of God. Lebret linked his major theme, development, to the creation of a life "worthy of man" - a life based on the dignity of the person, and oriented to the fulfillment of the needs of the person. Bigo emphasizes the human person's spiritual origin and destiny, and the person as a subject of rights. He believes that economic systems should be evaluated primarily in terms of their ability to secure the rights of persons. The anthropology of Bigo includes a recognition of human dignity and human rights, and the social nature of the person. The anthropology of Paul VI does the same. But where Bigo's anthropology is philosophically oriented, the pope's is based on a biblical theology of creation.

Although they did not reject capitalism outright, Maritain, Lebret, and Bigo were explicit about its limitations. Maritain said that it reduced the humanity of both the rich and the poor, while Lebret stressed its inappropriateness as a model for development. Bigo criticized its absolute individualism for being opposed to Christian thinking. It was not surprising, therefore, that the social teaching of Paul VI was more critical of capitalism than any of the previous social popes.

A sea-change in the Catholic attitude toward socialism occurred in the years after World War II, as socialism came to be evaluated more dispassionately and critically, and its merits acknowledged. Maritain said that it raised a needed protest against the evils of capitalism. Lebret praised socialism's call for a greater collectivization of production and ownership. Bigo notes socialism's recognition that the human person is social by nature, and the positive value it places on work. Paul VI's social documents promoted economic socialism to promote a more equitable distribution of goods.

In similar fashion Communism's positive characteristics were recognized by all three, even though they all ultimately disavowed it. Maritain cited as the merits of Communism its effort to liquidate the profit system, to give dignity to work, and to ally itself with the working class. Lebret viewed Communism as a kind of humanism in its attempt to liberate oppressed peoples. Bigo praises its belief in the demise of capital, money, and private property for the sake of the collective civilization. Although Paul VI repudiated Communism for its atheism and incomplete humanism, he attempted to initiate dialogue with a variety of Communist movements.

Each man envisioned the just social order somewhat differently. Maritain called for the "new Christendom," a Christian democratic state. Lebret cited the necessity for worldwide economic development to enhance the dignity of humanity. And Bigo rightly notes that the work of building the new social order is a demand of justice more than a voluntary act of charity. In his social teaching Paul VI combined elements of all three of these positions.

Paul VI's view of the relationship of the religious and secular was taken primarily from Lebret, who believed in the autonomy of the secular world and the need for Christians to bring their values and spirit to that world. This was not far removed from Bigo's notion that the secular and the religious, while independent of each other, are not completely autonomous. The "new Christendom" concept of Maritain, which promoted the regulation of society by the Church, was outdated and unworkable by the 1960s.

Given the sweeping developments in technology and communications after the Second World War, it is no surprise that Màritain, Lebret, Bigo, as well as Paul VI grasped the international range of application of the social teaching. The implications of this newfound awareness were developed over time by Paul VI in his various social documents.

All three thinkers accepted the traditional relationship of the right of ownership and the social function of property, while placing greater stress on the social function. Maritain stressed the collectivization of property - that the right of ownership should be ordered to the common good. Likewise, Lebret emphasized that goods are ordered to use by persons, and are intended for use by all persons. Bigo calls for the socialization of property based on work and need, as well as for nationalization, or the expropriation of property for the common good. The social teaching of Paul VI likewise emphasized property's social function. He applied the traditional teaching on the social function to greatly expand the definition of property and to demand a more just distribution of goods worldwide.

While Maritain, Lebret, and Bigo each added to the definition of property in his own way, Paul VI incorporated only the ideas of Lebret - raw materials and finished products - into his social teaching in *Populorum Progressio*.

Similarly all three thinkers, and Paul VI, agreed that the role of the state was to promote the right of ownership of property. The pope also adopted Bigo's acceptance of expropriation in order to correct the abuses of property.

It is surprising that Habiger gives so little consideration to the contributions of Maritain, Lebret, and Bigo in the formation of Paul VI's social and property teachings. As this chapter has shown, these three thinkers helped to shape the thought and practice not just of Paul VI, but of the Church in general regarding the social question.

For example, Habiger makes no reference to Maritain's interaction with Paul VI on issues surrounding the social question, even though the relationship between the two men is well known and easily documented, and Maritain's writings on the social question were considerable. And the only citation of Maritain in the bibliography - *The Things That Are Not Caesar's* - was published in 1931, long before his more well developed work on political and social philosophy.[136]

Lebret's involvement in *Populorum Progressio* is noted by Habiger, but only in passing.[137] This study has detailed several aspects of Lebret's work on the social question because a number of them, such as his concepts of development, solidarity, and the uneven distribution of goods worldwide, were incorporated in some manner into the social documents of Paul VI.

As with Maritain, the contribution of Pierre Bigo to the property teaching of Paul VI is not mentioned by Habiger, and none of his books is listed in the bibliography. Bigo's analysis of Marxism and his writings on the theme of liberation are certainly noteworthy. This merely illustrates the difference between Habiger's more general examination of the modern papal property teaching and this study.

The past three chapters of this paper have explored the significant background issues surrounding the property teaching of Paul VI. In chapter four the major focus of this essay will be dealt with: the examination of Pope Paul VI's social teaching - and in particular, his teaching on the property issue. With thinkers like Maritain, Lebret, Bigo and others showing the way, and with John XXIII's opening of the Church to genuine dialogue with the modern world in the *aggiornamento*, the time was ripe for the kind of social teaching proposed by Pope Paul VI.

NOTES - CHAPTER THREE

1 "Divino Afflante Spiritu" , in *Acta Apostolicae Sedis 35* (October 20, 1943), 297-326. English text in *Catholic Mind 42* (May 1944), 257-83.

2 Joseph Gremillion, pres., *The Gospel of Peace and Justice* (Maryknoll, New York: Orbis, 1976), 5-13.

3 William E. Barrett, *Shepherd of Mankind: A Biography of Pope Paul VI* (Garden City, New York: Doubleday, 1964), 206-7.

4 John Coleman, S.J., "Development of Church Social Teaching," in *Readings in Moral Theology No. 5*, Charles E. Curran and Richard A. McCormick, S.J., eds. (New York: Paulist Press, 1986), 178. The statement by Bigo concerning Lebret's inspiration of *Populorum Progressio* was made in a letter to the author dated August 27, 1990.

5 Julie Kernan, *Our Friend Jacques Maritain* (Garden City, New York: Doubleday, 1975), 15-16.

6 Yves R. Simon, "Jacques Maritain: The Growth of a Christian Philosopher," in *Jacques Maritain: The Man and His Achievement*, ed. Joseph W. Evans (New York: Sheed and Ward, 1963), 6.

7 Joseph Amato, *Mounier and Maritain* (University, Alabama: University of Alabama Press, 1975), 45-46.

8 Amato, 53.

9 Simon, 14-15.

10 Simon, 17.

11 Kernan, 111-12.

12 Kernan, 107.

13 Kernan, 108-9.

14 John Dunaway, *Jacques Maritain* (Boston: Twayne, 1978), 133.

15 Kernan, 120-22.

16 Bernard E. Doering, *Jacques Maritain and the French Catholic Intellectuals* (Notre Dame, Indiana: University of Notre Dame Press, 1983), 207.

17 Kernan, 142.

18 Kernan, 142.

19 Doering, 226.

20 Doering, 208.

21 Dunaway, 127-28.

22 Kernan, 187.

23 Jacques Maritain, *True Humanism*, 4th ed. (London: Centenary Press, 1946), xii.

24 Jacques Maritain, *The Rights of Man and the Natural Law* (1942), 90.

25 Jacques Maritain, *Christianisme et Democratie* (Paris: Hartmann, 1947), xv.

26 Maritain, *The Rights of Man and the Natural Law*, 91.

27 Maritain, *The Rights of Man and the Natural Law*, 94.

28 Maritain, *The Rights of Man and the Natural Law*, 126.

29 Dunaway, 81.

30 Dunaway, 74.

31 Maritain, *True Humanism*, 108.

32 Dunaway, 68.

33 Maritain, *True Humanism*, 81.

34 Maritain, *True Humanism*, 80-81.

35 Dunaway, 68.

36 Maritain, *True Humanism*, 45.

37 Maritain, *True Humanism*, 51.

38 Maritain, *Christianisme et Democratie*, 34.

39 Maritain, *True Humanism*, 34.

40 Charles O'Donnell, "Jacques Maritain: Political Philosopher," in *Jacques Maritain: The Man and his Achievement*, 167-68.

41 Dunaway, 71.

42 Maritain, *True Humanism*, 168.

43 O'Donnell, 168-70.

44 Maritain, *True Humanism*, 159.

45 Maritain, *True Humanism*, 65-86.

46 Maritain, *Christianisme et Democratie*, 7.

47 Maritain, *Christianisme et Democratie*, 8.

48 Dunaway, 83.

49 O'Donnell, 176.

50 Maritain, *The Rights of Man and the Natural Law*, 150.

51 Maritain, *The Rights of Man and the Natural Law*, 158, 162.

52 Maritain, *True Humanism*, 178.

53 Maritain, *True Humanism*, 182.

54 Dunaway, 73.

55 Maritain, *True Humanism*, 158, 186.

56 Dunaway, 73.

57 Maritain, *True Humanism*, 179.

58 Vincent Cosmao, O.P., "Louis-Joseph Lebret, 1897-1966," *New Blackfriars 51* (February 1970), 62.

59 Cosmao, 63.

60 Cosmao, 63.

61 Cosmao, 63.

62 Louis-Joseph Lebret, O.P., in *Economie et Humanisme 89* (1954).

63 F. Malley, *Esquisse pour un portrait du Père Lebret*, in *Etudes religieuses* 785 (Brussels: La Pensee Catholique, 1969).

64 Cosmao, 64.

65 Cosmao, 65.

66 F. Malley, *Le Père Lebret: L'Economie au Service des Hommes* (Paris: Les Éditions du Cerf, 1968), 10.

67 Cosmao, 65.

68 Cosmao, 66.

69 Cosmao, 66.

70 Malley, *Esquisse pour un portrait du Père Lebret*, 47.

71 Louis-Joseph Lebret O.P., *Human Ascent* trans. Robert and Martha Faulhaber (Chicago: Fides Publishers, 1955), 20.

72 Louis-Joseph Lebret, O.P., *The Last Revolution*, trans. John Horgan (New York: Sheed and Ward, 1965), 102-3.

73 Lebret, *The Last Revolution*, 104-5.

74 Louis-Joseph Lebret, O.P., *Pour Une Civilisation Solidaire* (Paris: Editions ouvrieres, 1963), 50.

75 Lebret, *Pour Une Civilisation Solidaire*, 52.

[76] Lebret, *Pour Une Civilisation Solidaire*, 39.

[77] Lebret, *Human Ascent*, 27-28.

[78] Lebret, *Human Ascent*, 49.

[79] Lebret, *Human Ascent*, 179.

[80] Lebret, *Pour Une Civilisation Solidaire*, 59.

[81] Lebret, *Human Ascent*, 2.

[82] Lebret, *Pour Une Civilisation Solidaire*, 37.

[83] Lebret, *Human Ascent*, 19.

[84] Lebret, *The Last Revolution*, 208.

[85] Lebret, *Human Ascent*, 19.

[86] Lebret, *Human Ascent*, 11.

[87] Lebret, *Human Ascent*, 19.

[88] Lebret, *Pour Une Civilisation Solidaire*, 26-28.

[89] Lebret, *The Last Revolution*, 194.

[90] Lebret, *The Last Revolution*, 159.

[91] Lebret, *Human Ascent*, 65.

[92] Lebret, *Human Ascent*, 103-4.

[93] Lebret, *Human Ascent*, 19.

[94] Lebret, *Pour Une Civilisation Solidaire*, 9.

[95] Lebret, *Human Ascent*, 10.

[96] Lebret, *The Last Revolution*, 5.

[97] Lebret, *Pour Une Civilisation Solidaire*, 34.

[98] Lebret, *Human Ascent*, 19.

[99] Lebret, *Pour Une Civilisation Solidaire*, 35, 40.

[100] Lebret, *Human Ascent*, 72.

[101] Pierre Bigo, S.J., Letter to the author, August 27, 1990.

[102] Bigo, Letter of August 27, 1990.

[103] Bigo, Letter of August 27, 1990.

[104] Bigo, Letter of August 27, 1990.

[105] Bigo, Letter of August 27, 1990.

106 Pierre Bigo, S.J., *La Doctrine Sociale de L'Eglise* (Paris: Presses Universitaires de France, 1966), 182-183.

107 Pierre Bigo, S.J., *Marxisme et Humanisme*, 3rd ed. (Paris: Presses Universitaires de France, 1961), 217.

108 Bigo, *Le Doctrine Sociale de L'Eglise*, 65-86.

109 Bigo, *Le Doctrine Sociale de L'Eglise*, 132.

110 Bigo, *Le Doctrine Sociale de L'Eglise*, 134-39.

111 Bigo, *Le Doctrine Sociale de L'Eglise*, 123-31.

112 Bigo, *Le Doctrine Sociale de L'Eglise*, 143-55.

113 Bigo, *Le Doctrine Sociale de L'Eglise*, 162-83.

114 See, among others, Bigo's *The Church and The Third World Revolution*, trans. Sr. Jeanne Marie Lyons (Maryknoll, New York: Orbis, 1977); *Le Doctrine Sociale de L'Eglise*; *Marxisme et Humanisme*; "Analisis Marxista y Materialismo Dialectico," in *Medellin 12* (March 1986), 96-102; "Meditacion Sacerdotal Sobre El Marxismo," in *Christus (Mexico) 36* (November 1971), 36-41.

115 Bigo, *Marxisme et Humanisme*, 125.

116 Bigo, *Marxisme et Humanisme*, 142.

117 Bigo, *Marxisme et Humanisme*, 142.

118 Bigo, *Marxisme et Humanisme*, 150.

119 Bigo, *The Church and Third World Revolution*, 204-7.

120 Bigo, *Le Doctrine Sociale de L'Eglise*, 297. An extended treatment of the relationship between justice and love in traditional Catholic theology is found in chapter 4, endnote 133.

121 Bigo, *The Church and Third World Revolution*, 20.

122 Bigo, *Le Doctrine Sociale de L'Eglise*, 101.

123 Bigo, *Le Doctrine Sociale de L'Eglise*, 76.

124 Bigo, *Le Doctrine Sociale de L'Eglise*, 57-64.

125 Bigo, *The Church and Third World Revolution*, 6.

126 Bigo, *Le Doctrine Sociale de L'Eglise*, 237-38.

127 Bigo, *Le Doctrine Sociale de L'Eglise*, 143-50, 426-27.

128 Bigo, *Le Doctrine Sociale de L'Eglise*, 248.

129 Bigo, *Le Doctrine Sociale de L'Eglise*, 252-54.

[130] Bigo, *Le Doctrine Sociale de L'Eglise*, 241.

[131] Bigo, *Le Doctrine Sociale de L'Eglise*, 246.

[132] Bigo, *Le Doctrine Sociale de L'Eglise*, 247.

[133] Bigo, *Le Doctrine Sociale de L'Eglise*, 39.

[134] Bigo, *Le Doctrine Sociale de L'Eglise*, 236.

[135] Bigo, *Le Doctrine Sociale de L'Eglise*, 268-69.

[136] Matthew Habiger, O.S.B., *Papal Teaching on Private Property: 1891-1981* (Lanham, Maryland: University Press of America, 1990), 390.

[137] Habiger, 263.

THE PROPERTY TEACHING OF POPE PAUL VI IN THE CONTEXT OF HIS SOCIAL TEACHING

I. INTRODUCTION TO CHAPTER

Chapters one, two, and three of this study have provided a background to its main focus - Pope Paul VI's social teaching on property. The first chapter briefly reviewed the history of the papal social teaching from Pope Leo XIII to the Second Vatican Council. It examined the historical context in which each document took shape, the thinkers and movements which influenced the social theology of the popes, and the content of the principal social documents. Significant categories surrounding the property teaching were analyzed, and the property teaching itself was examined in detail.

Chapter two was a biographical sketch of Giovanni Battista Montini prior to his becoming pope in 1963. This sketch showed that social involvement was always an important part of his personal experience, education, career as a bureaucrat and bishop, and in his interaction with influential Catholic social thinkers.

Chapter three summarized the positions of some of the thinkers who most influenced the social thinking of Montini before and after he became pope. It was shown how the social, economic, political, philosophical and theological thinking of Jacques Maritain, Louis-Joseph Lebret, and Pierre Bigo interacted with, and helped to shape the social thinking of Montini.

This chapter will examine in detail Paul VI's property teaching as it is found in his four major social documents - the encyclical *Populorum Progressio*

(1967), the pastoral letter *Octogesima Adveniens* (1971), and the post-synodal statements *De Iustitia in Mundo* (1971) and *Evangelii Nuntiandi* (1975). It will follow the same thematic development as the previous three background chapters. Each document will be framed in the context of the world socioeconomic situation and the situation in the Church from which it sprang. The anthropology of Paul VI's social documents will be detailed, since it forms the methodological framework of his social teaching. Several topics related to the property question, such as a critique of socioeconomic systems, principles and strategies for the actualization of the social teaching, and the geographic range of application of the property teaching, will be analyzed. And the principal focus of the chapter will be a detailed exposition of the property teaching itself. Each document will be examined in light of the thinkers and movements which helped shape it, other speeches and pronouncements of Paul VI on the social teaching, and critical reaction to the document.

II. *POPULORUM PROGRESSIO* (March 26, 1967)

A. Historical setting

The 1960s were a time of both great promise and threat in the world. With the end of European political colonialism scores of new nations were created in Asia and Africa. Yet many of these new nations remained economically dependent on the First World. In this relationship known as economic imperialism the developed nations of the First World exercised considerable economic control over the developing nations by purchasing raw materials from them at deflated prices, and selling them high-priced finished goods in return.

A number of international agencies, such as the Food and Agricultural Organization, the World Health Organization, UNESCO, and the International Labor Organization worked with limited resources to alleviate poverty and human suffering.[1] Yet there continued to be an ever-growing disparity of wealth between the developed, mostly capitalistic countries of North America and Western Europe, and the developing nations of Latin America, Africa, and Asia. Some areas of the world suffered from extreme poverty; Riga reported that no less than 1.5 billion people were living in poverty in 1967.[2] Great disparities of wealth existed within some regions of the world as well. In Latin America, for example, just five percent of the population owned 70% of the arable land.[3]

The Cold War continued apace, as the Soviet Union and the United States competed for influence in various part of the world, most notably in Vietnam, South America, and Egypt. Another manifestation of the Cold War was the ongoing escalation of both the conventional and nuclear arms races, which threatened world peace and drained valuable economic and human resources.

Political tensions were high in several parts of the world. Israel and the Arab nations fought their third war in twenty years in 1967 over territorial and sovereignty claims in the Middle East. In Rhodesia and South Africa racial tensions periodically exploded into violence. The war in Vietnam escalated rapidly in the mid-1960s, and American military involvement peaked at 550,000 troops. India and Pakistan fought a border war over the province of Kashmir in 1965. Serious border disputes were also contested by China and India, and China and the Soviet Union.

Within the Church the Second Vatican Council was being implemented on many fronts, among them liturgy, religious life, and the relationship of the Church to the modern world. In this regard *Populorum Progressio* echoes and carries forward the thrust of the social teaching in *Gaudium et Spes*, the Pastoral Constitution on the Church in the Modern World.

At this time Paul VI was fast becoming the most well-travelled pope in history. He was the first pope ever to visit the Holy Land, India, Africa, Latin America, and the United States. His one-day visit to the United States in 1965 included an address to the United Nations General Assembly.

Populorum Progressio, the first social encyclical of Paul VI, was issued in March 1967. He placed the encyclical squarely in the tradition of the previous social popes since Leo XIII, and in the spirit of *Gaudium et Spes*. At the same time he set out to expand the previous social teaching by broadening its application in light of the economic and social situation of the time.

B. Anthropology

The critical theological principle underlying the property teaching in *Populorum Progressio* is its anthropology. The positive anthropology of Paul VI's social teaching is rooted in the anthropology of *Gaudium et Spes*. Georges Jarlot, S.J., who was said by Bigo to have been one of the authors of the encyclical,[4] comments that the development of a positive anthropology, a vision of the human person and the world, is the Church's proper role in economic and social development.[5]

The anthropology of *Populorum Progressio* is founded on a theology of creation which holds that the human person is created by God in his image and likeness - in the *imago Dei* (Genesis 1:27), and given his/her destiny by God (##15-16). Each person is created with intelligence and freedom, with the capacity for moral discernment, with a spiritual dimension unlike any other creature, and endowed with infinite worth and dignity. This does not imply that every person has equal abilities. It does mean, though, that all persons are entitled to equal respect and opportunity.

The dignity of the individual makes him/her as well the subject of a whole host of rights. Among these are rights related to economic fulfillment. Human dignity, and the rights that accrue because of it, demand that each person have a minimum of social and economic goods,[6] and be able to participate in his/her own development.

Populorum Progressio goes on to say that the person is social by nature, according to the created order of God. Here the encyclical reveals a Trinitarian dimension. In the Christian tradition the Trinity is understood as a unity of three divine Persons. The Trinity is *in se* social, and the nature of the person in *imago Dei* includes this social dimension. Among other things, the international emphasis in *Populorum Progressio* is an application of the principle of the social dimension of human nature.

It is noteworthy that Bigo, Maritain, and Lebret all proposed an anthropology based on the dignity of the human person, and geared to human rights.[7]

The anthropology of *Populorum Progressio* is illustrated in the teaching on work. Every person, created in the image of God, is called to cooperate with God in the ongoing work of creation: "Everyone who works is a creator" (#27). When it is performed with intelligence and freedom, work is considered truly human. And the goal of work is to build up the person and the human community.[8]

The doctrine of the Incarnation, along with a theology of creation, are the backdrops to the anthropology of *Populorum Progressio.* And the anthropology, in turn, forms the theological framework for the property teaching.

A principal paradigm of the anthropology of *Populorum Progressio* is the Incarnation (##12, 14, 15-16, 21, 28, 32, 74, 80-81). Riga maintains that the Incarnation is the central theme of the encyclical, in that it requires Christians to take the Incarnation seriously, to deal with people in all dimensions in their concrete existence, to identify Christ with every person and with all persons.[9]

Indicative of its incarnational thrust, *Populorum Progressio* calls humanity to live in total fashion - socially, politically, economically, culturally, morally, spiritually.[10] Dogma and social teaching, the spiritual and the temporal, are two sides of the same coin.

Riga points out that two conceptions of God are at stake in Paul VI's incarnational theology. The first conception he calls illusory: the God who is understood as he exists in himself, whose existence is verbalized in eternal verities and abstracted from concrete reality. The other conception comes to grips in faith with the God who is a hidden reality. This God is revealed in an act of love and commitment expressed in concrete ways, such as feeding, clothing, housing, and sexuality, in which one comes to discover oneself and the neighbor.[11]

The incarnational humanism of *Populorum Progressio* is opposed to Marxist humanism. Marxism espouses a monistic, materialistic humanism which seeks the material and social advancement of humanity, but denies its spiritual dimension. Christian humanism, on the other hand, seeks a synthesis of the human and divine.[12]

The incarnational emphasis in Paul VI's theology is found in some of his addresses prior to *Populorum Progressio*. For example, in an address on the 75th anniversary of *Rerum Novarum* on May 22 1966 he said: "The Church has not been afraid to descend from its own religious sphere to that of the concrete conditions of social life (such as labor contracts, salary, welfare, family rights, private property, savings)." [13]

C. Topics related to property

1. Economic systems and property

As in previous social encyclicals, *Populorum Progressio* evaluates the capitalist, socialist, and Communist systems. Paul VI's assessment, unlike that of the social popes before John XXIII, was not made on purely ideological grounds. Rather, in keeping with the focus of the encyclical, economic systems are judged by their promotion of development in the spirit of solidarity. In particular, their ability to secure a more just distribution of goods and to foster equality and participation are scrutinized.

The encyclical attacks liberal capitalism as the ruling force of the international economy (##7, 26, 34, 52, 54, 59, 63, 70). The major fault of capitalism is seen as an excessive individualism which makes ownership of goods an absolute right, regardless of the needs and rights of society and the world as a whole. The encyclical declares, therefore, that capitalism should be modified by the principles of solidarity and dialogue.[14]

Maritain had rejected capitalism as a viable economic system because he believed it to be bound to antihumanist aims: productivity, technology, and money.[15] Lebret, in similar fashion, concluded that capitalism is powerless as a means of effective world development, because it tends toward the profitable rather than toward what is necessary for true development to take place.[16]

While the encyclical is critical of capitalism's overemphasis on the profit motive, competition, and the absolute right of ownership of the means of production, it nevertheless acknowledges that capitalism is the system most likely to foster industrialization. It maintains that it is wrong to attribute the evils of capitalism to industrialization, since industrialization properly applied has a positive role to play in integral development (#26).

The greatest evil of capitalism, as well as Communism, is considered to be materialism (#41). Exclusive concentration on the material aspect of development is fatally closed to the spiritual possibilities of integral development.

Riga notes that the critique of capitalism was one of the most controversial aspects of *Populorum Progressio*.[17] Wolf, for example, accuses Paul VI of "shrill overstatement" in his criticism of liberal capitalism,[18] and Pallenberg refers to the critique of capitalism as "extremely severe."[19] Yet Riga points out that the pope's criticism is directed mostly at the under-regulated capitalism of the Latin American countries rather than the American capitalist system as it had evolved since 1929.[20] On the whole the encyclical does not reject capitalism, as Masse notes: "*Populorum Progressio* is no more anticapitalist, or pro-Socialist - no more inimical to private property, the profit motive, and competitive markets - than any other socio-economic documents of the Popes."[21]

The whole of *Populorum Progressio* advocates a moderate socialism of goods that is fundamentally opposed to capitalist individualism (##6, 17, 20, 26, 28, 34, 47, 65). Riga comments that "one of the most striking aspects of (*Populorum Progressio*) is its frankly socialistic tone," and Pallenberg agrees with this assessment.[22] Its evaluation of socialism is entirely consistent with the encyclical's incarnational thrust and its call for worldwide solidarity,[23] and paves the way for its strong emphasis on the priority of the social function of material goods over the right of ownership.

The encyclical accepts the socialistic principle of state planning for development (#50),[24] while emphasizing the freedom which countries must have in choosing their own economic system. For example, it argues for the legitimacy of expropriation of land when huge estates are underutilized or significantly deter the common good in some other way (#24), because the owners of this land disregard the social function of property. Yet expropriation is not equated with revolution, and those who expropriate land are to do so whenever possible without resorting to violence. Also, those whose land is taken are expected to receive just compensation.

It is important to point out that the type of socialism advocated in the encyclical is economic socialism, which focuses on concrete actions to promote the equitable ownership and distribution of goods. *Mater et Magistra* had done the same, in its advocacy of the socialization of goods. This represents a rather dramatic shift in the Church's attitude toward socialism. *Rerum Novarum* had condemned every form of socialism. And Pius XI, while he distinguished atheistic from economic socialism, still declared in *Quadragesimo Anno* that "no one can be at the same time a sincere Catholic and a true socialist" (#120).[25]

Populorum Progressio's evaluation of Communism is relatively benign, especially given the history of the social teaching prior to John XXIII. Communism is criticized for its atheism and its incomplete humanism, because these deny the Absolute, and thus prevent the realization of the fullness of integral development (#39).[26] Paul VI's negative assessment of Communism is milder even than in his encyclical *Ecclesiam Suam*, in which he repudiated Communism for denying God and also for oppressing the Church.[27]

Bigo's lengthy assessment of Marxism in his book *Marxisme et Humanisme* was positive overall, although in a similarly qualified way. He included among its contributions "the birth of a collective civilization of work" which would generate "the promotion of the masses into a universal solidarity."[28] Maritain, while critical of Marxism's dialectical materialism and thoroughgoing atheism, also praised it for its liquidation of the profit system and restoration of the dignity of work.[29] Lebret had referred to Marxism as illusory because, even though he found it to be viable as an ideology of development, it was still based on an atheistic and materialistic humanism.[30]

Populorum Progressio likewise acknowledges what it considers to be the positive aspects of Marxism. It points out that some Marxists are concerned for the true welfare of persons, and that some are not exploiting the desire of the masses for liberation as an excuse to grab power.

The economic problem of poverty, and the conflict between the rich and poor nations, are viewed in the encyclical as bigger threats to peace than Communism. In fact both capitalism and Communism come under the same criticism - their tendency to materialism (#41). Materialism in both systems prevents the realization of integral development, because materialism's greed and selfishness close off persons from each other.

Riga believes that Paul VI's acceptance of land expropriation in no. 24 comes close to Communism. But he points out that this position must be understood in the context of the situation in Latin America in the mid-1960s.[31] *Populorum Progressio*'s position on the expropriation of land is based on the theological principle of the social function of property rather than on the Communist principle of absolute equality in the distribution of wealth.

2. Principles and strategies of actualization

In *Populorum Progressio* there are four themes having to do with the actualization of the property teaching which need to be addressed.

The first two themes are solidarity and development, which are built upon the theological paradigm of the Incarnation and upon the encyclical's anthropology, and are the major principles for the realization of the social teaching in *Populorum Progressio* (##1, 6, 15, 17, 20, 22, 27-28, 34, 39, 42, 47, 65, 79, 86). Solidarity is the eventual goal of a worldwide society afflicted with many social, economic, and spiritual ills. Development is the concrete means of achieving the goal of global solidarity.

Riga notes correctly that "the whole of the encyclical is based on universal human solidarity and fraternity," [32] and Burnham believes that Paul VI's call for human solidarity was "unquestionably historic." [33]

The notion of solidarity is based on Paul VI's complete humanism or transcendent humanism (##1, 16), which is a reflection of the doctrine of the Incarnation. Transcendent humanism is the fulfillment of humanity in all its dimensions - not just economic and social, but artistic, cultural, educational, moral and spiritual.[34]

The concept of transcendent humanism is also found in *Pacem in Terris* (##11, 45), and in *Gaudium et Spes*. Number three of *Gaudium et Spes*, for example, declares that "the pivotal point of our total presentation will be man himself, whole and entire, body and soul, heart and conscience, mind and will." The theme of transcendent humanism also appears in the writings of Maritain and Lebret.[35]

Populorum Progressio views transcendent humanism as the Church's answer to Marxist and atheistic humanism. The latter are viewed as incomplete because they deny the necessary spiritual dimension of human existence (#16).[36]

The theme of solidarity is also rooted in the encyclical's anthropology, which affirms the dignity of the person and the social dimension of human nature. Human dignity implies that all persons are equal, and entitled to the opportunity to advance and fulfill themselves, while the social dimension of human nature means that people have the duty to work together for the fulfillment of all.

Populorum Progressio makes an earnest plea for that solidarity which is needed for full development (#1), and which must accompany development (#43). Solidarity calls all people to the duty to work for the development of all (#17). Well-off nations have the duty to build solidarity through aid for the weak - by feeding the hungry, but also by engaging in the work of building a fully human life. The international scope of the social problem in the 1960s makes solidarity all the more important: "Today the principal fact that we must all recognize is that the social question has become worldwide" (#3). *Gaudium et Spes* had made a quite similar plea for solidarity when it said that "the destiny of the human community has become all of a piece" (#5).

Solidarity calls for sacrifice, both by individuals and by nations. The encyclical gives several specific suggestions to the nations of the world on this point. Foremost among them is the establishment of a World Fund to assist in the development of the poorer nations of the world, to be funded from monies that would have been spent on the arms race (#51). Lebret earlier had called for just such a world fund, to be diverted from the arms race.[37]

Paul VI's call for a World Fund was motivated in part by what Burnham calls his "anguish and alarm before the hunger and wretchedness which he himself witnessed in Africa, Latin America, the Near East, and India."[38] The pope first mentioned the idea of a World Fund in Bombay in 1964, in a talk to members of the press: "Would that the nations could cease the armaments race, and devote their resources and energies instead to the fraternal assistance of the developing countries!" "Would that every nation . . . would contribute even a part of its expenditure for arms to a great world fund for the relief of the many problems of nutrition, clothing, shelter, and medical care which affect so many peoples!"[39] He brought it up again in his address to the United Nations General Assembly in 1965,[40] and in an address to the Administrative Council of the United Nations Development Program on June 25, 1966, in which he noted how the idea of the World Fund had evolved into the United Nations Development Program.[41]

Paul VI insists that the building of a worldwide system of cooperation through solidarity would require the elimination of nationalism and racism (##62, 63), which serve to divide peoples rather than to bring them together, and hinder economic solidarity.[42] He also calls for improved trade relations (##56-65), declaring that the liberal principle of free trade should no longer govern international trade relations, but that free trade should be subject instead to the demands of social justice for the sake of solidarity.

Solidarity had been one of the important themes of Paul VI's addresses on the social question even before *Populorum Progressio*. He highlighted it in his address to the United Nations General Assembly on October 4, 1965: "Let no one as a member of your union be superior to others: not one over the other."[43] And he noted the importance of solidarity in an address to leaders of non-Christians during his trip to Bombay in 1964: "Are we not all one in this struggle for a better world, in this effort to make available to all people those goods which are needed to fulfill their human destiny and to live lives worthy of the children of God?"[44]

Solidarity had also been an important theme in Lebret's work. In *Human Ascent*, for example, he noted that, in light of nature and the natural world, "man has felt his vision expand and has felt responsible for the whole order and harmony of the world." "All men are bound together in the same world."[45]

Social justice means that human rights, including the right of trade, are secured by law in the institutions of public authority.[46] This ensures, for example, that trade is more human and moral - that it provides equality of opportunity, rather than concentrating wealth and economic power in the hands of a few wealthy nations. Likewise, the profit motive should be abandoned as the foundation of international social justice in favor of the goal of world solidarity (##3, 5, 44, 48).

Dorr points out that one of the major advances in the social teaching in *Populorum Progressio* is its call, in the spirit of international social justice, for these types of specific structural changes in society.[47] Where previous social teaching tended to be moralistic in tone, *Populorum Progressio* calls for change in the very structures of society.

Coming to the aid of the poorer nations is a duty of worldwide solidarity (##45-55). The encyclical encourages developing nations to organize and work together for the universal common good. Each nation has an absolute obligation to contribute to the international society according to its abilities.[48] The whole international community will benefit as a result of these cooperative efforts.

Solidarity does not mean, however, that the developed nations should impose formulas or plans for economic and social advancement on the developing nations in a condescending or paternalistic manner. *Populorum Progressio* emphasizes that peoples should become the artisans of their own destiny (#65), and not have economic solutions imposed on them by other nations.

The encyclical suggests universal, international charity as the motivating force for building worldwide solidarity (##66-75). Colin Clark comments on this point: "The principle stated in the past by some moralists, of *caritas ordinata*, of one's duty of first giving help to those countries near at hand, or with whom one has political or historical connections - should be regarded as obsolete, so far as all new commitments are concerned."[49]

Several concrete steps toward the achievement of universal charity are listed. The peoples of the world should welcome each other in the spirit of hospitality (#67). Industrialists, merchants, and businesspersons should go to developing nations and offer their expertise (#70). Sincere dialogue between civilizations should be initiated in order to create brotherhood (#73). Lay missionaries should continue to volunteer their services in foreign countries (#74).

Worldwide organizations with political and juridical authority should grow and flourish "until finally there is established an order of justice which is universally recognized" (#78). Charity is seen as the way of overcoming the lack of brotherhood in the world, and of building universal solidarity.

Development is the second important principle for the fulfillment of the social teaching in *Populorum Progressio.* In light of the goal of worldwide solidarity, development is understood as the means of achieving solidarity in the economic and social spheres.

Jarlot states that the notion of development grew up among those European economists in the 1940s who had been involved in the war effort.[50] By the 1950s Lebret had already termed development "the problem of the century."[51]

Paul VI had identified with the poor and their plight throughout his life (see chapter 2), and he continued to do so as pope. He was deeply moved by the poverty he saw in India during his trip there in 1964. In a symbolic gesture shortly before his departure for India he gave away his papal tiara to be sold, and the proceeds given to the poor.[52]

Populorum Progressio calls attention constantly to the needs of the poor (##4, 9, 12, 18-19, 21, 41, 45). In fact, Riga comments that "it is evident that the whole encyclical is one great appeal for the poor throughout the world."[53]

Part I of *Populorum Progressio* concentrates on social and economic development in the context of integral development, which is defined as the will "to do more, know more, and have more in order to be more" (#6). Reflecting incarnational theology and its principle of the social nature of the human person, integral development "promote(s) the good of every man and of the whole man" in every dimension of human life (#14).

Integral development is possible for individuals and societies, but it is not without obstacles. Greed, avarice, materialism, and the desire for power are ever-present temptations to pervert the kind of social order intended by God. They can and do impede the realization of integral development (#18).

Development should ascend along a hierarchical ordering from less human to more human conditions. Less human conditions are the lack of material necessities for people lacking the minimum essentials of life, moral deficiencies of persons imprisoned by selfishness, and oppressive social structures brought about by abuses of wealth or power. The more human conditions are passage from misery to possession of necessities, triumph over social ills, the growth of knowledge, the acquisition of culture, cooperative efforts to promote the common good, the desire for peace and, at the pinnacle of the hierarchy of development, acceptance of the gift of faith and unity in the charity of Christ (#21).

Populorum Progressio places the concept of integral humanism in the context of the unequal pace of worldwide development in the distribution of goods, wealth, and power (#8). Although individual Christians have long been involved in the development effort, local, individual work is no longer enough. What is needed is "concerted action based on a clear vision of all economic, social, cultural, and spiritual aspects" (#13). As important as the economic component may be, therefore, development must involve more than just economic advancement.

Paul VI had spoken about integral development on other occasions, as in his letter to the Latin American Bishops' Conference at Mar del Plata. In the letter he said that development, although it demands enough material goods for all, is not identified with a purely material increase in goods. Rather, it must be integral: "It must be an elevation of the person from all points of view and universal elevation of all mankind." [54]

Maritain had used the term "integral humanism" to describe the force in history that "essentially tends to render man more truly human and to make his original greatness more manifest by causing him to participate in all that can enrich him in nature and in history." [55] In a similar vein, Lebret wrote of the need for the "human ascent" of all people so that "every person can be more." [56]

Integral development includes both personal and societal dimensions. Personal development involves the self-fulfillment of one's God-given aptitudes and qualities. It requires intelligence and freedom, and each person is responsible for his/her own development (#15). Self-fulfillment is not something one may take lightly or ignore, because it is part of one's calling from God, and it leads to transcendent humanism, the highest goal of personal development, by reason of one's union with Christ (#16).

The notion of personal development is also found in *Pacem in Terris* (#34), where John XXIII noted the responsibility each person has to fulfill him/herself.

Yet integral development is not to take place only on the personal level. Societal development is called for as well (#17). Human solidarity imposes a duty upon all to work for the development of all, so that humanity can advance together.

Societal development necessarily includes economic progress. In this regard the encyclical assigns an important role to the private sector. A prominent place is given to the process of industrialization: "The introduction of industry is a necessity for economic growth and human progress; it is also a sign of development and contributes to it" (#25). It is assumed that the developing nations will have to become industrialized if they are to achieve the levels of material and social progress necessary for full development. However, Paul VI warns of the dangers of industrialization - over-reliance on the profit motive, competition, and private ownership as an absolute right - which are brought on by what he calls "unchecked liberalism." But he says it would be wrong to attribute to industrialization itself the evils of liberal capitalism which all too often accompany it.

While *Populorum Progressio* concentrates heavily on the importance and the benefits of economic development, it extols as well the need for social progress (#34), the promotion of the dignity and rights of persons and groups in society. Not only do the two go hand in hand, but "it can even be affirmed that economic growth depends in the very first place upon social progress" (#35). This assertion is entirely consistent with the incarnational thrust of the encyclical, and with the notion of integral development. Economic, material development is never sufficient in itself for the fulfillment of persons and societies. It must be accompanied by social development for the fulfillment of the whole person.

Primary among the measures of social development is education (#35). The role of professional organizations such as unions is noted (#38), as is the need to respect local cultures and cultural heritage (#40). Here the encyclical deals with the sensitive issue of the relationship between population and development. Acknowledging that overpopulation hinders social progress, *Populorum Progressio* recognizes the right of governments to supply birth control information to their people (#37).

The culmination of authentic development is found in the spiritual realm (##41-42). Paul VI had previously mentioned this aspect of development in his letter to the Latin American Bishops' Conference at Mar del Plata, when he wrote that development should result in the spiritualization of humanity.[57] *Populorum Progressio* expands on this theme by noting that developing nations must discern what is true and good about material prosperity and reject the bad, so that complete humanism can be achieved (#42). Development, if it is to be integral, must be open to the Absolute, to the Spirit (#42). This theme would assume greater prominence in the later social documents of Paul VI, especially *Evangelii Nuntiandi*.

States and governments have an important role to play in the development effort (#33). Public authorities should select development objectives to be pursued, ends to be achieved, and the means to achieve them. Governments should ensure the participation of both private initiative and intermediary bodies in order to avoid the hazards of collectivism and arbitrary planning, and to guarantee that all social programs are placed in the service of people (#34).

Part II of the encyclical offers a set of strategies for governments to accomplish the goal of development in the spirit of solidarity (##43-80). Here the implications of the development theme for the property teaching are spelled out.

The premise of this section is that the social function of property has often been abused, resulting in an unjust distribution of material goods worldwide. To help remedy this situation, wealthy nations and individuals are called to heroic generosity, sacrifice, and effort to alleviate the almost overwhelming problems of the poor. Nations must take care of their own people, but they must also advance the universal common good. They should not impose heavy debts on the developing nations, nor hinder development by creating trade imbalances (##54, 57). Developed nations are called to share their technical competence, but in a spirit of love, so as not to create new relationships of dependency (#72). Their superfluous wealth must be placed at the service of the developing nations (#49). The aforementioned world fund should be established to relieve the most serious examples of destitution (#51). In these ways development will lead to a "civilization founded on world solidarity" (#73).

Populorum Progressio seeks to dispel the notion that development is an inevitable, even if gradual, march of progress. Development always entails the surmounting of the sinful propensities of individuals and sinful societal structures. The acknowledgement of the presence of social sin, and the need for redemption from sin in individuals and societies, would later become important themes of *Evangelii Nuntiandi.*

John XXIII's attitude toward the possibilities of progress had been quite positive, perhaps unrealistically so. But in *Populorum Progressio* Paul VI calls attention to a certain ambivalence to development (#19). Development, he argues, is essential, yet imprisoning if it is considered to be the supreme good. The worldwide development effort requires technicians, but also persons with wisdom who embrace the values of love and friendship, prayer and contemplation, so that the fullness of authentic development can be realized (#20).

Still, the major weakness of the concept of development in the encyclical is its implicit assumption that the Third World would achieve economic development in a gradual and steady manner, like the First World. This assumption overlooks an important historical fact - that the development of the First World was accomplished, in part, at the expense of the Third World. Typically, the developing nations provided raw materials at depressed prices, as well as markets for the higher-priced manufactured goods of the industrialized world. As Gudorf points out, the First World's economic exploitation of the Third World was a critical factor in its development.[58] The Third World has no such ready-made source of raw materials and markets. Lebret and Jarlot also called attention to this economic imperialism which allowed the developed nations to dominate the developing world economically, even after the end of the era of political colonialism.[59]

The final goal of development is peace - or in the famous words of the encyclical: "Development is the new name for peace" (#76).[60] Development culminates in the restoration of the temporal order to the condition intended by God at the time of creation, and is the means of achieving that universal solidarity which brings about peace.[61]

The social teaching since John XXIII had promoted the positive concept of peace based on the theology of Augustine and Aquinas. In

Pacem in Terris peace was defined not just in negative terms as the absence of war, but as "an order founded on truth, built according to justice, verified, and integrated by charity, and put into practice" (#167). *Gaudium et Spes* defined peace in similar words: "Peace is not merely the absence of war. Nor can it be reduced to the maintenance of a balance of power between enemies. Nor is it brought about by dictatorship. Instead, it is rightly and appropriately called 'an enterprise of justice' (Is. 32:7). Peace results from that harmony built into society by its divine Founder, and actualized by men as they thirst after ever greater justice" (#78).

Paul VI had alluded to the positive notion of peace prior to *Populorum Progressio*, in his address to the United Nations General Assembly: "You are working here not just to eliminate conflicts between States, but to make it possible for States to work for one another."[62]

The achievement of peace is closely tied to a more just distribution of material goods. Peace is incarnated in positive work to achieve justice, development, and solidarity among all people. Yet peace, like solidarity and development, cannot be measured merely in economic and material terms. Its fulfillment is found in the realm of the spiritual. Earthly peace is a participation in the one, true peace of God. The absence of war is merely a result, not a cause of this peace (#81).[63]

Populorum Progressio implies that the biggest obstacles to peace are economic in nature, rather than political or ideological. Inequalities of all kinds are a threat to peace, and the greatest of these is poverty, especially the disparity between the rich and poor nations.[64] It is noteworthy, and a reflection of Paul VI's faith in the benefits of economic development, that in the context of the Cold War the encyclical cites economic disparity as the biggest threat to peace, and not the ideological struggle between Communism and the so-called "free world."[65]

Third, Leo XIII and Pius XI believed that the Church and its moral principles should be given the leading role in the transformation and regulation of society. *Populorum Progressio* represents an almost complete reversal in the understanding of this relationship. Based on the demands of the Gospel, the Church should "put herself at the service of all" in order to convince them of the seriousness of the prevailing situation, and of the urgent need for solidarity in action to overcome it (#1).

A fourth theme, one which underlies the plea for international solidarity and worldwide development, is the urgency of the problems facing humanity. This theme appears often in *Populorum Progressio* (##1, 3, 29, 44, 55, 80).

Although development is urgently needed because "too many are suffering, and the distance is growing that separates the progress of some and the stagnation, not to say the regression, of others," and even though the failure to pursue development poses a threat to civil peace around the world, it should still proceed smoothly (#29). The strategy of gradualism is preferred over violent revolution.

Riga states that the urgency of development is one of the encyclical's outstanding characteristics.[66] Paul VI had called attention to the sense of urgency on other occasions, for instance in a letter to United Nations General Secretary U Thant of May 26, 1966.[67]

3. Geographic area of application

Another important theme in *Populorum Progressio*, one which is alluded to throughout the encyclical, is the worldwide range of application of the social question. Riga states that its global vision is one of the outstanding features of the encyclical.[68] Similarly, Calvez notes that "what is remarkable in (*Populorum Progressio*) is the Pope's grasp of the global dimensions" of development.[69]

The encyclical states that the Church, characterized by its global vision of the human person and the human race, and with its long history of outreach to the poor, is in a position to exercise moral leadership in the task of worldwide development (##12-13). Because its goal is to "carry forward the work of Christ" the Church is compelled to work for development, and to proclaim its international implications (#13).

Since human beings are social by nature, worldwide development in a spirit of solidarity requires international collaboration and dialogue, especially between "those who contribute wealth and those who benefit from it" (#54). Before sincere collaboration and dialogue can take place, and solidarity achieved, there is a need for conversion from a national to an international outlook (#62). Masse notes in this regard that *Populorum Progressio* "brings to a climax an evolution of the Church's social teaching that started with Pius XII during World War II and was noticeably enriched by Pope John XXIII and the Fathers of the Vatican Council, an evolution that has proceeded from an almost exclusive emphasis on justice within nations to an overriding concern for justice among (all) men."[70]

Lebret, Bigo, and Maritain had all acknowledged the worldwide scope of the social question,[71] and it was recognized as well by John XXIII in *Mater et Magistra* (##200-202) and *Pacem in Terris* (#130).

D. The property teaching

Populorum Progressio's property teaching is best understood in light of the encyclical's anthropology - the creation of the person in *imago Dei*, the dignity, rights and social duties which follow therefrom, the equality of all persons, and the right of each person to participate in his/her own development. The most noteworthy aspect of the property teaching is its forceful emphasis on the social function of material goods in God's plan of creation (##22-24, 48, 49).[72] Paul VI uses the traditional property teaching, and places a timely emphasis on the social function of property. In line with Aquinas' teaching, *Populorum Progressio* asserts that the use of material goods is a fundamental, primary right, and that the right of ownership is secondary and derived.[73] The right of ownership is secured by *ius gentium*, while the right of use follows directly from the natural law.[74] Ownership exists so that an order can be established in which the right of usage is assured. Therefore ownership is seen merely as the means to an end - "The right to property exists so that the right of usage may be assured and guaranteed."[75]

The heart of the property teaching is found in nos. 22-24, entitled "The Universal Purpose of Created Things." *Populorum Progressio* develops and expands the teaching in *Gaudium et Spes*, which had declared that "created goods should abound for (all people) on a reasonable basis" (#69). This principle is founded on the traditional teaching which states that the world exists for the livelihood and growth of all persons, that created things are intended for use by all people. All other property rights, such as the right of ownership, freedom of commerce,[76] and the right of nationhood,[77] are subordinated to the right of all to use the good things of the earth.

Number 23 restates in unambiguous terms the traditional teaching on the primacy of the social function of material goods: "Private property does not constitute for anyone an absolute and unconditional right. No one is justified in keeping for his exclusive use what he does not need, when others lack necessities." Property ownership is primarily a social responsibility (#3). Absolute ownership, defined as the right to own, control, and dispose of as much property as one can, is considered a "grave social aberration."[78] Riga states that when the Wall Street Journal reacted to *Populorum Progressio* by labelling it "warmed-over Marxism," it was because the newspaper failed to understand that goods and capital are social by nature.[79]

This teaching is a complete reversal of *Rerum Novarum*'s position on the priority of ownership and use of goods. Leo XIII had declared ownership to be a natural right rather than a derivative right, in a way that implied absolute discretion over the disposition of property (see chapter 1).

Paul VI breaks new ground in that he declares the teaching on the priority of the social function of property in the context of the call to worldwide development and solidarity. No previous social document had taken this aspect of the traditional teaching to such a sweeping and dramatic conclusion.

An obvious implication of this principle is the need for a more equitable distribution of goods worldwide. Lebret had made this point forcefully: "Only a balance in the distribution of material (and spiritual) goods, only a balance between needs and resources will assure world peace by cooperation in justice."[80] *Populorum Progressio* maintains that the ownership of material goods makes one responsible for their proper distribution, based on the needs of all, especially the poor of the world, in the context of the universal common good. This is because the earth has been given to all persons for their use as incarnate beings.

The property teaching in *Populorum Progressio* differs somewhat from the position of Bigo, who held that ownership, like use, is a "primary right" rather than a secondary and derived right.[81] Maritain, on the other hand, was more in agreement with Paul VI in that he called for a purification and ennoblement of property by means of its greater socialization, so that it might be better ordered to the common good.[82]

The understanding of the person as social by nature and the awareness of the international scope of the social question lead to a broadening of the definition of property in *Populorum Progressio*. For the first time in the social teaching the property of nations - raw materials, exports, and agricultural products - are considered forms of property (#57). This internationalization of the definition of property would expand even more in Paul VI's later social documents.

The ownership of property is a legitimate end of development, and material goods are not evil in themselves. Paul VI makes a plea for a modicum of goods for all, which persons need for their dignity (#19). Lack of material possessions is listed as one of the less human conditions which development should alleviate, and possession of material goods is one of the more human conditions leading toward integral development (#21).

But property is fraught with temptation to the sins of avarice, greed, and materialism. Therefore "increased possession is not the ultimate goal of nations nor of individuals" (#19). Rather possessions are understood as an opportunity to promote the more important aims of human fulfillment and solidarity. *Populorum Progressio* views ownership as ambivalent: it helps persons develop as persons, but it imprisons them if they make possession the supreme good. When this happens possessions become an obstacle to development.

Paul VI reaffirmed this aspect of the property teaching in his address on the first anniversary of *Populorum Progressio* on March 27, 1968, when he stated that religion reminds "the rich man that he is an administrator, and not the despotic master of his possessions, whose fruits should be in some fair measure at the service of the needy."[83]

Populorum Progressio teaches that nations have a duty to secure for their own people a level of ownership which will satisfy their basic needs, secure their freedom in society, and promote civil peace. This requires, and at times even demands strong measures. For instance, agrarian reform is badly needed in many of the developing nations (#24). In regions such as Latin America, expropriation may be the only way to secure a just distribution of land. But expropriation, as Masse points out, is not to be taken as a condemnation of ownership itself - only the abuse of ownership, because land that is not used to promote the common good violates the social function of property.[84] Measures may also be taken to prevent wealthy citizens from taking their wealth out of their home country and investing it in other countries (#24).

In this context the encyclical raises the possibility of violent revolution, and acknowledges that revolution may be justified when long-standing oppressive regimes violate human rights and the common good (#31).[85] Still, it condemns violent revolution in general,[86] and points out the danger that revolutions may very well lead to other injustices.[87] Andrews sums up this problematic section best when he states that "in urging social reform, Paul VI spurned violence. However, reluctantly, he did admit its value as a last resort."[88]

Paul VI's position on revolution in *Populorum Progressio* is new to the social teaching. In *Pacem in Terris* John XXIII had advocated the strategy of gradualism: "It must be borne in mind that to proceed gradually is the law of life in all its expressions. Therefore, in human institutions, too, it is not possible to renovate for the better except by working from within them" (#162). Paul VI stopped well short of advocating violent revolution, and *Populorum Progressio* espouses a consensus model for social change (#64). But the pope warns that without massive aid for development from the rich countries revolution might break out all over the world.[89]

Paul VI had advocated gradualism over revolution prior to *Populorum Progressio*. In a letter to the Latin American Bishops' Conference at Mar del Plata, Argentina in 1966, for example, he called for gradualism, while still acknowledging the need for profound structural reforms in Latin America.[90] Yet gradualism was not to be identified with tokenism; it involves, as Riga points out, "bold transformation, innovations that go deep."[91]

The encyclical also takes up the issue of the international common good. It says that the superfluous wealth of rich countries - that which remains after basic needs are satisfied - should be used to help the poor countries (#49). A nation's property must be subordinated to the worldwide common good. But the transfer of wealth from the rich to the poor nations should be accomplished without what Vermeire calls "providentialism," or in a paternalistic or condescending fashion. Rather, there should be respect for the self-determination of the poor nations.[92]

The encyclical suggests some ways that property and wealth might be distributed more evenly worldwide. It calls for the establishment of a World Fund (#51); a tax on luxury items (#84); and a progressive income tax to help redistribute wealth worldwide (#47). These measures are needed because "the world is sick" due to the lack of brotherhood among individuals and peoples as regards property distribution (#66).

The inevitable conflicts that occur between property ownership and the common good should be settled by public authorities, with the participation of individuals and social groups (#23). To this end the encyclical calls for the establishment of a worldwide political authority to plan for the just distribution of the world's goods.[93]

Paul VI had the utmost regard for the United Nations and its potential to build a worldwide society. He hailed it as a potential world authority in his address to the United Nations General Assembly: "You are in existence and you are working to unite nations, to associate states. Let us use this formula: to bring them together with each other."[94]

Gaudium et Spes had also called for the formation of some kind of universal public authority which would be "endowed with effective power to safeguard, on the behalf of all, security, regard for justice, and respect for rights" (#82). In his later writings Maritain had also envisioned an international society as part of the "new Christendom."[95]

Populorum Progressio's teaching on property in the context of the universal common good compares with that of *Pacem in Terris* and *Gaudium et Spes*. But here again Paul VI demonstrates what is new about his property teaching. He takes the traditional teaching on superfluous wealth and the common good, which were originally applied on the interpersonal and intranational levels, and expands them in dramatic fashion to the international level.

E. Conclusion of section

Populorum Progressio is a landmark social document, and one of the reasons why is its property teaching. In the encyclical Paul VI spells out his property teaching in great detail, and makes some dramatic and progressive applications of the traditional teaching on property. These applications are made in light of the document's historical setting and theological principles.

A sense of optimism pervades *Populorum Progressio*. This was reflective of the optimism within the Church in the years immediately following the Second Vatican Council, and the optimism of those involved in the worldwide economic development effort.

A key to understanding *Populorum Progressio* is found in its theological anthropology. Its exalted concept of the human person, which framed the social teaching since John XXIII, is an outgrowth of the doctrines of the Incarnation and the Trinity, and a theology of creation. The incarnational thrust means that, for human fulfillment to be integral, it must include both the temporal and spiritual dimensions of the person. Christianity therefore necessarily involves a commitment to this world and to the material advancement of people. The social nature of the person is understood as a reflection of the social nature of the Trinity. The theology of creation provides the backdrop for what the document views as the goal of development and human solidarity - the re-establishment of the world order intended by God.

The anthropology of *Populorum Progressio* shapes its social teaching. The human person, because he/she is created in *imago Dei*, possesses absolute worth and dignity. As an individual, the person is the subject of human rights. As a social being, the person is bound to a set of social duties. Human dignity leads to the assertion of the equality of all persons, and the right and duty of each person to participate in his/her own development.

The document examines the prevailing socioeconomic systems in light of their ability to promote worldwide solidarity through economic development. Capitalism is faulted for its tendency toward individualism, which is contrary to the principle of solidarity. When they promote the socialization of property and state planning for development, socialist systems can be beneficial. Communism is not condemned, but its atheism and humanism make it unacceptable as an ideology because these deny the Absolute.

The encyclical proposes several important strategies and principles for the actualization of the social teaching. Solidarity involves the fulfillment of the human person in all dimensions, and its goal is the achievement of a worldwide community. The work of international social justice builds solidarity by establishing laws and institutions which secure human rights, and international charity is the motivating force for solidarity.

Another key theme in *Populorum Progressio*, understood as the means of achieving solidarity, is economic development. If it is to be effective economic development must be integral, promoting the material and spiritual fulfillment of persons, and it requires state planning. The encyclical sees development as ambivalent, since it is a force for good and a source of temptation to sin. And the ultimate goal of development is peace, the ongoing achievement of a just social order motivated by charity.

Despite its optimistic tone the encyclical sounds a note of urgency about the serious social and economic problems facing the human community.

The guiding principle of the property teaching in *Populorum Progressio* is the priority of the social function of property over the right of ownership. Paul VI echoes the traditional teaching on this relationship, but in a way that draws out the implications of his anthropology and demonstrates a sophisticated understanding of the international range of application of the social teaching.

Human dignity and the social nature of the person require that the material goods of the earth be distributed in such a manner that each person has the opportunity to fulfill him/herself, and make a contribution to the international common good. The definition of property is expanded to include the property of nations, such as raw materials, exports, and agricultural products. Solidarity and the promotion of human fulfillment are seen as the primary purposes of property. States are given wide authority to promote the just distribution of property within their borders, and are called upon to work together to further worldwide solidarity.

Populorum Progressio favors economic measures of development, and believes that spiritual fulfillment follows from material progress. This would remain the basic orientation of Paul VI's social teaching until *Evangelii Nuntiandi* in 1975.

III. *OCTOGESIMA ADVENIENS* (May 14, 1971)

A. Historical setting

Several important developments in world affairs took place in the years between *Populorum Progressio* and *Octogesima Adveniens* (1967-71). The Vietnam War took a fateful turn after the Tet offensive in 1968, U.S. bombing incursions into Cambodia, and a shift in public opinion in the United States against the war. Tensions remained high in the Middle East, as the Arab countries continued to put military pressure on Israel. World attention was focused anew on Northern Ireland, where political and religious factionalism exploded in acts of violence. Cruel tribal warfare ravaged the country of Nigeria, accompanied by genocidal starvation and suffering in the Biafran region there. The civil rights movement in the United States was dealt a terrible blow when Dr. Martin Luther King, Jr. was assassinated in April 1968. And just two months later Sen. Robert F. Kennedy was felled by an assassin's bullet in the midst of his campaign for the presidency. These two killings contributed to widespread and violent urban rioting in the United States in the summer of 1968. One of the most positive accomplishments of the 1960s was the landing of two American astronauts on the moon in July 1969.

The late 1960s and early 1970s were years of dramatic change in the Church, as Catholics continued to implement the pronouncements of the Second Vatican Council. Economically and spiritually developing nations of the Third World captured the attention of the Church and of Pope Paul VI. He made pastoral visits to Africa in 1967 and again in 1969, attended the International Eucharistic Congress in Bogota, Colombia in 1968, and addressed the historic meeting of the Latin American Bishops' Conference (CELAM) at Medellin, Colombia that same year. The Medellin conference was a watershed for the Church in Latin America in that it endorsed the newly emerging liberation theology. Paul VI demonstrated his ongoing commitment to the task of worldwide development by creating the Pontifical Commission for Justice and Peace in 1968, and by instituting the World Day of Peace on January 1, 1968.

A critical event for the Church and for Paul VI was his promulgation of the encyclical *Humanae Vitae* in 1968.[96] The issue of artificial contraception had been studied by the Church for several years, and in *Humanae Vitae* Paul VI adopted the findings of the minority report which had concluded that artificial contraception constitutes a violation of the nature of sexual activity and procreation.

Humanae Vitae created a storm of controversy among Catholics, and lasting divisions within the Church over the contraception issue. It also highlighted, in two ways, the issue of magisterial authority in relation to the freedom of individual Catholics. First, the response required of Catholics to the encyclical was debated, because *Humanae Vitae* was not an infallible pronouncement. As a teaching of the ordinary magisterium, it was to be taken seriously in the moral decision-making process; still, it was not to be separated from the concrete situation of each particular couple and become the sole basis for decisions on the use of artificial contraceptives.[97] Second, *Humanae Vitae* brought to light a change in the attitude of many Catholics toward the authority of God and the Church. Greeley has concluded on the basis of his research that the decline in religious behavior on the part of American Catholics from the early 1960s to the mid-1970s is attributable solely to the birth control issue.[98] *Humanae Vitae* was to be the last encyclical issued by Paul VI, most likely due to the authority problems he encountered because of it.

Humanae Vitae would have a bearing on the social teaching of Paul VI in its assertion that birth control is not the solution to the problem of overpopulation in the developing countries (#24). Commenting on this matter, Riga points to empirical evidence which shows that couples will not limit the number of children they bear without some kind of incentive to do so. What is needed is economic aid and technical help from the rich to the poor countries of the world. Birth control information should not substitute for concrete financial assistance to the developing world.[99]

The focus of *Octogesima Adveniens* is different from *Populorum Progressio* in one major respect - where *Populorum Progressio* focused primarily on the need for economic activity to create a world of solidarity, justice, and peace, *Octogesima Adveniens* calls for political activity in the quest for justice and solidarity. Paul VI observes in *Octogesima Adveniens* that economic activity for development is stifled or rendered ineffective without the ability to exercise political power and influence to create structures of justice in society. And the pope, in a departure from previous papal teaching, acknowledges the limitations of universal solutions, proclaimed by the Holy See, to the many complex problems faced by those who work for justice among their own people. Without abandoning the call for economic and social development, *Octogesima Adveniens* shifts the emphasis to the need for engagement in political activity at the local level. In this way *Octogesima Adveniens* draws out an important implication of the belief in the dignity of the human person - the right of persons and groups to actively participate in their own development.

While *Populorum Progressio* was a papal encyclical, *Octogesima Adveniens* was written in the less authoritative form of a pastoral letter. It was addressed to Cardinal Maurice Roy, President of the Council of the Laity and of the Pontifical Commission for Justice and Peace.[100] One possible reason for this has already been noted - that Paul VI wanted to avoid the authority problems he had faced in the wake of *Humanae Vitae*. Higgins suggests that there are other reasons for Paul VI's use of a pastoral letter to present his social teaching in *Octogesima Adveniens*. First, the pope wanted to depart from the pontifical style of teaching that so often characterized papal documents, in favor of a pastoral style which is tentative in its discussion of social and economic problems, and encourages dialogue among persons of good will. Second, the tone of *Octogesima Adveniens* is collegial. It was meant as a kind of interim report prior to the 1971 Synod of Bishops, not the final word on any of the matters it discussed.[101]

B. Anthropology

The anthropological basis of his social teaching is not directly addressed by Paul VI in *Octogesima Adveniens*, as it had been in *Populorum*

Progressio. Still, the same anthropological principles - the person as created in the image of God, the human dignity and human rights which flow from this belief, and the duties which prescind from the social nature of the person - are assumed and applied in *Octogesima Adveniens*. They are reflected, for example, in the call for local solutions (##3-4, 42, 50); the section on new social problems (##8-21); and the assertion of the right of each country to promote its own development (#43).

C. Topics related to property

1. Economic systems and property

Octogesima Adveniens deals briefly with capitalism, socialism, and Marxist Communism in a way that reflects a weariness with their unfulfilled promise. Schall suggests that Paul VI's analysis of these systems in the letter is pragmatic, even anti-ideological.[102]

Liberal capitalism is criticized for its tendency toward absolute individualism (#26). Although capitalism promotes personal initiative, which is needed for development, its individualism is also its greatest weakness (#35).

Bigo was a critic of the early liberalism of the nineteenth century for its absolute individualism, but he saw the weakness of twentieth century neo-liberalism more in its pretension that market mechanisms are sufficient to assure the regulation of production and exchange.[103]

The letter admonishes Christians to be careful in evaluating socialist ideologies. Too often socialism is idealized in very general terms, for its will to justice, solidarity, and equality. Care should be exercised in making distinctions among, and commitments to, socialist aspirations and movements (#31).

Marxist Communism is faulted for its atheistic materialism, its tendency to violence, its absorption of the individual into the collectivity, and its denial of transcendence (#26). But rather than dismiss Marxism outright, the letter points out that there are several ways of analyzing it: as the active practice of the class struggle; as a one-party, totalitarian state; as a materialist ideology; and as a scientific method of analysis (#33). *Octogesima Adveniens* concludes that Marxism has some merit as a method of analysis, and that collaboration with Marxists is possible under some conditions (#30).[104] Hollenbach notes that Paul VI's pragmatic attitude toward Marxism was occasioned in part by the need to clarify Church-Marxist relations in Latin America and eastern Europe.[105]

2. Principles and strategies of actualization

Ten topics in *Octogesima Adveniens* relating to the actualization of the property teaching are examined in this section.

First, the call to justice is consistent, and insistent, throughout *Octogesima Adveniens.* "From all sides there rises a yearning for more justice" (#2). "There is a need to establish a greater justice in the sharing of goods, both within national communities and on the international level." "The most important duty in the realm of justice is to allow each country to promote its own development, within the framework of cooperation free from any spirit of domination, whether economic or political" (#43). *Octogesima Adveniens* is referring here to social justice, defined as the establishment of structures of law and social institutions which make justice a permanent fixture within societies and in the world community, and which empower persons to be the artisans of their own development and make a contribution to the common good.

The pastoral letter lists a series of new social problems that have led to a variety of injustices:

Urbanization - The phenomenon of urbanization had been noted in *Gaudium et Spes* without elaboration (#6). *Octogesima Adveniens* makes several observations about urbanization and the problems connected with it. Urbanization is affecting the industrialized and the developing nations alike (#8). A lack of attention to agrarian problems is driving more and more people into the cities, creating a new urban poor working class (#10). Thus, urbanization tends to create two socioeconomic classes - a wealthy consumer class and a large poor class "unable to satisfy their primary needs" (#9).

The problems of urbanization are related to the issue of property in three ways. First, the agrarian problems which help cause urban overcrowding involve the misuse of arable land in the developing nations, the undervaluation of raw materials, and fluctuations in the price of farm products. Second, the near-poor working class created in the cities often lacks the material necessities of life, and is denied its right to material development. Third, urbanization exacerbates the maldistribution of wealth within cities and nations.

Prior to *Octogesima Adveniens* Bigo had called attention to the injustices caused by urbanization, and Lebret had listed the problems of urbanization as obstacles to international development.[106]

Youth - The letter states that youth should be empowered to participate in a meaningful way in society (#13).

Women - Based on the belief that each person possesses absolute dignity, the letter cites the need to establish relationships of equality between men and women (#13).

Workers - Every person has the right to work, to a just wage, and to assistance when sick or old. Consistent with previous papal social teaching, *Octogesima Adveniens* acknowledges these as property rights (#14). The importance of unions is reaffirmed, but the letter notes that unions, because of strikes and abuses of power, sometimes place excessive burdens on society (#14).

Victims of changes - Attention is drawn to the "new poor" - the handicapped, the maladjusted, and those who survive on the margins of society - who have been victimized by the many social changes brought about by industrialization and development (#15). These persons often are deprived of their property rights, because their dignity and their right to participate in economic, political, and social life are denied.

Discrimination - Among the victims of injustice are those who have been discriminated against on the basis of race, origin, color, culture, sex, or religion (#16). Equality demands that all persons be allowed to exercise their rights, including the right to property and participation.

Right to emigrate - In order to establish a universal brotherhood, all people should be granted freedom of movement among the nations of the world so that they can pursue their rights, including the right to use and own property, fulfill themselves as persons, and make a contribution to the universal common good.

Creating employment - Nations should distribute the benefits of development more equally by developing employment, investment, trade, production, and education policies that will promote greater justice (#18).

The media - The communications media are viewed as beneficial, but they constitute at times a "new power" to influence politics, ideology, education, and public opinion (#20).

The environment - The exploitation of nature risks its being destroyed (#21). In *Octogesima Adveniens* the environment is considered a form of property on the international level, since it belongs to all people for their well-being, is oriented toward social use rather than private possession, and the duty of preserving it belongs to all people.

Second, a shift in emphasis in the social teaching from a call to economic activity to political activity is a critical factor in *Octogesima Adveniens*. Paul VI understood that successful development depends to a large extent on the possession and exercise of political power, and that political forces can impede or help economic growth. In many Latin American countries, for example, much of the wealth generated by development efforts benefitted only a very wealthy and privileged few, and usually the wealthy elite had close ties to the political leadership within their own countries.

How is political activity defined? It is, first of all, an activity rather than adherence to an ideology (#25). Political activity "should be the projection of a plan of society which is consistent in its concrete means and in its inspiration, and which springs from a complete conception of man's vocation and of its differing social expressions" (#25). The aim of political power should be the common good on the personal and societal level, and also the universal common good (#46). When conducted properly, political activity creates the conditions required for attaining humanity's true and complete, or integral good, including its spiritual good (#46). Political activity should not deprive persons and groups of their proper autonomy. Rather, it should maximize freedom to build the good "of the city and of the nation and of mankind" (#46). Political activity is a way of living out the Christian call to service. It should give witness to the faith through service (#48). Finally, political activity is part of the proper vocation of the laity, to complement the hierarchy's role of teaching and interpreting Christian morality. Here an important point made is made: the laity should take the initiative in their engagement in political activity, and not wait for orders from the hierarchy (#48). This is an allusion to perhaps the most radical teaching in *Octogesima Adveniens* - the legitimacy of local solutions in the struggle for justice and peace.

As important as it is, however, political activity should never become an absolute value. For example, states should not impose a political ideology on their people.[107] Rather, cultural and religious groupings should develop ideologies which are consistent with, and which will fulfill the nature, origin, and end of the person and society (#25). In other words, ideologies should be grounded in the truth. In this venture "the Christian must make a wise and vigilant choice and avoid involving himself in collaboration without conditions and contrary to the principles of a true humanism, even in the name of a genuinely felt solidarity" (#49). This implies that any ideology that excludes any of the facets of integral development is unacceptable.[108] Therefore political activity should avoid the tendencies toward "selfish particularism," which is the shortcoming of liberal capitalism, and of "oppressive totalitarianism," a shortcoming of Marxism and socialism (#49).

The encyclical calls for political activity because of what it terms the "radical limitation of economics." Economic activity is seen as necessary because it can be a source of brotherhood, a sign of God's activity in the world, and it involves a recognition of rights, of services rendered, of dignity affirmed in work and of dialogue and cooperation. "Yet (economic activity) always runs the risk of taking up too much strength and freedom" - it can become absorbing to the detriment of other human values, and it can deprive persons of freedom if they make economic advancement their sole aim in life. "That is why the need is felt to pass from economics to politics" (#46).

Populorum Progressio calls for new forms of democracy which will give more people a share in political responsibility and decision-making, in order to counteract technocracy, or the domination of economic forces. In this way persons can more easily fulfill themselves, and peoples can achieve greater freedom (#47). The Christian has the duty to promote equality and participation in society by engaging in political activity (#24).

Land comments regarding the shift in the pastoral letter to the call for political activity that "(Paul VI) recognized that most social problems are at bottom political problems. This was in notable contrast to papal tradition." Land also notes that Paul VI acknowledged in *Octogesima Adveniens* that "Christian commitment to the transformation of the world requires a commitment to the political order." [109]

Paul VI had addressed the issue of political activity on other occasions prior to *Octogesima Adveniens*. For instance, in a message to a general audience on the first anniversary of *Populorum Progressio* in 1968, he said that development was leading to the struggle for political independence first, then economic development.[110]

Octogesima Adveniens places greater importance on political activity than even the Medellin documents.[111] Medellin had mentioned the need for political reform as part of the necessary transformation of unjust societal structures, but without much elaboration.

A third important theme in *Octogesima Adveniens*, one which had been an established part of the social teaching since John XXIII, is the right of participation. The letter notes that the aspiration to equality and participation is growing in the minds of many people (#22). Participation is seen as a necessary expression of human dignity and liberty.

The principle of participation is at the heart of the critical theme of local solutions in *Octogesima Adveniens*. This theme implies that persons at the local level possess the dignity, competence, and integrity to develop solutions consistent with the Gospel and the Church's social teaching. One of the principal motivations for the shift in emphasis from economic to political activity in *Octogesima Adveniens* is to ensure greater participation (#47). Land notes that one of the important contributions of Paul VI to Catholic social thought is "his insistence on actual engagement in the struggle for human development." [112]

Fourth, Paul VI's invitation to local communities to develop and implement solutions to their own social and political problems represents a major breakthrough in the social teaching. The notion of local solutions runs contrary to previous papal social teaching, which had advocated reliance on the Holy See for solutions claiming universal applicability.[113]

The letter acknowledges that local solutions are needed because of the wide diversity of situations people find themselves in (#3). "In the face of such widely varying situations it is difficult for us to utter a unified message and to put forward a solution which has universal validity. Such is not our ambition, nor is it our mission. It is up to the Christian communities to analyze with objectivity the situation which is proper to their own country, to shed on it the light of the Gospel's unalterable words and to draw principles of reflection, norms of judgment and directions for action from the social teaching of the Church." "It is up to these Christian communities, with the help of the Holy Spirit, in communion with the bishops who hold responsibility and in dialogue with other Christian brethren and all men of goodwill, to discern the options and commitments which are called for in order to bring about the social, political, and economic changes seen in many cases to be urgently needed" (#4). The social teaching of the Church is helpful to persons in their search for solutions to their problems, but by recalling general principles, not by proposing "ready-made models" (#42).

Implicit in the call for local solutions is the acknowledgement of the complexity of social and economic problems around the world, and a genuine recognition of the ability and the duty of persons at the local level to deal with their own social, economic and political problems. This is a logical outgrowth of Paul VI's anthropology, which stresses the dignity of the human person and the right of all to participate in their own development and fulfillment.

Two other observations need to be made about the teaching on local solutions. First, the Gospel is cited as the authoritative source in the search for solutions, rather than the social teaching itself. Second, Christians are encouraged to work with their local bishops, fellow Christians, and persons of goodwill rather than turning to the Holy See for answers.

Land states that as a result of the teaching on local solutions "Rome would stop handing down solutions to specific questions Christians faced in their local communities."[114] Higgins also notes the importance of local solutions in *Octogesima Adveniens*, since Paul VI himself could not offer definitive answers to all the complex economic and social problems in the world.[115]

A fifth theme, liberation, is treated only briefly in *Octogesima Adveniens*. This is somewhat surprising, given that liberation was the major focus of the Medellin conference in 1968. Medellin had viewed liberation primarily from the temporal perspective. For example, it cited Jesus as the Liberator from the effects of the sins of hunger, misery, oppression, and ignorance.[116]

Octogesima Adveniens preserves the temporal thrust of the liberation theme. It calls for liberation from physical need and dependence, and holds that liberation begins with the interior freedom to place one's goods and powers at the service of the world (#45).

Gudorf believes that in *Populorum Progressio* and *Octogesima Adveniens* Paul VI is trying to push the Church in the direction of liberation theology.[117] In many ways this seems to be true. Both documents emphasize the temporal aspect of development and the right of participation. But after *Octogesima Adveniens* and *Justice in the World* Paul VI would move no closer to liberation theology, and *Evangelii Nuntiandi* would approach the liberation theme from a far different point of view.

Sixth, *Octogesima Adveniens* confronts the question whether revolution is justifiable in the pursuit of justice. Is revolution an acceptable local solution to injustice? Is revolution an acceptable form of political activity?

The document takes a negative view toward revolution and violence (##3, 28, 43), and Paul VI appears to back off his conditioned acceptance of the possibility of revolution in *Populorum Progressio*. Actually, Paul VI seems to have been backing off his position in *Populorum Progressio* well before the issuance of *Octogesima Adveniens*.[118]

Octogesima Adveniens calls violence a temptation for Church persons who "allow themselves to be beguiled by revolutionary ideologies which promise them, not without delusion, a definitively better world" (#3). Unless they are liberated from an attitude of greed toward their possessions people turn to revolutionary ideologies which initiate new injustices and forms of oppression (#45). In order to prevent violence, the formation of international relationships based on the common good is advocated (#43).

The issue of violence and revolution in the letter is addressed mainly to the Church in Latin America, where violence was advocated and practiced at times in the name of justice and the Gospel. *Octogesima Adveniens* reaches the same conclusion about the inadvisability of violence and revolution as the Latin American bishops at Medellin in 1968.[119]

Seventh, the teaching on utopianism in *Octogesima Adveniens* is remarkably positive, even though its general tone is less optimistic than any social document since *Mater et Magistra*. The letter's utopianism seems to correspond with the recognition of the failures of bureaucratic socialism, technocratic capitalism, and authoritarian democracy. These systems had historically deprived persons of freedom and participation, and had focused exclusively on material development. What is needed is "the forward looking imagination both to perceive in the present the disregarded possibility hidden within it, and to direct itself to a fresh future." Utopianism need not always be identified with escapism; it can appeal, rather, to the "inventive powers of the human mind and heart" (#37).

Paul VI had dismissed utopianism as unrealistic in *Populorum Progressio*. Pius XI in *Quadragesimo Anno*, and Pius XII in *Divini Redemptoris* had also taken a dim view of utopianism. Likewise Maritain, in the late-depression and pre-war climate of the late 1930s, had rejected utopias as ideals incapable of being realized.[120] Lebret, on the other hand, writing in the far more optimistic milieu of the late 1950s and early 1960s, had concluded that "the world has reached a stage where the only realistic answer is a Utopian one."[121]

The critical reaction to Paul VI's call for utopianism was generally favorable. Alves, for example, views the utopianism of the letter as "a constellation of symbols which, as they are transformed in action, tend to break the status quo open for new possibilities."[122]

An eighth theme, development, is important in *Octogesima Adveniens*, but is emphasized less than in *Populorum Progressio.* Herein lies the most obvious evidence of the shift from economic activity to political activity. By the time *Octogesima Adveniens* was issued in 1971 there was a general consensus that the international development effort was at best a mixed blessing. *Octogesima Adveniens* reflects this by noting the ambivalence of progress, in that progress is needed but is often mindlessly pursued, and too often becomes an ideology in modern society. Genuine progress, on the other hand, is found first of all in the development of moral consciousness (#41). Progress manifests itself concretely in allowing countries to develop themselves with the cooperation - not the domination - of the world community (#43). This would counteract the economic colonialism which continued to hinder the international development effort.

Industrialization continues to be viewed as important for development, but it too is considered ambiguous because it has helped cause the problems of urbanization, abuse of workers, and consumerism (#9). In general *Octogesima Adveniens* is more negative about industrialization than *Populorum Progressio*.

Racism and nationalism continue to be seen as obstacles to development (##16-17). The letter's position on racism and nationalism is consistent with *Populorum Progressio*, and Paul VI had restated it on several occasions between 1967-71.[123]

Nations and international agencies are called upon to develop investment, trade, production, and education policies (#18). The relationship of population control and development is discussed in this context. The letter quotes *Populorum Progressio*'s assertion that families may control their size naturally in order to improve their economic situation, and that governments may distribute family planning information, as long as it is in conformity with the moral law (#18).

Ninth, Hollenbach raises the question whether the acknowledgement of ideological pluralism in *Octogesima Adveniens* relativizes the fundamental principles of the Church's social teaching. He answers by pointing out that, rather than relativize Church principles, the relativization of ideologies may actually serve to affirm the "concrete transcendence" of those principles. Christianity is not judged by any ideology; rather, all ideologies are judged by Christian standards. From *Rerum Novarum* to Pius XI the model of society determined what the demands of justice were to be. But in *Octogesima Adveniens* the demands of justice are the norms by which all economic and social models are evaluated.[124]

This transcendence, Hollenbach points out, is found in the Church's principle of the dignity of the human person. The "concrete transcendence" of human dignity, and the claims that flow from it, are the standards by which ideologies are to be judged.[125]

Tenth, while *Populorum Progressio* had used the word "urgent" to describe the world's social and economic problems, *Octogesima Adveniens* uses the even stronger word "grave" to describe the social and economic situation. The new social problems listed in nos. 8-21, for example, "put the very future of man in jeopardy" (#7). Clearly Paul VI detects a deterioration in the world's social and economic condition, and an even greater urgency in improving it.

Octogesima Adveniens was not the first time the pope used such strong language in this context. In an address to the Vatican Diplomatic Corps on January 11, 1968, he said "it is the very destiny of the world that is at stake" if the world's economic problems were not resolved.[126] And in an address to the College of Cardinals on June 23, 1970 he warned the cardinals of "lethal consequences" if the world failed to bridge the gap between the rich and poor nations.[127]

3. Geographic area of application

The international range of application of the social question is an accepted fact in *Octogesima Adveniens* (see ##2, 23, 43). Even the letter's call for a pluralism of options and for local solutions to social, political, and economic problems presumes the internalization of a mature sense of the international reach of the social teaching.

D. The property teaching

While the property teaching in *Octogesima Adveniens* is conceptually consistent with the traditional teaching on the ownership and social function of property, its application is broadened once again to address the changing social and economic situation.

The document restates much of the property teaching of *Gaudium et Spes* and *Populorum Progressio*. It notes the need for more justice in the sharing of goods, both within and among nations (#43). The unequal distribution of goods worldwide is lamented (#7). Racism and nationalism deny the fundamental equality of all persons and the right of all to participate in their own development, and thus impede the just distribution of wealth (##16-17). Individualism, which is the foundation of liberal capitalism, should be renounced for the sake of the common good (#23).

The definition of property in *Octogesima Adveniens* is considerably broader than in the previous social teaching, due to the strong emphasis on the social function of property and on the international scope of the social question. Land, wages, social insurance, the right to work, and the right to develop skills continue to be included (#14). But the letter adds several new forms of property, forms which are under the control of nations, but which rightly belong to humanity as a whole.

The first of these is a country's productive capability (#43). A key element in any nation's development is its ability to manufacture goods. All nations should manage their productive potential in such a way that the goods they produce serve the genuine material needs of people, and not the superfluous needs of consumerism (#9). Developing nations should engage in economic planning to ensure an equitable distribution of the benefits of economic production. And nations have the duty to use their productive capacities to promote the universal common good.

A nation's trade policies (#43) deeply influence the pace of economic development both internally and in relation to other countries. Trade agreements negotiated justly by nations work to the benefit of both countries, by ensuring a just return for the products of each. The people of each nation, in turn, will share in the economic benefits resulting from these agreements.

The principles of co-management and the socialization of property apply to corporate profits (#43). Paul VI, in agreement with the teaching of John XXIII, calls for the just allocation of profits among those who supply capital, as well as those who supply their labor to the process of production. This socialization of profits is contrary to capitalist thinking, which holds that the greater share of profits accrues to those who supply capital to production.

A stable monetary system (#43) on the national and international levels is another key to economic development. The value of a country's currency affects the standard of living of its people, because it determines their ability to acquire goods and to accumulate wealth.

Multinational corporations can also be considered a form of property in *Octogesima Adveniens*, even though they are independent of states and nations, "and therefore not subject to control from the point of view of the commonwealth" (#44). The multinationals are criticized for their tendency to lead to an excessive concentration of the means of production. But because they are a form of property, all people are entitled to participate in multinationals - by contributing their labor, by participating in management, by having access to the goods they produce, and by sharing in their profits.

Another newly recognized form of property in the letter is the environment (#21). His inclusion of the environment in the definition of property is a logical outgrowth of Paul VI's emphasis on the social function of property and the international scope of the property question. The environment is viewed as the common possession of humanity, to be used for the good of all. Yet "man is suddenly becoming aware that by an ill-considered exploitation of nature he risks destroying it and becoming in his turn the victim of this degradation" (#21). The entire human family is called to assume responsibility for the preservation of the environment.

Although it does not deny the right of ownership of property, *Octogesima Adveniens* highlights those ends of property which are consistent with its social function. Because material possessions are properly ordered to use by all persons, "the more fortunate should renounce some of their rights so as to place their goods more generously at the service of others" (#23). Similarly, no. 43 makes a strong call for greater justice in the sharing of goods both within nations and on the international level.

Octogesima Adveniens addresses the relationship of justice and love in the context of the property teaching. Though there is a need for structures which establish true relationships of justice and equality, the law alone is not enough to protect property rights. Charity goes beyond social justice by teaching preferential respect for the poor and the renunciation of rights by persons and nations who are more well-off materially.

E. Conclusion of section

World events in general were less hopeful in the years immediately after 1967. The Vietnam War, the reaction among Catholics to Paul VI's encyclical *Humanae Vitae*, and a growing sense that the international development effort was failing, all contributed to the less than optimistic tone of *Octogesima Adveniens*.

The property teaching in *Octogesima Adveniens*, as in *Populorum Progressio*, is based on a theological anthropology. The letter highlights the dignity and social nature of the human person, which means that all persons possess a fundamental equality and the right to participate in their own development and liberation (##22-36). The letter's anthropology leads to a call for the self-fulfillment of individuals and nations (##42-47), including the fulfillment of property rights.

Socioeconomic systems are likewise evaluated in a manner similar to *Populorum Progressio*. Capitalism's tendency toward individualism is cited, and Christians are cautioned to exercise care in committing themselves to socialist movements. Collaboration with Communist movements may also be appropriate at times.

The letter refutes the charge that its critique of socioeconomic systems relativizes Christian principles. It maintains that its assessment of these ideologies demonstrates instead the concrete transcendence of Christianity.

Several new themes related to the creation of a just social order are introduced in *Octogesima Adveniens*. The letter's call for the work of justice is insistent. Persons have the right and the duty to participate in their own fulfillment. Believers are encouraged to engage in political activity, because economic activity alone has proven to be insufficient to create the just society. Economic democracy, in other words, is difficult to achieve without political democracy. Groups should formulate and pursue solutions to their social and economic problems at the local level, based on Christian principles. And the letter introduces the theme of liberation, understood primarily in economic terms, to the social teaching.

Economic development is viewed with ambivalence in *Octogesima Adveniens*. Worldwide development is needed, but all too often it is pursued mindlessly, without regard for personal dignity.

As in *Populorum Progressio*, the worldwide scope of the social question is a given in *Octogesima Adveniens*. And it projects an even greater sense of urgency regarding the world's social and economic problems than *Populorum Progressio*.

The property teaching in *Octogesima Adveniens* is traditional and consistent with the teaching in *Populorum Progressio*, and the social function of property remains the key to the application of the teaching. In the letter the social function of property is discussed as it relates to the worldwide distribution of goods, racism and nationalism, and the absolute individualism of many in the world.

The definition of property is again expanded to include the productive capability, trade policies, and monetary systems of nations, corporate profits, multinational corporations, and the environment. And the duty of the wealthy to share their goods with the poor is highlighted as a purpose of property. States should continue to promote social justice, but they are reminded that charity has a more important function to play than law and justice.

Octogesima Adveniens' call for political activity in the pursuit of fulfillment and peace, and its advocacy of local solutions to social and economic problems, are its major contributions to the social teaching of Paul VI. Both are based on his anthropology, which highlights human dignity, human rights, and social duties flowing from the creation of each person in the image of God.

IV. *DE IUSTITIA IN MUNDO* (November 30, 1971)

A. Historical setting

The Third Synod of Bishops convened in September 1971 with the directive from Pope Paul VI to address the subjects of the ministerial priesthood and justice in the world. Two documents were produced by the synod after a month of deliberations, and they were approved for publication by the pope on November 30, 1971.

Because *De Iustitia in Mundo* (the document is commonly known in English as *Justice in the World*, and will be referred to in this study by that title) is a synod document rather than an encyclical or pastoral letter of the pope himself, the question may legitimately be asked: in what sense can it be considered a part of Paul VI's social teaching?

In the first place, the two topics taken up by the synod had been assigned to the synod by Paul VI himself.[128] Second, the working draft of *Justice in the World* was prepared by the Pontifical Commission for Justice and Peace, whose formation had been authorized by Paul VI in 1969 as an outgrowth of *Populorum Progressio*. Third, Paul VI indicated his acceptance of the document in a rescript of November 30, 1971 signed by Vatican

Secretary of State Cardinal Villot.[129] Coleman considers this the most compelling reason of all, noting that "the ultimate promulgative authority of (*Justice in the World*) depended on papal approval." [130] Fourth, the content of *Justice in the World* is consistent with the previous social teaching of Paul VI, and generally reaffirms the teaching of *Populorum Progressio* and *Octogesima Adveniens*.

Justice in the World followed on the heels of *Octogesima Adveniens*, and does not depart from it in any significant way. It reflects as well the continuing influence of the Medellin documents and the liberation theology that was prominent in the Latin American Church.

B. Anthropology

Justice in the World contains the same anthropological framework as the previous social teachings of Paul VI, although it is not spelled out in as much detail (##5, 77). The human person in the *imago Dei*, with its implications for human dignity, human rights, and the social nature of the person, are again affirmed. The document focuses in particular on three implications of this anthropology - participation, the right to development, and solidarity.

While *Justice in the World* contains elements of creation theology, its basic perspective is a theology of redemption. The two theologies are juxtaposed in nos. 5 and 6. In no. 5 the unjust systems and structures of the world are called contradictions to the plan of the Creator. The next paragraph notes that these injustices must be understood in light of God's plan of salvation and liberation as these are revealed in the Paschal Mystery.

The theme of liberation is also presented in the context of redemption theology. The document points out that God revealed himself in the Old Testament as the "liberator of the oppressed and defender of the poor" (#30). And the fullness of liberation and salvation have come to light in the person of Christ, through his preaching and witness of life (#31). From its earliest days the Church has understood the death and resurrection of Christ as a call to love (*agape*) all persons in the totality of their existence, including their material well-being (#32).

The document's redemption theology allows it to deal directly with the reality of sin in the world. Sin is described in the Augustinian sense of the word, as a perversion of the order intended by God (#5). The liberation and salvation of Christ are needed to transform a world permeated with sinful injustices. Some of the more serious injustices are spelled out in nos. 21-25, and these injustices are viewed as sinful situations. The Church herself is called to purification from her sinfulness in matters of economics and justice (##40-60).

C. Topics related to property

1. Economic systems and property

Justice in the World contains no detailed examination of the capitalist, socialist, or Communist systems. Rather, the document notes that new ways of understanding human dignity, based on the analysis of existing economic, political, technological, and ecological systems, are emerging in the world (#12). As with *Octogesima Adveniens*, the demands of human dignity are the standard by which all economic systems are evaluated.

2. Principles and strategies of actualization

There are seven topics related to the actualization of the property teaching in *Justice in the World* which are discussed in this section.

First, the primary focus of *Justice in the World* is the need for action on behalf of justice. This theme is stated emphatically in the introduction: "Action on behalf of justice and participation in the transformation of the world appear to us as a constitutive dimension of the preaching of the Gospel, or, in other words, of the Church's mission for the redemption of the human race and its liberation from every oppressive situation" (#6). This statement is the strongest in the entire modern papal social teaching about the duty of Christians to act for justice in the world. There has been considerable debate over the meaning of the term "constitutive" in the document.[131] It is obvious, in any case, that justice is seen by the Synod fathers as a necessary and indispensable dimension of Christian living, and the statement sets the tone for the rest of the document.

Justice in the World calls specifically for social justice - the establishment of structures of law, economics, politics, and culture which guarantee the rights of all persons in society.

Maritain's description of justice was strikingly similar to that of *Justice in the World.* Maritain wrote that justice, in simplest terms, meant that in internal and external affairs political decisions should aim at giving each citizen, group, or nation its due. Concretely, this involved securing the common good, racial nondiscrimination, religious tolerance, economic welfare, and political freedom.[132]

The document cites a list of injustices which deserve special attention. Migrants are often treated badly in the country in which they work (#21). Refugees and many other persons suffer from persecution (#22). In some parts of the world believers are persecuted for their faith (#23). The rights of persons are restricted because of violence or torture (#24). Legalized abortion and the imposition of contraceptives deny persons the freedom to bear children and form a family (#25).

Justice, however, is not an absolute value. The supreme value, that to which all others are subordinated, is love. "Christian love of neighbor and justice cannot be separated;" "Love implies an absolute demand for justice" (#34); "Justice attains its inner fullness only in love" (#34). *Justice in the World* reflects traditional Christian thinking on the relationship of justice and love.[133]

While the document calls for justice *ad extra*, in the world as a whole, it adds that justice should also be practiced *ad intra*, within the Church (#40). This is a courageous and humble acknowledgement on the part of the Church. It was inspired by the Medellin documents, which had explicitly called for the Church in Latin America to live in spiritual and material poverty, to be a "poor Church."[134] *Justice in the World* explicitly acknowledges the need for witness on the part of persons in the Church as an essential aspect of the work for justice.

The need for education for justice (#49) is also a reflection of Medellin. This process of education for justice is what the Medellin documents referred to as *concientizacion* - the need for social education to awaken the social conscience of all strata of society[135]. Education for justice is designed to lead to that renewal of heart which alone can make action for justice genuine (#51).

The document cites a special need for action for justice on the international level. All nations are called to promote the worldwide justice effort in several ways: by ratifying and adhering to the United Nations Declaration of Human Rights (#64); by supporting the United Nations (#65); and by fostering the aims of the Second Development Decade (#66).

Second, the teaching on participation is in many respects a continuation of that theme in *Populorum Progressio.* Human dignity demands that persons have the right to participate in the economic, social, and political arenas (#18). Developing nations should be guaranteed the economic and political autonomy to develop themselves, so that they can "take their future into their own hands" (#17). In order to accomplish this "a certain responsible nationalism" is allowed as a transitional measure (#17), in order to build a sense of national solidarity for the promotion of the common good, and to allow developing nations the autonomy to develop themselves as they see fit. This approach is consistent with the call to local solutions in *Octogesima Adveniens*, but differs from *Populorum Progressio*'s view of nationalism as an obstacle to world solidarity.

Third, in *Justice in the World* the teaching on solidarity is not as optimistic as in *Populorum Progressio*, nor is it given as much emphasis. The document notes a paradox involving solidarity: that the forces working for world solidarity - technology, science, communications, economic interdependence, the environment - are stronger than ever, but that the forces of division and antagonism -

nations, empires, classes, the arms race - are also increasing in strength (##8-9).

Fourth, the notions of justice and liberation are interrelated in *Justice in the World*, reflecting the influence of liberation theology and the theology of redemption. God is viewed as the liberator of the oppressed in the performance of the duties of justice (#30), and Christ is acknowledged as liberator and savior from sin and injustice (#31).

The treatment of the theme of liberation is much the same as in *Octogesima Adveniens*, which had viewed liberation primarily as deliverance from the sins of economic and social oppression. Medellin had alluded to this same point, by noting that Christ proclaimed the intervention of God's justice on behalf of the poor.[136] All three documents reflect the influence of Latin American liberation theology.[137]

Actually the term "liberation" predates *Justice in the World*, the Medellin documents and *Octogesima Adveniens* by several years. It appeared in the writings of Lebret as early as 1955. Lebret used the phrase "Christian Liberation" to describe deliverance from oppression in economic and social terms.[138]

Justice in the World preserves the understanding of the priority of liberation in the temporal realm. It points out that the Old Testament reveals God as the liberator of the oppressed and defender of the poor (#30), and that the Gospel dictates that the Church work for the liberation of humanity so that "the Christian message of love and justice shows its effectiveness through action in the cause of justice in the world" (#35). From this biblical perspective the document calls for the liberation of the human race from every oppressive situation (#6), and it specifically refers to the need for nations to achieve liberation through development (#16). While there are references to liberation from sin (##6, 31, 77), they are secondary to the call for temporal liberation.

Fesquet is critical of what he calls the synod's obsession with the concept of temporal liberation.[139] Rubio also claims that the term "liberation" was understood in strictly economic terms by the synod fathers, and not in its transcendent, supernatural sense as the Scriptures understand it.[140]

In *Justice in the World* the concept of liberation seems to be related, at least negatively, to the concept of integral development as it was understood in *Populorum Progressio.* Liberation implies the elimination of all those oppressive and unjust conditions which hinder the complete development of all persons.

Fifth, *Justice in the World* continues to employ "development" as the predominant paradigm. But the document reflects Paul VI's disenchantment with the failing worldwide development effort. Walsh and Davies, for instance, note that by 1970 "not only had economic growth failed to bring about a more equitable distribution of wealth, it had mitigated against such a distribution."[141] Still, development remains an important theme, perhaps because the working draft of *Justice in the World* was prepared by the Pontifical Commission Justice and Peace.[142]

The document states that the hope of sufficient economic growth so that all could at least be fed "has proved a vain hope" (#10). Yet it advocates the "right to development" (#13), defined as "a dynamic interpretation of all those fundamental human rights upon which the aspirations of individuals and nations are based" (#15). In the fulfillment of the right to development individual cultures should be respected. The peoples of the world should be the principal architects of their own development, and there should be equality of participation for all peoples (#71).

Justice in the World reflects the same discouragement with the worldwide development effort as *Octogesima Adveniens.* It notes that the industrial and technological order favors a concentration of wealth, power, and decision making in the hands of small public or private groups. This new order had been caused in part by development efforts in the Third World, and by the industrialized nations of the First World. Its results had fallen far short of the hopes expressed in *Mater et Magistra* and *Populorum Progressio*.

There are two solutions offered to rectify this situation. The first is the establishment of systems and structures of social justice which will allow for increased participation. A second solution is the adoption of a simpler lifestyle on the personal level: "Those who are already rich are bound to accept a less material way of life, with less waste, in order to avoid the destruction of the heritage which they are obliged by absolute justice to share with all other members of the human race" (#70).

There is a lingering confidence in the possibilities of economic development, expressed in language which is reminiscent of *Populorum Progressio*. Number 16, for example, states that "the right to development is above all a right to hope according to the concrete measure of contemporary humanity." And in the same vein no. 18 notes the impossibility of achieving true progress without economic development and participation "and the necessity too of an increase in wealth."

Sixth, in *Justice in the World* the temporal and religious dimensions of existence are seen as independent, yet inseparable from each other. Because God identifies himself with all people, especially the poor, and because every person is created in God's image, the document concludes that response to God in faith and response to the neighbor in love are fundamentally the same. The Christian faith is at the root of the idea of justice, and by the same token the demands of justice are religious obligations.

Finally, while *Justice in the World* reflects Paul VI's discouragement with the worldwide development effort, this is not its primary affective tone. The document is meant to be a word of hope for the kind of radical transformation needed "to build a world which will reach the fullness of creation only when it becomes the work of man for man" (#77).

3. Geographic area of application

The worldwide scope of justice and human solidarity had become a standard part of Paul VI's social teaching, so that in *Justice in the World* there is no need to spell it out in great detail. The international range of application of the document appears throughout the document (##1, 7-28, 63-71).

D. The property teaching

The document restates a number of ideas which were firmly entrenched in Paul VI's previous property teaching. There is a clear call for individuals to share their material wealth with those in need out of respect for the social function of property. This is coupled with a call for renewal in attitudes, personal lifestyle, and institutional practices within the Church regarding property rights and material goods.

There is a strong emphasis in *Justice in the World* on the property issue within the Church, most likely due to the influence of Medellin. It recalls the practice of the early Church, in which fraternal love was practiced in a voluntary sharing of material goods (#32). Persons in the Church are entitled to property rights such as fair wages and social security, and lay persons should help to administer Church property (#41). The institutional Church is called to give evangelical witness in its use of temporal possessions: "Our faith demands of us a certain sparingness in use, and the Church is obliged to live and administer its own goods in such a way that the Gospel is proclaimed to the poor" (#47). Churches of the rich and poor nations are encouraged to divide and share their material and human resources (#59).

Rubio reacted negatively to this whole discussion of possessions and property rights within the Church, saying that *Justice in the World* employed exclusively "human" language when speaking about the Church and its attitude toward the use of temporal goods.[143]

Justice in the World contains a very broad definition of property, reflecting the internationalization of the social teaching and the anthropology of Paul VI. Property, understood as those material goods and rights whose function is to serve the common good, and which persons and nations have a right to possess for their fuller development, includes several new elements in *Justice in the World.* The economic and political power of nations (##9-10) determine to a great extent the distribution of the material wealth of nations, and the exercise of these powers should be ordered to the common good. Housing (#10) is a prerequisite to integral fulfillment for individuals and families. Energy (#11), raw materials (#66), and markets (#66) are necessities for the economic and social development of nations.

The most important contribution of *Justice in the World* to the property teaching lies in its broader understanding of what constitutes property. Since *Rerum Novarum* the definition of property in the social teaching expanded in two ways: from the strictly material and tangible, such as land, wages, and insurance, to the intangible and immaterial, such as economic and political power; and from personal and class-oriented property, like wages and social insurance, to national and international property, like economic and political power, markets, energy, and raw materials.

Justice in the World focuses on the implications for the Church of the social function of property. The Church is called to give evangelical witness in its use of temporal possessions: ". . . our faith demands of us a certain sparingness of use, and the Church is obliged to live and administer its own goods in such a way that the Gospel is proclaimed to the poor" (#47).

Consistent with Paul VI's belief in the need for nations and international institutions to build worldwide solidarity, and his enduring allegiance to the United Nations, *Justice in the World* promotes the aims of the Second Development Decade (#66):

- The transfer of a certain unspecified percentage of the annual incomes of the rich nations to the developing nations. A draft of *Justice in the*

World had stipulated that one percent of gross national product should be donated, but this was deleted from the final draft because the bishops could not reach agreement on this point.[144] This transfer of wealth is dictated by the social function of property in order to ensure a more just distribution of goods worldwide.

- Fairer prices for raw materials of the developing nations.
- The opening of the markets of the richer nations.
- Preferential treatment for exports of manufactured goods from the developing nations (#66). Steps 2, 3, and 4 must be taken to overcome the economic exploitation of the underdeveloped Third World countries by the developed First World.
- A graduated, or progressive income tax. Progressivity in taxation is a means of distributing fairly the tax burden of each nation, and of the world.
- An economic and social plan for the whole world, in order to promote the universal common good.

In addition, in order to balance the concentration of power between the richer and poorer nations, governments are exhorted to contribute to a development fund (#69). This is a reiteration of the World Fund concept in *Populorum Progressio*, but stated less emphatically. The World Fund envisioned by Paul VI never did gain acceptance among the international community despite, or perhaps because of the fact that by 1971 the world was spending some $300 billion on arms.[145]

E. Conclusion of section

Because *Justice in the World* appeared the same year as *Octogesima Adveniens* it was framed by the same historical events, with the exception that *Justice in the World* was produced by the Synod of Bishops. Its anthropology is also consistent with the previous social documents of Paul VI, except that the juxtaposition of redemption theology and creation theology allows *Justice in the World* to deal more effectively with the reality of sin in the world.

Nor does the treatment of topics related to the property teaching in *Justice in the World* depart from the previous teaching of Paul VI. Socioeconomic systems are evaluated in terms of their effect on human dignity. Individuals and nations are called to participate in their own fulfillment. Liberation in the social and economic spheres is advocated. There is dissatisfaction with economic development, but still the right to development for all people is affirmed. The temporal and religious spheres, viewed in terms of love of God and love of the neighbor, are seen as inseparable. Only two points of emphasis in *Justice in the World* distinguish it from its predecessors. First is its strong endorsement of action for justice as a constitutive dimension of the Church's mission. Second, its tone is somewhat more hopeful than *Octogesima Adveniens*.

The property teaching in *Justice in the World* affirms the basic principles of the traditional teaching, while expanding in some ways the implications of those principles. It continues to assert the primacy of the social function of property. In light of this principle individuals are encouraged to adopt new attitudes towards their wealth, and the property issue within the Church is examined in detail. Some new forms of property, which are more intangible and international in scope than previous social documents, are added to Paul VI's ever-growing list: the economic and political power of nations, housing, energy, and markets. Believers are admonished to give evangelical witness in their use of goods, in light of the purposes of property. States are encouraged to promote the right of property by fulfilling the aims of the Second Development Decade.

It should be noted that some commentators reacted quite negatively to *Justice in the World.* M. Delecluse of IRFED (Institut international de recherche et de formation en vue du développement harmonis), which had been founded by Lebret, criticized the document for not being serious enough. Delecluse maintained that although the document mentioned the presence of injustices in the world, it failed to identify them. It failed to mention, for instance, such problems as the inequality of the opportunity for development, the inequality of the international monetary system, the problem of employment, international firms, equality of access to culture and knowledge, and access to the power to make decisions.[146] Rubio faulted *Justice in the World* for lacking unity, saying that it was merely "a mosaic, a compromise" of previous teachings.[147] While Rubio's criticism is valid to a certain extent, the same can also be said of any of the papal social documents, since each was formed through compromise and consensus.

V. *EVANGELII NUNTIANDI* (December 8, 1975)

A. Historical setting

There was considerable turbulence and rapid change in many parts of the world during the years between *Justice in the World* (1971) and *Evangelii Nuntiandi* (1975). American involvement in the Vietnam War came to an end in April 1975, according to the terms of a peace treaty concluded in 1973. Cambodia, which had been a part of the Vietnam conflict since the early 1970s, became embroiled in a civil war which would lead to the terrible carnage inflicted by the Khmer Rouge regime. Hostilities continued in Northern Ireland, as resistance to British occupation forces increased. The Middle East was the focus of world attention in two ways. Yet another regional war, between Israel and Egypt, erupted briefly in 1973. And the industrialized world was dealt a stunning blow in late 1973 when the Organization of Petroleum Exporting Countries (OPEC), acting in unison, dramatically raised the price of crude oil. Famine and drought in 1974 killed thousands in East Africa, from Mauritania to Ethiopia, and a bloody civil war broke out in the still-colonized African countries of Angola and Mozambique.

The Church remained unsettled into the mid-1970s, as Catholics continued the struggle to interpret and implement the teachings of Vatican II, *Humanae Vitae*, and the social teaching of Pope Paul VI. A prime example of this struggle was the 32nd General Congregation of the Jesuits, which took place shortly after the conclusion of the 1974 Synod and before the promulgation of *Evangelii Nuntiandi*. Debate at the Congregation over the issues of the "grades" and the mission of the Society gave Paul VI an opportunity to articulate his position on the relationship between faith and justice, the same position he would espouse in *Evangelii Nuntiandi*.[148]

Paul VI's ambitious international travel schedule was drastically curtailed after an attempt was made on his life in Manila during a pastoral visit to the Far East in 1972. Although he survived an injury he suffered in the attack, he never travelled outside Italy again after the incident.

Evangelii Nuntiandi was the product of the Fourth Synod of Bishops, who met in Rome in September 1974. By the close of the Synod the bishops failed to agree on a major text on the subject of evangelization. They handed their draft over to Paul VI, who reworked it and issued *Evangelii Nuntiandi* on December 8, 1975.

Evangelii Nuntiandi reflects the ongoing influence of liberation theology and liberation movements, especially those in Latin America. But it also reveals the Church's growing disaffection of these movements, many of which seemed to be politically motivated exclusively and to be breaking their connections with the Church. For example, the document devotes a whole section to the *communidades de base* which had become so much a part of Church life in Latin America. The document admonishes them to maintain a spiritual orientation, and to work closely with their local bishops and with the Church in Rome in their political activities.

It can legitimately be asked whether *Evangelii Nuntiandi* is really a part of the papal social teaching. Walsh and Davies maintain that the document is "not primarily a statement of Catholic social teaching."[149] There are a number of factors in support of this contention:

- The primary paradigm in *Evangelii Nuntiandi* is evangelization, understood in the context of the Church's mission to proclaim the Gospel, rather than development. Most of the principal themes of Paul VI's previous social teaching - development, justice, human rights, property, liberation - are secondary in the document, and discussed only as they relate to the paradigm of evangelization.

- The document's treatment of the liberation theme differs markedly from *Octogesima Adveniens* and *Justice in the World*. In *Evangelii Nuntiandi* liberation is defined first and foremost as liberation from sin and death, rather than from oppressive economic, political, and social conditions.
- *Evangelii Nuntiandi* stresses the need for interior change and renewal (*metanoia*) over external renewal of economic, social and political structures, which is the work of international social justice.
- The primacy of the spiritual dimension of the Church's mission is stressed in *Evangelii Nuntiandi*, rather than economic activity (*Populorum Progressio*), political activity (*Octogesima Adveniens*), or the work of justice (*Justice in the World*). For example, no. 36 notes the need to build up structures that are more human, more just, more respectful of rights, and less oppressive, but these structures should be the outgrowth of interior conversion of heart more than the external concretization of social justice.

During the synod, on October 23, 1974 the bishops had issued a statement which used stronger development and human rights language than would eventually appear in *Evangelii Nuntiandi*. The statement mentions human dignity rooted in the *imago Dei*, integral development, and that "the promotion of rights is required by the gospel and is central to (the Church's) ministry." [150]

- *Evangelii Nuntiandi* greatly downplays the anthropology of Paul VI's previous social teaching (see ##26, 33).

Despite their reservations, Walsh and Davies still conclude that *Evangelii Nuntiandi* "is a profound theological statement of the Church's commitment to the struggle for justice." [151] In its own way *Evangelii Nuntiandi* can be considered a genuine part of the social teaching of Paul VI. It deals with many of the central themes of his previous social teaching: the integral development of humanity, economic development, social justice, liberation, and property. But these themes are approached from a different theological perspective than *Populorum Progressio*, *Octogesima Adveniens*, and *Justice in the World*. This is due to the shift in *Evangelii*

Nuntiandi from creation theology to a theology of redemption which focuses on the Paschal Mystery, the salvation of humanity and the world from sin and death through the death and resurrection of Christ. Redemption theology has two important implications in the document. First, there is a more acute awareness of sin, and the need for salvation and liberation from sin on the personal and societal levels, than in Paul VI's previous social documents. Second, strong emphasis is placed on spiritual renewal as the necessary preliminary step to the renewal of the temporal order. Paul VI's previous social documents had made temporal renewal the steppingstone to spiritual fulfillment.

In general the social teaching in *Evangelii Nuntiandi* shifts from an emphasis on temporal themes to spiritual themes. The document's central paradigm of evangelization is indicative of this shift. For example, evangelization is linked with liberation from anything that oppresses humanity, but first and foremost "liberation from sin and the evil one" (#9). Primary among the methods of evangelizing are proclamation of the Word and personal witness of life rather than action for economic and political development. Salvation as it is proclaimed in the evangelization effort is more eschatological and transcendent than imminent and temporal. Although the temporal mission of the Church is not overlooked, in *Evangelii Nuntiandi* it assumes a subordinate role to the spiritual mission.

The shift to the spiritual even affects the property teaching. While the social function of property and the duties that attend to it are preserved, the document places greater emphasis on simplicity of life and personal service to the poor than on structural social justice and international collaboration.

B. Anthropology

The theology of *Evangelii Nuntiandi* emphasizes the primacy of salvation, where Paul VI's prior social teaching had been written primarily from the perspective of a theology of creation.[152] Some salvation theologies stresses the importance of the action of Christ in saving humanity from sin and death. This salvation is what enables the social, economic, and political order to be transformed. Faith's role in the theology of salvation is to transform the world from "the inside out." Interior, spiritual renewal leads to the transformation of the temporal order.

Paul VI's previous social teaching, on the other hand, stressed the importance of restoring the order intended by God at the time of creation. There the function of the faith was to transform the world from the "outside in." The renewal of the temporal order allows persons and nations to fulfill themselves in material terms first, so that they can fulfill themselves spiritually. Creation theology is behind such themes as the *imago Dei*, world solidarity, participation, and the positive concept of peace.

The traditional property teaching is also better understood in the context of the plan of creation, as part of the restoration of the order intended by God at the time of creation. It implies that material goods should be available for use by all persons for their development and for social peace, according to the plan of God.

Another way of making this distinction is that *Evangelii Nuntiandi* is primarily soteriological in tone, where Paul VI's previous social teaching had been primarily incarnational. The transformation of the temporal order is seen mostly as a result, an extension, and an outgrowth of the saving action of Christ, where his previous teaching tended to view the temporal order as the concrete manifestation of the love of God in the world.

C. Topics related to property

1. Economic systems and property

Evangelii Nuntiandi contains no systematic analysis of capitalism, socialism, and Communism. Rather it admonishes Christians to adhere to the timeless tenets of the Gospel rather than any temporal ideology. Evangelizers in the Church should preach the Gospel, and not "their own selves or their personal ideas" (#15). The notion that salvation is first of all transcendent and eschatological (#27) can be construed as a criticism of the limitations of Marxist and many socialist humanisms, which restrict themselves to the purely temporal. If her mission were reduced to "initiatives of the political or social order" the Church would lose her fundamental meaning, and "her message of liberation would no longer have any originality and would easily be open to monopolization and manipulation by ideological systems and political parties" (#32). Evangelization and liberation are based on a concept of the person which can never be sacrificed "to the needs of any strategy, practice, or short-term efficiency" (#33).

Paul VI would continue to express his dissatisfaction with socioeconomic ideologies after *Evangelii Nuntiandi*. For example, in an address to a general audience in 1975 he said that the Christian solution to development is not a compromise between liberal capitalism and communistic socialism, but "an original, organic, dynamic expression of authentic social fellowship" based on moral, spiritual, and religious values.[153] And in a message delivered by Cardinal Villot to the 30th Spanish Social Week in 1976 the pope noted that the economy, if it is to be humanized, must avoid becoming the servant of either capitalist or Marxist ideology.[154]

2. Principles and strategies of actualization

In this section seven themes having to do with the fulfillment of the property teaching in *Evangelii Nuntiandi* are analyzed.

First, in a major departure from the social teaching since Leo XIII, *Evangelii Nuntiandi* employs evangelization as its principal paradigm and organizing theme. This represents a change in the teaching from the paradigm of development, which is anthropologically-based and has economic and political overtones, to the paradigm of evangelization, which is ecclesiologically-based and has strongly spiritual overtones.

Paul VI had made known his shift to evangelization in April 1974 in an address to the Council of the Secretariat of the Synod of Bishops: "But now a new topic of the highest importance urgently confronts you for the first time - the topic of evangelization." "This subject is of the greatest interest to the Church, pertaining as it does to its nature and deeply rooted as it is in its life." [155]

Laurentin discusses the evolution of the term "evangelization," noting its ever-expanding implications. Before Vatican II it referred to "the first announcing of the Good News (*kerygma*)." At the Council it came to mean "the whole ministry of the Word." And by the 1974 Synod it meant "the whole mission of the Church." [156]

Evangelii Nuntiandi describes itself as a "meditation on evangelization" (#5). Evangelization is described as the Church's essential mission, because it was the mission of Christ (#6). The main question it addresses is how well the Church is equipped to evangelize, to proclaim the Gospel "with conviction, freedom of spirit, and effectiveness" to the modern world (#4).

Numbers 8-15 discuss the essential aspects of evangelization. The first is the Kingdom of God, which is to be considered an absolute value (#8). The second is salvation, which is "liberation from everything that oppresses man but which is above all liberation from sin and the evil one" (#9). Both the Kingdom of God and salvation are gained "by force" - through toil and suffering, through fidelity to the Gospel, abnegation, the cross, the beatitudes, and *metanoia*, or interior change of heart (#10).

The document then explains why and how "the task of evangelizing all people constitutes the essential mission of the Church" (#14). It states that "evangelizing is in fact the grace and vocation proper to the Church, her deepest identity. She exists in order to evangelize, that is to say in order to preach and teach, to be the channel of the gift of grace, to reconcile sinners with God, and to perpetuate Christ's sacrifice in the Mass, which is the memorial of his death and glorious resurrection" (#14). The Church receives her vocation and motivation to evangelize from Christ: "It is above all (Jesus') mission and his condition of being an evangelizer that (the Church) is called upon to continue" (#15).

An explanation of the meaning of evangelization is then detailed. First, evangelization means bringing the good news to all strata of humanity, transforming humanity from within (#18). The message of the gospel involves "upsetting, through the powers of the gospel, mankind's criteria of judgment, determining values, etc." (#19). Second, the gospel is proclaimed both by witness and by word (#22). Third, it involves the reception of the word by the hearer, and adherence to a new way of life (#23). Fourth, those who have been evangelized go on to evangelize others (#24).

The content of the message of evangelization is presented in nos. 25-30:

- Evangelization attests to God who is Father, which means that all persons are brothers and sisters. Here the anthropology of previous papal social teaching is alluded to (#26).
- In Christ, salvation has been offered to all - not an imminent, temporal salvation first of all, but a transcendent, eschatological salvation (#27).

Numbers 40-48, on the methods of evangelization, again demonstrate how different *Evangelii Nuntiandi* is from Paul VI's previous social documents. The methods of evangelization include witness of life, preaching, catechetical instruction, mass media, the sacraments and the word, and popular religion. There is no mention of work for justice, which in *Justice in the World* was described as a "constitutive dimension" of Christian activity.

The discussion of the Church's missionary work (##49-58) is mindful of the perceived dangers of some Third World missionary efforts. Therefore it holds that the missionary effort must be religious first of all (#53), and that the role of the laity, but not of religious men and women, includes political, social, and economic activity. Qualities which should be exhibited by the evangelist (##76-82) include witness of life, simplicity of life, prayer, charity, obedience, detachment, and humility. Nowhere does the document say that missionaries should work for justice, or for the creation of the structures called for by social justice. Personal and interior qualities of the missionary are seen as more important than social, external qualities.

Second, Laurentin maintains that the consensus of the Synod was that "the Gospel is a message of liberation." [157] This assertion is true, but only given *Evangelii Nuntiandi*'s understanding of liberation - that liberation is understood first and foremost as deliverance from sin rather than from oppressive economic and political situations. Liberation is subsumed under the theme of evangelization. Thus, liberation is from "all that oppresses man," but is above all liberation "from sin and the evil one" (#9).

Both before and after the 1974 Synod Bigo wrote of a different concept of liberation, one more in line with Paul VI's social teaching prior to *Evangelii Nuntiandi*. For example in *The Church and Third World Revolution* (1977), he wrote that one of the characteristics of the Third World is its striving for liberation "from a lack of basic necessities." In the book he discussed liberation at some length, using language which referred to liberation more in economic and political terms than in spiritual terms. For example: "(Liberation) is the very coming of the Kingdom in its temporal form." He concluded his discussion of this issue with these words: "Everyone of us will be judged by whether or not we gave bread to the hungry, water to the thirsty, freed the captive." Bigo mentioned only once that the "third revolution" which he foresaw is not just an economic revolution, but also a spiritual revolution.[158]

Evangelii Nuntiandi points out that some persons in the Church want to reduce the Church's mission to the purely temporal, in the name of liberation. Walsh and Davies note in this context that "Pope Paul establishes a firm link between salvation and liberation, but he is concerned that the former be reduced to the latter: that the Church's role be reduced to a purely temporal one." [159] Paul VI made this same point on other occasions, as in his message to the 84th German Katholikentag in 1974: "To wish to limit the responsibility of Christians in the service of men and the world merely to the economic, social, and cultural spheres would mean betrayal not only of the Church's real mission, but also of man himself. Man's complete human development necessarily requires the religious dimension. The real evil that enslaves and threatens man is not this or that unjust social system, but sin, man's alienation from his creator. Even if man were to succeed in creating an earthly paradise, eliminating all enslavement and all poverty, he would still need God's saving message above all."[160]

A third issue, the use of violence, is related in the document to the property question. Consistent with his position since *Octogesima Adveniens*, Paul VI rejects violence in unambiguous terms: "The Church cannot accept violence, especially the force of arms - which is uncontrollable once it is let loose - and indiscriminate death as the path of liberation." "We must say and reaffirm that violence is not in accord with the gospel, that it is not Christian" (#37). Paul VI's intention is to distance himself and the Church from the violence of some of the liberation movements in Latin America. Clearly violence is not an acceptable recourse in the pursuit of rights, including the property right.

Walsh and Davies maintain that Paul VI was worried that his acceptance of liberation would be construed as an acceptance of violence,[161] and the language of *Evangelii Nuntiandi* bears out this claim. The document is careful to assert the primacy of the spiritual dimension of liberation, and to reject violence in the name of liberation. This rejection of violence had been an established part of Paul VI's social teaching since *Octogesima Adveniens*, and it is not surprising to find it once again in *Evangelii Nuntiandi*. Still, the fact that it receives only the briefest mention is indicative of the new direction of the social teaching in *Evangelii Nuntiandi*. One implication of this position for the property teaching is that Christians should be more concerned with interior spiritual renewal than with the expropriation of land.

Fourth, although the principal paradigm in *Evangelii Nuntiandi* is evangelization, it deals as well with the "development" concepts and themes of Paul VI's earlier social documents. In particular the document explores the ways in which evangelization and development are related to each other.

The language of development and human rights is found in *Evangelii Nuntiandi*, but is given far less emphasis than in Paul VI's previous social teaching. Number 29 notes, at the end of a lengthy list of what constitutes the content of evangelization, "the unceasing interplay of the gospel and of man's concrete life, both personal and social." It goes on to say that evangelization is explicit about "the rights and duties of every human being;" evangelization is about "life in society, about international life, peace, justice, and development." This is a far cry from the language of development in *Populorum Progressio*, *Octogesima Adveniens*, and *Justice in the World*.

Fifth, *Evangelii Nuntiandi* deals briefly with the issue of the primacy of the Holy See in relation to the local church. *Octogesima Adveniens* had emphasized the need for local solutions to economic and social problems based on the Gospel and the social teaching.[162] In *Evangelii Nuntiandi* the primacy of the universal Church, and the primacy of the pope, are stressed (##62-67). Paul VI's position is a response to some of the Latin American liberation groups which were acting with increasing independence, and at times even in defiance of Rome.

Paul VI would continue to emphasize papal and Roman authority after *Evangelii Nuntiandi*. In a *motu proprio* on the Pontifical Commission for Justice and Peace in 1976 he defined the commission's function in terms of study to foster action for evangelization, "with fidelity to the supreme authority of the Church as their primary guide and pledge of effectiveness."[163]

Sixth, in *Evangelii Nuntiandi* development is seen as a necessary part of evangelization - but only a part. "Between evangelization and human advancement - development and liberation - there are in fact profound links." These links are anthropological, because the person to be evangelized is subject to social and economic questions; theological, because the "plan of redemption" touches the very concrete situations of injustice to be combatted and justice to be restored; and evangelical - a "link of charity" (#31). The question is then posed: "How in fact can one proclaim the new commandment without promoting in justice and in peace the true, authentic advancement of man?" (#31).

Given these links between evangelization and development, the document spells out the proper relationship between the two. First, both must take in the "whole man," including humanity's openness to the absolute. Second, they relate to a concept of the human person which cannot be sacrificed to any ideology. Third, they must preserve the primacy of the spiritual mission of the Church (##33-34).

Bigo had compared what he called "civilization" and evangelization, and found a complementarity between the temporal and spiritual orders which they symbolize. "Civilization (which involves work for the promotion of human rights) is for the growth of man, evangelization (which involves the relationship between the life of grace and the temporal life, and whose goal is, using Pope Pius XII's phrase, 'the consecration of the world') is for the growth of Christ."[164] He concluded that although civil society and religious society are independent of each other, they nevertheless resemble each other closely.[165]

Paul VI had addressed this subject in his opening remarks to the 1974 Synod: "It will be necessary to define more accurately the relationship between evangelization properly so called and the whole human effort toward development, for which the Church's help is rightly expected even though this is not its specific task." He said that evangelization's aim is strictly religious, but added that "this by no means implies that evangelization could or should ignore the importance of worrisome current problems concerning justice, liberation, development, and world peace."[166] In the same vein Bishop Eduardo Pironio, President of CELAM in 1974, said in his report to the Synod about the state of evangelization in Latin America: "Evangelization has a direct relation to the promotion of humanity, and the full liberation of peoples."[167]

The relationship between evangelization and development in *Evangelii Nuntiandi* can be summed up in four points. First, the mission of the Church involves both evangelization and work for development. Second, the spiritual dimension of the Church's mission, the transcendent dimension of salvation, has priority over the temporal work of economic and social development. Third, the clergy should focus its energies on the spiritual work of evangelization, and the laity should concentrate on the economic and political tasks of development. Fourth, the personal and internal signs of human advancement are emphasized over the social and external. Evangelization transforms humanity "from within," through conversion, where development transforms humanity "from without." In *Evangelii Nuntiandi* the paradigm of human progress is subsumed under the paradigm of evangelization.

Paul VI would continue to speak and write on the relationship between evangelization and development after *Evangelii Nuntiandi*, giving greater emphasis to the primacy of the spiritual. For example, in an address to the International Congress on Missiology in 1975: "We must get back to the idea of God and to the positive fact of religion; we must give our religious faith the place and role that belong to it in a wise and organic vision of human life. Religion does not impede our secular activity; rather, it respects, fosters, rectifies, and sanctifies it." [168]

He did not stop speaking about economic or political problems, but he addressed his concerns in these areas to temporal authorities, and focused on the religious dimension when addressing Church leaders. In a message to U.N. Secretary General Kurt Waldheim in 1974, he stressed such traditional development issues as the importance of bridging the gap between the rich and poor nations, the need for international collaboration, solidarity, just structures, and the use of property for the common good.[169] Likewise, in an address to the Rome World Food Conference in 1974 he stressed the importance of industrialization in the world development effort, and the continuing gap between the rich and poor nations.[170] But in a September 1975 address to the members and consultors of the Pontifical Commission for Justice and Peace, which had been set up to study and help promote the world development effort, he said: "The role of the Commission is to show, patiently, courageously, and lucidly, that evangelization in the full sense of the word is the means by which the Church contributes in its own way 'to establishing peace and laying the foundation of human and international brotherhood' (*Gaudium et Spes*, #89)." [171] Likewise, in an address to the Episcopal Conferences of Africa and Madagascar in 1975, he declared that the conference should be geared toward studying the meaning of evangelization in Africa: "Despite the many difficult problems calling for your attention, Bishops of Africa - underdevelopment, social disparities based on class, illiteracy, lack of personal material means, etc. - the faith must always be the principle guiding your action and the supreme motive for the Church's activity in society." [172]

Finally, Paul VI's skepticism of purely material progress is evident in *Evangelii Nuntiandi*. The fact that the document employs the paradigm of evangelization rather than of development is indicative of the pope's change in attitude. *Evangelii Nuntiandi* cites a seventh theme, the need for spiritual development accomplished through the work of evangelization, "to make the Church of the twentieth century even better fitted for proclaiming the Gospel to the people of the twentieth century" (#2).

3. Geographic area of application

Evangelii Nuntiandi preserves the international perspective of Paul VI's previous social documents. The major difference is that the document is addressed more to the universal Church than to all of humanity. Proclaiming the Gospel is seen as a service rendered to the Christian community and "to the whole of humanity" (#1). Non-Christians are viewed primarily as objects of the evangelization effort, where in the previous social documents they were considered equal partners in the worldwide development effort.

D. The property teaching

Because the primary paradigm in *Evangelii Nuntiandi* is evangelization rather than development, it contains no explicit delineation of the property teaching. Rather it undertakes a more general discussion of poverty and the duties of believers to relieve the suffering of the poor.

All references to the property teaching in the document are indirect. This is consistent with its emphasis on the primacy of spiritual fulfillment through evangelization over material fulfillment through development. Jesus' mission to the poor and humble is highlighted (##6, 12). Number 26 notes that the message of the Gospel includes the proclamation that God is Father, and that therefore all persons are brothers and sisters. One of the implications of this doctrine concerns the property teaching, since the primary property right is the right of use, which is based on the principle that all persons are brothers and sisters.

The discussion of *communidades de base* in no. 58 also has an indirect relationship to the property teaching. *Evangelii Nuntiandi* points out that some of these communities are based on a common aim, like age, culture, or "the struggle for justice, brotherly aid to the poor, human advancement," and these model what the Christian community should be like.

Bishop Pironio, President of CELAM, had proposed four criteria for authentic base communities in his report to the Synod on evangelization in Latin America. First, they should be homogeneous groups which find the presence of God in fraternal communion, in the light of the Gospel. Second, they should be centered in the Word of God and the Eucharist. Third, they should serve the needs of the local Church. Fourth, they should be in communion with the bishops and all the people of God.[173] The spiritual tone of Bishop Pironio's criteria does not overshadow the fact that property, and the securing of an amount of material goods sufficient for freedom, self-fulfillment, and peace, are among the "needs of the local Church" which the base communities are expected to pursue.

After *Evangelii Nuntiandi* Paul VI would continue to stress the primacy of the social function of material goods over the right of ownership, as in his message to the UN Conference on Trade and Development (UNCTAD) at Nairobi, Kenya in 1976: "The world's goods are meant for all; the peoples of the earth are dependent on one another, and that all together are responsible for organizing trade in the interests of all." "You must constantly keep alive the flame of your conviction that the purpose of material wealth is to enable men to have food, clothing, lodging, and education, to help one another and, by developing a sense of solidarity, to build authentically fraternal communities which experience a real joy in living."[174]

The scarcity of direct references to the property teaching does not mean that Paul VI abandoned or backed away from the traditional teaching. The broad definition of property which had developed in his previous social documents is not considered null and void in *Evangelii Nuntiandi*.

The document mentions the sins of hedonism, consumerism, the desire for power and domination, and discrimination (#55). These are sinful because they abuse the social function of property. Individuals and groups both within and outside the Church need to be purified of these temptations to abuse the primary end of property.

Even though evangelization is primarily a spiritual activity, it still bears a relationship to the property issue. *Evangelii Nuntiandi* notes that the message of evangelization is explicit about "the rights and duties of every human being," and the right to the use of material goods, as well as the right to own property, are among these rights (#29). It condemns everything which forces persons "to live on the margin of life: famine, chronic disease, illiteracy, poverty, injustices in international relations and especially commercial exchanges, situations of economic and cultural neo-colonialism sometimes as cruel as the old political colonialism" (#30).

But where previous papal social documents had called for the establishment of structures and institutions of social justice as a principal remedy to social and economic problems, *Evangelii Nuntiandi* exhorts Christians to a personal and individual response, the "witness of poverty and detachment" (#41).

E. Conclusion of section

Evangelii Nuntiandi is different than Paul VI's other social documents, so much so that some have questioned whether it belongs in the corpus of his social teaching. The conclusion reached in this study is that *Evangelii Nuntiandi* is a legitimate part of the Pauline teaching, primarily because it deals with many of the same themes as Paul VI's previous social documents. What sets it apart are its anthropology and its major paradigm.

There is a shift in the anthropology of *Evangelii Nuntiandi* from creation theology to a theology of redemption. Redemption theology focuses on the reality of sin in the world and on the primacy of the spiritual dimension, where Paul VI's creation theology had stressed personal dignity and the restoration of the temporal world. As a result *Evangelii Nuntiandi* teaches that spiritual renewal and salvation lead to the salvation of the material world.

This shift in emphasis is reflected throughout the document. Believers are advised to adhere to the Gospel rather than to any ideology or socioeconomic system. Evangelization, the principal paradigm in *Evangelii Nuntiandi*, is presented as a primarily spiritual activity, where the previous paradigm of development had focused on temporal progress and fulfillment. Liberation is understood first as freedom from sin rather than from economic or social oppression. The call for local solutions to social and economic problems in *Octogesima Adveniens* is abandoned in favor of greater reliance on the Holy See.

The traditional property teaching is not denied in *Evangelii Nuntiandi*; it is merely downplayed. This is due to the document's shift in emphasis from the paradigm of development to evangelization, and from the primacy of temporal development to the primacy of spiritual fulfillment. For instance, the principle of the social function of property remains intact. Yet the implications of the social function in *Evangelii Nuntiandi* differ greatly from the past social teaching of Paul VI. Nothing is denied, yet nothing is added to the definition of property from the previous social documents. Those who own property are admonished to avoid the sins of hedonism, consumerism, desire for power and domination, and discrimination in order to uphold the proper purposes of property. *Evangelii Nuntiandi* recommends the personal witness of poverty and one-on-one service to the neighbor rather than a strong role for the state in securing the right of property.

VI. CHAPTER CONCLUSION

The modern papal social teaching tradition, of which the property teaching is an integral component, is a tapestry of principles, themes, and strategies. Pope Paul VI's own social teaching is an interwoven set of ideas, most of which were already well established within the Christian tradition. His greatest contribution to the property teaching is the shading he gives to the tapestry of traditional principles in the way he applies them in light of the world of his time.

The social teaching and property teaching of Paul VI underwent a noticeable evolution from *Populorum Progressio* in 1967 to *Evangelii Nuntiandi* in 1975. This chapter has spelled out the course of that evolution in several areas.

Two events which were quite different in nature stand out as perhaps the most influential in the ongoing formation of Paul VI's social teaching. First was the general failure of the worldwide economic development effort in the late 1960s and early 1970s, and the second was the promulgation of *Humanae Vitae* in 1968. These events transformed the content and tone of Paul VI's teaching in several respects. Development, the primary paradigm of the first three social documents, changes to the paradigm of evangelization in *Evangelii Nuntiandi*. In the same vein his social teaching shifts from the priority of economic measures of progress to spiritual fulfillment. And the authority problems he encountered over *Humanae Vitae* led Paul VI to abandon the encyclical as a vehicle of communication with the Church in favor of less authoritative documents.

Throughout Paul VI's social teaching anthropology provides the theological framework for his social and property principles. Yet the anthropology of *Evangelii Nuntiandi* differs significantly from his previous social documents. *Populorum Progressio*, *Octogesima Adveniens*, and *Justice in the World* contain a biblical anthropology based on a theology of creation. The human person is viewed primarily as a creature of God, made in his image and likeness, and is therefore the subject of dignity, rights, and social duties. In *Evangelii Nuntiandi*, however, Paul VI shapes his anthropology more around a theology of redemption. Here the reality of sin and the role of Christ as Savior are given primacy. Salvation is understood first in terms of the spiritual, and only secondarily as salvation or liberation from sinful social and economic structures.

Paul VI's treatment of topics related to the property teaching reveals his anthropological shift from the primacy of the temporal realm to the spiritual. His evaluation of socioeconomic systems in *Populorum Progressio*, for example, is generally positive about their potential to promote economic development in the spirit of solidarity. Yet *Evangelii Nuntiandi* projects a weariness with all socioeconomic systems, and advocates the primacy of the Gospel over all ideologies. Similarly, the principal paradigm of economic development gives way to the paradigm of evangelization. In general there is a shift in emphasis from economic activity (*Populorum Progressio*), to political activity (*Octogesima Adveniens* and *Justice in the World*), to spiritual activity (*Evangelii Nuntiandi*). One of the few consistent features of all four documents is their acknowledgement of the worldwide range of application of the social teaching. Paul VI was the first pope to articulate a sophisticated understanding of the implications for the social teaching of this global awareness.

The property teaching itself evolved considerably in the documents of Paul VI, but almost always in the direction of greater expansion of its application. While the primacy of the social function of property is always affirmed, this principle is applied in various ways by Paul VI. In *Populorum Progressio* he advocates the concepts of expropriation and a world fund for development for the sake of worldwide solidarity and peace. The implications of the social function of property on the worldwide distribution of goods, racism, nationalism, and economic individualism are explored in *Octogesima Adveniens.* He calls for new attitudes toward wealth and for new approaches to the property issue within the Church in *Justice in the World.* And *Evangelii Nuntiandi* encourages increased help for the poor out of respect for the social function of property.

The definition of property was expanded considerably by Paul VI, in recognition of the many new ways humanity had come to relate to the material world. He includes the property of nations - raw materials, exports, agricultural products (*Populorum Progressio*), productivity, trade policies, corporate profits, monetary systems, multinational corporations, the environment (*Octogesima Adveniens*), economic and political power, housing, energy, markets (*Justice in the World*) - within the scope of property. While *Evangelii Nuntiandi* does not add to the forms of property, neither does it deny any of those previously proposed.

Paul VI describes the purposes of property in various ways, all of which are related to property's social function. Whether it be the promotion of human fulfillment and solidarity in *Populorum Progressio*, the sharing of wealth with the poor in *Octogesima Adveniens*, the call to evangelical witness in the use of goods in *Justice in the World*, or the avoidance of the sins of hedonism, consumerism, and discrimination in *Evangelii Nuntiandi*, property's relationship to the world community is always emphasized.

There is a certain ambivalence on the part of Paul VI concerning the role of the state in promoting the property right. In *Populorum Progressio* and *Justice in the World* he advocates an expanded role for governments, whether it be in agrarian reform, expropriation, the formation of a worldwide political authority, or the fulfillment of the aims of the Second Development Decade. Yet in *Octogesima Adveniens* the pope favors charity over justice as embodied in law, and *Evangelii Nuntiandi* promotes the personal witness of poverty over the structures and institutions of social justice.

The most obvious difference between Habiger's book and this essay has to do with the documents which each considers to be part of Paul VI's property teaching. In his fifth chapter Habiger includes *Gaudium et Spes* and *Dignitatis Humanae* from Vatican II, because of Paul VI's influence in their formation, and also *Populorum Progressio* and *Octogesima Adveniens*. This study treated *Gaudium et Spes* in chapter one, because the document bears the imprint of John XXIII as much as Paul VI. Besides *Populorum Progressio* and *Octogesima Adveniens*, this study has dealt with *Justice in the World* and *Evangelii Nuntiandi*. Even though the latter two are synodal statements their content is unmistakenly Pauline. In fact *Evangelii Nuntiandi* was reworked extensively by the pope before it was issued.

There are differences also in the analyses of *Populorum Progressio* and *Octogesima Adveniens*. In his discussion of *Populorum Progressio* Habiger notes in passing the anthropology behind the property teaching.[175] This study has considered it at length, since the anthropology provides the theological framework for the property teaching. While both note the importance of the concept of development,[176] this study has examined the notion of solidarity as the goal of development, because solidarity for Paul VI has such a strong bearing on the principle of the social function of property. This study has noted Paul VI's critique of capitalism, socialism, and Communism because it is within these systems that property is defined and distributed. Habiger makes only scattered references to these socioeconomic systems.[177]

The treatment of *Octogesima Adveniens* by Habiger is quite brief, covering just two pages.[178] The reason for the brevity of his remarks is that he believes *Octogesima Adveniens* neither affirms nor denies what Paul VI said about property in *Gaudium et Spes* or *Populorum Progressio*.[179] *Octogesima Adveniens* has been examined in far greater detail in this study. Its call to political activity and local solutions, its treatment of revolution and the use of violence, its discussion of liberation, and its expansion of the definition of property all have a bearing on the property teaching, and make the document an important milestone in the social teaching.

In general this study has dealt more extensively than Habiger with the historical setting of Paul VI's social documents, the pope's speeches and writings related to the property question, thematic parallels in Maritain, Lebret, and Bigo, and the critical reaction to Paul VI's social teaching. This is to be expected, given that the main focus of this paper is the property teaching of Paul VI, while Habiger concentrates on the papal property teaching from Leo XIII to John Paul II.

NOTES - CHAPTER FOUR

1 Peter J. Riga, *The Church of the Poor* (Techny, Illinois: Divine Word Publications, 1968), 138.

2 Riga, 117.

3 Riga, 92.

4 Letter of Fr. Bigo to the author, August 27, 1990.

5 Georges Jarlot, S.J., "L'Eglise et le développement l'encyclique '*Populorum Progressio*,'" in *Etudes* 326 (May 1967), 679.

6 Riga, 24.

7 See Bigo's *La Doctrine Sociale de L'Eglise* (Paris: Presses Universitaires de France, 1966), 70-71. For Maritain, see John Dunaway, *Jacques Maritain* (Boston: Twayne, 1978), 80-81. For Lebret, see *Human Ascent*, trans. Robert and Martha Falhaber (Chicago: Fides Publishers, 1955), 11.

8 See also Christine E. Gudorf, *Catholic Social Teaching on Liberation Themes* (Lanham, Maryland: University Press of America, 1980), 127-28.

9 Riga, 3, 6.

10 Riga, 5.

11 Riga, 5.

12 Riga, 6.

13 *The Pope Speaks*, vol. 11 (1966), 327.

14 Dorr, 143.

15 Dunaway, 74.

16 Louis-Joseph Lebret, O.P., *The Last Revolution*, trans. John Horgan (New York: Sheed and Ward, 1965), 109.

17 Riga, 94.

18 Charles Wolf, "Beyond *Populorum Progressio*," *National Catholic Reporter 3* (May 10, 1967), 8.

19 Corrado Pallenberg, *Pope Paul VI* (New York: G.P. Putnam's Sons, 1968), 186.

20 Riga, 95.

21 Benjamin L. Masse, "The Pope's plea for poor nations," *America 117* (August 5, 1967), 131.

22 Riga, 27; Pallenberg, 185.

23 Riga, 14.

24 Riga, 29-30.

25 Riga, 29.

26 Riga, 27.

27 *The Pope Speaks*, vol. 10 (1965), 286.

28 Pierre Bigo, S.J., *Marxisme et Humanisme*, 3rd ed. (Paris: Presses Universitaires de France, 1961), 125.

29 Dunaway, 67-68.

30 Lebret, *The Last Revolution*, 179.

31 Riga, 92.

32 Riga, 30.

33 Philip Burnham, "The encyclical's challenge," *Triumph 2* (May 1967), 10.

34 Riga, 56.

35 See, for example, Maritain's *True Humanism*, 4th ed., trans. M.R. Adamson (London: The Centenary Press, 1946), xvi-xvii; also Lebret's *Human Ascent*, 10.

36 Bigo had also criticized Marxism for its atheism, and Maritain called atheism one of the cornerstones of Marxism. See Bigo, *Marxisme et Humanisme*, 142. For Maritain, see Dunaway, 67.

37 Lebret, *The Last Revolution*, 159.

38 Burnham, 10.

39 *The Pope Speaks*, vol. 10, 37.

40 *The Pope Speaks*, vol. 11, 55.

41 *The Pope Speaks*, vol. 11, 246.

42 Riga, 15.

43 *The Pope Speaks*, vol. 11, 51.

44 *The Pope Speaks*, vol. 10 (1965), 153.

45 Lebret, *Human Ascent*, 4, 12.

46 In the most basic terms, social justice is the justice of the common good. It has been recognized as a subspecies of the virtue of justice since *Quadragesimo Anno* in 1931, where it was applied to the relationship between the capitalist and the worker. Social justice envisions above all the community of persons established by God, the common family of humankind. The rights and duties

of social justice derive from the worldwide human community. Although it includes every human society, such as the family and civil government, since the mid-twentieth century social justice among the community of nations has come to the forefront. In this age of rapid technological advance, such issues as aid for development are not matters of charity. Rather, they are real demands of the social order and duties of justice for the sake of peace, and they should be institutionalized by law and everyday practice. See the *New Catholic Encyclopedia*, vol. 8 (New York: McGraw-Hill, 1967), 71-72.

47 Donal Dorr, *Option for the Poor* (Maryknoll, New York: Orbis, 1983), 142.

48 Riga, 11.

49 Clark, 401.

50 Jarlot, "L'Eglise et le développement l'encyclique '*Populorum Progressio*,' " 674.

51 F. Malley, ed., *Le Père Lebret: L'Economie au Service des Hommes* (Paris: Les Éditions du Cerf, 1968), 8, 38. See also Riga, 18.

52 *The Pope Speaks*, vol. 10, 145-60. See also William J. Wilson, *Paul: The Missionary Pope* (Maryknoll, New York: Maryknoll Publications, 1968), 24-32.

53 Riga, 18.

54 *The Pope Speaks*, vol. 12 (1967), 52.

55 Maritain, *True Humanism*, xii.

56 Lebret, *Human Ascent*, 10.

57 *The Pope Speaks*, vol. 12, 53.

58 Gudorf, 148.

59 Lebret discusses economic imperialism at length in *The Last Revolution*, chs. 9, 11, and 12. For Jarlot, see "L'Eglise et le développement l'encyclique '*Populorum Progressio*,' " 675.

60 *Populorum Progressio* was not the first document of Paul VI in which this phrase appears. He had used it in a letter to U.N. Secretary General U Thant on May 26, 1966. See *The Pope Speaks*, vol. 11, 245.

61 Riga, 15.

62 *The Pope Speaks*, vol. 11, 55.

63 See also Riga, 148.

64 The gap between rich and poor had been cited in *Gaudium et Spes* (#83). Paul VI also referred to it in his homily at the 50th anniversary celebration of the apparitions at Fatima. See *The Pope Speaks*, vol. 12, 96.

65 Riga, 15.

66 Riga, vii.

67 *The Pope Speaks*, vol. 11, 245.

68 Riga, 86.

69 Jean-Yves Calvez, "The Social Thought of Paul VI: from development to liberation," *Month* 11 (September 1978), 299.

70 Masse, 129.

71 In his later writings Maritain envisioned "the new Christendom" as an international society. See O'Donnell, 176.

The international range of application of the development question is a consistent feature of Lebret's writings. See, for example, *Human Ascent*, 4, 19; *The Last Revolution*, chs. 16-17; and *Pour Une Civilisation Solidaire* (Paris: Les Éditions ouvrières, 1963).

Bigo also viewed development from a worldwide perspective. See *The Church and Third World Revolution*, trans. Sr. Jeanne Marie Lyons (Maryknoll, New York: Orbis, 1977), 6; and *La Doctrine Sociale de L'Eglise*, ch. 24.

72 See also Riga, 34.

73 Gudorf, 127.

74 *Ius gentium* refers to that part of a legal system, whether international or national, which is derived from the general principles of law or from common customs prevailing among different peoples. It is positive common law, nearer in spirit to natural law than any particular civil law.

The term *ius gentium* is most likely of Roman origin. It dates from the usage of second century jurists dealing with the law of contract and with informal methods of acquiring property. Thomas Aquinas in the thirteenth century viewed every system of law as embodying two elements: *ius civile*, which consists in determinations of the natural law, and *ius gentium*, which is derived from the natural law as conclusions from its precepts (*Summa Theologiae*, 1a, 2ae, 95.4) *Ius gentium* comes into play in modern times when a court is faced with a question involving the rights of two states with no written law to guide its decision. In such cases the court has to avail itself of the experience of humankind or the customary practices of different peoples in their dealings with each other. There is a gradual formation of *ius gentium*, therefore, through the channel of human experience. See *The New Catholic Encyclopedia*, vol. 7, 774-75.

75 Riga, 34.

76 See also Gudorf, 127.

77 Riga, 9.

78 Riga, 35.

79 "A Blessing for Secular Error," editorial in *The Wall Street Journal*, March 30, 1967, 14; Riga, 36.

80 Lebret, *Human Ascent*, 19.

81 Bigo, *La Doctrine Sociale de L'Eglise*, 243.

82 Dunaway, 73.

83 *The Teachings of Pope Paul VI, December 29, 1967 - December 18, 1968* (Vatican City: Libraria Editrice Vaticana, 1969), 148.

84 Masse, 131.

85 See also Colin Clark, "The development of peoples; some implications of the papal encyclical," *Tablet 221* (April 15, 1967), 400-401.

86 Dorr, 146.

87 Riga, 45.

88 James Andrews, ed., *Paul VI: Critical Appraisals* (New York: Bruce, 1970), 38.

89 Riga, 45-46.

90 *The Pope Speaks*, vol. 12, 53.

91 Riga, 102-103.

92 Rik Vermeire, "Reflections on Development," *World Justice 8* (June 1967), 483.

93 Riga, 10.

94 *The Pope Speaks*, vol. 11, 51.

95 Charles O'Donnell, "Jacques Maritain - Political Philosopher," in *Jacques Maritain: The Man and His Achievement*, ed. Joseph W. Evans (New YorK: Sheed and Ward, 1963), 176.

96 "Humanae Vitae" (July 25, 1968), *Acta Apostolicae Sedis 60* (September 30, 1969), 481-518. English text in *The Gospel of Peace and Justice*, Joseph Gremillion, presenter (Maryknoll, New York: Orbis, 1976), 427-44.

97 Peter J. Riga, "Humanae Vitae," in *Catholic World 208* (December 1968), 109.

98 Andrew M. Greeley, *Crisis in the Church: A Study of Religion in America* (Chicago: Thomas More Press, 1979), 227.

99 Riga, "Humanae Vitae," 109.

100 Christine E. Gudorf explains: "In the classification of papal documents by content *litterae encyclicae* rank first. *Epistulae encyclicae* are second, and *epistulae apostolicae* (the category of *Octogesima Adveniens*) rank third. (*Index*

Documentorum of *Acta Apostolicae Sedis*)." The footnote goes on to say that apostolic letters concern affairs of the executive or administrative order, and that encyclicals are teaching instruments which explain, instruct, or admonish. See Gudorf, 457.

101 Msgr. George Higgins, "A Commentary on the Apostolic Letter," *Catholic Mind 69* (November 1971), 59-60.

102 James V. Schall, S.J., *The Sixth Paul* (Canfield, Ohio: Alba Books, 1977), 115.

103 Bigo, *La Doctrine Sociale de L'Eglise*, 139.

104 See also Gudorf, 227.

105 David Hollenbach, S.J., *Claims in Conflict* (New York: Paulist Press, 1979), 83.

106 Bigo, *La Doctrine Sociale de L'Eglise*, 260; Lebret, *The Last Revolution*, 67.

107 An ideology is more than just a set of economic or political doctrines or principles shared by a society or nation. Communist ideology, for example, is different in the Soviet Union than in China, and socialism is not the same in the Scandinavian countries as in Tanzania. This is because there are cultural, social, and political differences among peoples and nations. Nurnberger adds that an ideology is also a "conscious or unconscious self-justification mechanism of a social group," which means that it contains non-rational and, at times, irrational elements. Although the ideologies discussed in *Octogesima Adveniens* are fundamentally economic, they also reflect and include social, political, racial, and religious attitudes and assumptions. This makes it difficult to analyze a particular ideology as if it were a monolithic set of ideas clearly understood and put into practice by a group or nation. See Klaus Nurnberger, *Socio-Economic Ideologies in a Christian Perspective* (Durban, South Africa: Lutheran Publishing House, 1979).

108 Hollenbach, 83.

109 Philip S. Land, S.J., "The Social Theology of Pope Paul VI," in *America 140* (May 12, 1979), 394.

110 *The Pope Speaks*, vol. 13 (1968), 148.

111 "Medellin Documents" (September 6, 1968), *The Gospel of Peace and Justice*, Joseph Gremillion, presenter (Maryknoll, New York: Orbis, 1976), 445-76.

112 Land, 393.

113 Gudorf, 93.

114 Land, 394.

115 Higgins, 59.

[116] Medellin documents, #3 of the section on justice, in *The Gospel of Peace and Justice*, 446-47.

[117] Gudorf, 343.

[118] See, for example, Paul VI's message to a general audience on the first anniversary of *Populorum Progressio* (March 27, 1968), *The Pope Speaks*, vol. 13, 149; address to a general audience (August 21, 1968), *The Pope Speaks*, vol. 13, 232; address to Campesinos at San Jose, Colombia (August 23, 1968), *The Pope Speaks*, vol. 13, 236; homily at his "Development Day" Mass (August 23, 1968), *The Pope Speaks*, vol. 13, 240; or his address to the General Assembly of the Latin American Bishops' Conference (CELAM) (August 24, 1968), *The Pope Speaks*, vol. 13, 256.

[119] "Medellin Documents," in *The Gospel of Peace and Justice*, 445-76.

[120] Maritain, *True Humanism*, 254.

[121] Lebret, *The Last Revolution*, 5.

[122] Rubem A. Alves, "The Case Against the New Roman Catholic Spirituality," in *Paul VI: Critical Appraisals*, ed. James F. Andrews (New York: Bruce, 1970), 44.

[123] See Paul VI's message to the Catholic hierarchy of Africa and all the African people (October 29, 1967), *The Pope Speaks*, vol. 13, 11; or his Easter message (April 14, 1968), *The Pope Speaks*, vol. 13, 129.

[124] David Hollenbach, S.J., "Modern Catholic Teachings Concerning Justice," in *The Faith That Does Justice*, John C. Haughey, S.J., ed. (New York: Paulist Press, 1977), 223.

[125] Hollenbach, 83-84.

[126] *The Pope Speaks*, vol. 14 (1969), 31.

[127] *The Teachings of Pope Paul VI* (1970), (Washington, D.C.: United States Catholic Conference, 1971), 102.

[128] Pope Paul VI, "Address Delivered at the Opening of the Third International Synod of Bishops," in *Catholic Mind 70* (January 1972), 2.

[129] The rescript reads: "The Holy Father has carefully examined the two documents containing the proposals by the Second General Assembly of the Synod of Bishops on the themes, 'The Ministerial Priesthood' and 'Justice in the World,' which had been put before the Assembly for study. As he has already announced in his address at the General Audience of 24 November, the Holy Father desires that the aforementioned documents be made public. His Holiness now accepts and confirms all the conclusions in the two documents that conform to the current norms: in particular, he confirms that in the Latin

Church there shall continue to be observed in its entirety, with God's help, the present discipline of priestly celibacy. The Holy Father reserves to himself to examine carefully in due course whether the proposals - and which of them - contained in the recommendations of the Synodal Assembly should be convalidated as directive guidelines or practical norms." In *The Gospel of Peace and Justice*, 513 (footnote).

130 John Coleman, S.J., "Development of Church Social Teaching," in *Readings in Moral Theology No. 5*: *Official Catholic Social Teaching*, Charles E. Curran and Richard A. McCormick, S.J., eds. (New York: Paulist Press, 1986), 174.

131 Charles Murphy has thoroughly analyzed the debate over the term "constitutive", and maintains that the concept represents "the most notable development to date in the history of modern social teaching." He notes that the term forces Christians to ask the vital question whether working for justice is part of the very definition of Christianity, or whether action for justice is more on the level of an ethical deduction from the central truths of the Christian message. The sentence containing the phrase "constitutive dimension" was written by Vincent Cosmao, O.P., a member of the drafting committee for *Justice in the World.* After the phrase passed at the synod without debate, however, it was translated from the original French (*une dimension constitutive*) and the official Latin text (*dimensio constitutiva*) in a variety of ways. The Italian text read *la dimensione constitutiva*, but the German and Dutch translations used the word "essential" rather than "constitutive." Although it stimulated a considerable amount of social action, particularly in Latin America, the term was critically examined at the next synod in 1974. The Pontifical Commission for Justice and Peace issued a document of its own prior to the synod. In its introduction Bishop Ramon Torella Cascante, vice president of the commission and a member of the drafting committee for *Justice in the World*, said there was a need to correct some of the ambiguities and misunderstandings surrounding the term. He said that action for justice is a "constitutive" but not unique dimension of the gospel, and that action for justice should be seen as an "integral part" of evangelization. Other members of the drafting committee from the 1971 synod disagreed with Torella. Philip Land, S.J. said that "integral" in this context could mean that action for justice is either a substantial or an accidental part of the gospel, and that no one at the 1971 synod wanted to make justice an accidental part of the gospel. Juan Alfaro, S.J., believed that the 1974 synod attempted to weaken the term "constitutive." To Alfaro "constitutive" and "integral" dimensions were not the same. His position was that "constitutive" implies that justice is an essential element of the gospel, but not the only element. Cosmao said that "constitutive" was used by the synod to say that action for justice "is a very condition for the truth of the faith."

In *Evangelii Nuntiandi*, the document produced by Paul VI after the 1974 synod, the pope emphasizes the relationship between eschatological salvation offered through evangelization and temporal concerns. Temporal concerns, he says, as part of evangelization are entirely proper, and he notes the "profound links" between evangelization and human advancement (#31). Paul VI preferred to note these "links" rather than highlight justice as a "constitutive dimension" of the gospel.

For a more thorough treatment of this question see Charles M. Murphy, "Action for Justice as Constitutive of the Preaching of the Gospel: What Did the 1971 Synod Mean?", in *Readings in Moral Theology No. 5*, 150-66.

132 O'Donnell, 166.

133 From the point of view of traditional Christian theology, justice among persons is considered secondary to the sovereign justice of God by which sinners are justified by his grace. Justice among humanity is a genuine Christian virtue only when it is accomplished in thanksgiving and obedience to God. The traditional view takes as its point of departure the human person, with his/her dignity, and the solidarity of the human community. From this perspective love is seen as primary and justice is understood as the manifestation of love in the temporal order.

Justice also recognizes a hierarchy of personal rights. Property rights, as important as they may be, are secondary to personal dignity and personal rights. The fulfillment of the duties directly related to measurable values, such as property, clears away many obstacles that stand in the way of love. In other words, the basic ontological order is love, then justice; but in terms of the gradual achievement of the just society, the order may be justice, then love. See the *New Catholic Encyclopedia*, vol. 8, 68-72.

134 Medellin documents, #5 of the section on poverty in the Church, in *The Gospel of Peace and Justice*, 473.

135 Medellin documents, #15 of the section on justice, in *The Gospel of Peace and Justice*, 451-52.

136 Medellin documents, #3 of the section on justice, in *The Gospel of Peace and Justice*, 446.

137 Michael Walsh and Brian Davies, eds., *Proclaiming Justice and Peace* (Mystic, Connecticut: Twenty-Third Publications, 1985), xvi.

138 Lebret, *Human Ascent*, 43.

139 Henri Fesquet, *Le Synode et L'Avenir de L'Eglise* (Paris: Le Centurion, 1972), 128.

140 Andrés M. Rubio, *III Sínodo*, 3rd ed. (Madrid: Ediciones Palabra, 1972), 45-47.

141 Walsh and Davies, xvi.

142 Murphy, 152-53.

143 Rubio, 46.

144 René Laurentin, *Nouveaux Ministères en Fin du Clergé Devant Le Troisieme Synode* (Paris: Éditions du Seuil, 1971), 164.

145 Laurentin, *Nouveaux Ministeres*, 164.

146 Laurentin, *Nouveaux Ministeres*, 166.

147 Rubio, 44.

148 The 32nd General Congregation of the Jesuits met in Rome from December 2, 1974 to March 7, 1975. One of the congregation's primary concerns centered around the issue of "grades," in particular the fourth vow of special obedience to the pope, and whether it could be extended to non-priests in the order. Paul VI discouraged this move, and ultimately forbade it. There were some difficult communications and misunderstanding between the pope and the congregation before this issue was amicably resolved. Vincent O'Keefe, S.J. notes that "for the Holy Father, the question of the grades was connected with a thrust for promoting justice, and this could lead to an undermining of a direct priestly ministry . . ." O'Keefe holds that Paul VI was afraid that the distinction between the ordained priesthood and the common priesthood might be undermined if the grades were eliminated.

This same danger was feared by the pope in the congregation's discussions on the relationship between evangelization and justice. The pope feared the dilution of the properly spiritual and evangelical role of the ordained priesthood. O'Keefe says this role applies to the Society of Jesus in a special way because it was founded for a particularly spiritual and supernatural end: "The Holy Father felt that the congregation was over-emphasizing the horizontal dimension and that there should have been more emphasis on the principles of religious and ascetical life." Eventually the congregation issued a statement entitled "Our Mission Today: The Service of Faith and the Promotion of Justice." The statement defined the mission of the Jesuits as the promotion of justice, but in the context of, and subordinated to, the service of faith. It affirmed the basic religious and supernatural nature of the mission of the Jesuits in terms of the work of evangelization, and the promotion of justice was to be done in the context of this primary mission. Promotion of justice was seen as the main apostolic objective of the society in the present, but the promotion of justice was inseparably connected with the service of faith. O'Keefe maintains that this was done to correct a "socio-economic tendency" in the apostolate, and to ensure "a healthy integration of the religious and social dimensions of the Jesuit mission." The pope's position in favor of the primacy of the spiritual dimension of the mission of the Jesuits, which he communicated on several occasions to the congregation, is entirely consistent with his position on the relationship between evangelization and justice in *Evangelii Nuntiandi*.

See Vincent O'Keefe, S.J., "The Holy See, the Society of Jesus, and the 32nd General Congregation," in *Review for Religious 35* (January 1976), 33-45; and Francisco Ivern, S.J., "Faith and Justice," in *Review for Religious 35* (May 1976), 338-51.

[149] Walsh and Davies, 204.

[150] *Synod of Bishops 1974* (Washington, D.C.: United States Catholic Conference, 1975), 27.

[151] Walsh and Davies, xvii.

[152] Walsh and Davies, 205.

[153] *The Pope Speaks*, vol. 21 (1976), 137.

[154] *The Pope Speaks*, vol. 21, 329.

[155] *The Pope Speaks*, vol. 19 (1974), 46.

[156] René Laurentin, *L'Evangélisation après le quatrième Synode* (Paris: Éditions du Seuil, 1975), 16-17.

[157] Laurentin, *L'Evangélisation après le quatrième Synode*, 178.

[158] *The Church and Third World Revolution*, trans. Sr. Jeanne Marie Lyons (Maryknoll, New York: Orbis, 1977), 4, 61, 131.

[159] Walsh and Davies, xvii.

[160] *The Pope Speaks*, vol. 19, 203.

[161] Walsh and Davies, xvii.

[162] Land, 394.

[163] *The Pope Speaks*, vol. 22 (1977), 31.

[164] Bigo, *La Doctrine Sociale de L'Eglise*, 68.

[165] Bigo, *La Doctrine Sociale de L'Eglise*, 86.

[166] *The Pope Speaks*, vol. 19, 189-90.

[167] *Sínodo 1974* (Madrid: Ediciones Accion Catolica, 1975), 52.

[168] *The Pope Speaks*, vol. 20 (1975), 282.

[169] *The Pope Speaks*, vol. 19, 12-13.

[170] *The Pope Speaks*, vol. 19, 211.

[171] *The Pope Speaks*, vol. 20, 248.

[172] *The Pope Speaks*, vol. 20, 268-69.

[173] *Sínodo 1974*, 53-54.

[174] *The Pope Speaks*, vol. 21, 231-32.

[175] Matthew Habiger, O.S.B., *Papal Teaching on Private Property: 1891-1981* (Lanham, Maryland: University Press of America, 1990), 264.

[176] Habiger, 264-65, 273.

[177] Habiger, 271, 274.

[178] Habiger, 275-76.

[179] Habiger, 275.

CONCLUSION

This study has examined the property teaching of Pope Paul VI as it is found in his four major social documents. In order to place that teaching in its proper historical and theological context, it has been necessary to examine as well the papal social teaching since Leo XIII, the life of Giovanni Battista Montini prior to his assuming the papacy, and the three thinkers - Jacques Maritain, L.J. Lebret, and Pierre Bigo - who most helped to shape his social teaching. Paul VI's property teaching is contained in four documents which span eight years of his papacy, and the applications of the teaching evolved in order to address a rapidly changing world situation. The fluidity of the teaching itself, and of its application, makes it problematic to summarize the teaching as if it were a unified whole. Still, several points about the teaching can be made by way of conclusion.

1. The property teaching of Paul VI in general is consistent with the Christian tradition. It restates the ancient relationship of the social function of property and the right of ownership. Material goods are ordered primarily for use by all persons, and each person has by nature a right to a sufficient amount of goods for the satisfaction of personal and family needs, the fulfillment of personality, and the preservation of peace in society. The right of ownership is secondary to and derived from the right of use of material goods.

   Overall the fundamental principles of Paul VI's property teaching are consistent with the encyclicals of the previous social popes. The major exception is Leo XIII's encyclical *Rerum Novarum*, which reversed the priority of the social function of property over the right of ownership in such a way that ownership was viewed as an absolute right. *Rerum Novarum* considered ownership a natural right, which implied that the power of the individual to dispose of his/her property was absolute. The traditional teaching considers ownership a secondary right which derives from the natural right of all persons to use the goods of the earth. It should be recalled, however, that Leo XIII's intention in emphasizing the right of ownership over the social function of property was to refute the socialist theories and movements of his time.

Pius XI in *Quadragesimo Anno* restated the traditional priority of the social function of property over the right of ownership. Still, in his desire to protect the property rights of individuals from the threat of totalitarianism, he strongly affirmed the right of ownership and the absolute right to dispose of possessions.

The traditional relationship of property ownership and use was faithfully adhered to by Pope Pius XII. By placing his teaching in the context of an anthropology which stressed the dignity of the person, Pius XII established a precedent which would be followed by all his successors.

The social encyclicals of John XXIII, *Mater et Magistra* and *Pacem in Terris*, emphasized the social function of property within the context of his notion of socialization. At the same time, he strongly affirmed the right of ownership, more so than would Paul VI.

The Second Vatican Council gave a detailed exposition of the traditional property teaching and its implications for the modern world in *Gaudium et Spes*. Paul VI's property teaching, particularly in *Populorum Progressio*, would be modelled in some ways after *Gaudium et Spes*.

Paul VI affirms the traditional property teaching in nos. 22-24 of *Populorum Progressio*, and then spells out its implications. Number 48 points out that the advanced nations have an obligation to help the developing nations in their material advancement. Number 49 states that the superfluous wealth of countries should be placed at the service of the poor nations. And no. 51 calls for the establishment of a world fund to help destitute peoples. In *Octogesima Adveniens* the traditional property teaching is discussed in no. 23, where those who are more well off are called to place their goods at the service of others; and in no. 43, which cites the need to establish a greater sharing of goods on the international level. *Justice in the World* extends the application of the property teaching even further. It calls Christians to a sparingness in use of goods, and the Church to live and administer its own goods in such a way that the Gospel is proclaimed by example to the poor (#47). Also it recommends the sharing of human and material resources among the churches of the rich and poor regions (#59). In *Evangelii Nuntiandi* the traditional property teaching is alluded to, but primarily in the context of the personal witness of evangelical poverty rather than the worldwide economic development effort. The document states that authentic development and liberation are necessarily linked with evangelization (#31), because liberation must include not just the economic, political, social, and cultural spheres, but also an openness to the Absolute (#33). Numbers 41 and 76 affirm the importance of the witness of poverty and detachment, the need for simplicity of life, and charity towards all, especially the poor and lowly.

2. The geographic perspective from which the papal property teaching was proclaimed changed dramatically from *Rerum Novarum* in 1891 to *Gaudium et Spes* in 1965, and it continued to evolve during the papacy of Paul VI. *Rerum Novarum* and *Quadragesimo Anno* were written from a European perspective, and were meant to be applied only to European problems. In the social teaching of Pius XII the beginnings of the international worldview were detectable. John XXIII's social teaching acknowledged directly the worldwide scope of its application - for example, in *Mater et Magistra* (##200-202), and *Pacem in Terris* (##7, 130). *Gaudium et Spes* expanded on this to the point where the entire document was addressed to the modern world.

Pope Paul VI draws out the implications of the worldwide range of application of the property teaching. *Populorum Progressio* begins by pointing out that the global range is the principal fact that must be acknowledged in the consideration of the social question (#3). In *Octogesima Adveniens* the worldwide scope is a given, and some of its implications are spelled out. Number 2 notes great inequalities around the world in the pace of development and the levels of material prosperity, and no. 43 points to the need for greater justice in the sharing of goods on the international level. *Justice in the World* alludes to the international scope several times. All persons in the world are said to comprise a family of persons (#55), and to share a common destiny (#7). Number 8 calls attention to worldwide communications, economic interdependence, and natural resources as the patrimony of humanity. Injustices on the international level are noted (#20), as well as the Church's right and duty to proclaim justice on the international level (#36). In nos. 63-71 several specific recommendations for international action for justice are listed.

In *Evangelii Nuntiandi* the focus of the international scope shifts, so that the worldwide range of the task of evangelization is highlighted. The document states that the message of evangelization is for all people of the world (##49-50), and that the Church has the duty to preach salvation to all people (#57).

3. The definition of property in the papal social teaching, which had expanded gradually from Leo XIII to Vatican II, was greatly enlarged by Paul VI. *Rerum Novarum*, written from the perspective of Italy's agrarian economy in the late nineteenth century, defined property strictly as land, and advocated a diffusion of ownership of land for the sake of social peace. As a consequence of the rapid and widespread growth of the union movement in Italy and much of Western Europe, *Quadragesimo Anno* broadened the scope of property to include employment wages and social insurance benefits. In the social teaching of Pope John XXIII the definition of property changed again, as the largely industrialized world economy measured wealth in increasingly intangible terms. *Mater et Magistra* viewed economic power (#92), professional skill, and information (##106-107) as property, since they were primarily ordered to use by all persons, persons had the right to possess them in order to satisfy basic needs and fulfill themselves, and they could help build social peace.

Paul VI's expansion of the definition of property reflects above all his awareness of the international scope of the social question. *Populorum Progressio* focuses on the worldwide economic development effort, and it calls attention to the forms of property associated with that effort - exports, raw materials, and agricultural products (#57). *Octogesima Adveniens* broadens the definition of property in three directions. First, in continuity with *Populorum Progressio*, it lists more forms of property associated with economic development - a nation's productive capability, trade policies, and monetary system (##43, 44). Second, it calls attention to the fact that multinational corporations, and the profits of all corporations, should not exacerbate the already unjust distribution of the world's goods (##43, 44). Third, it reminds humanity of its obligation to protect one of its most fundamental and most endangered common possessions, the environment (#21). *Justice in the World* continues in the same vein, by adding the economic and the political power of nations (##9-10), energy (#11), and markets (#66) to the growing list of the forms of property. The property teaching in *Evangelii Nuntiandi* is consistent with the document as a whole. It shifts the focus of the social teaching away from economic and social - temporal - development, toward the spiritual dimension of development, evangelization. Although the property teaching itself is not directly addressed in *Evangelii Nuntiandi*, it neither denies the forms of property from the previous social documents nor expands the definition of property.

4. There is a shift in the methodological framework of the property teaching from a fundamentally philosophical, natural law approach to one which retains the basic principles of the natural law, but is built upon a theological, biblically-based anthropology.

Leo XIII and Pius XI both maintained a traditional natural law perspective. Pius XII did the same, although he also incorporated a faith-centered emphasis on the dignity of the human person. John XXIII continued the natural law tradition, while giving a far more scriptural and theological orientation to the social teaching (*Mater et Magistra* ##2-3; *Pacem in Terris* #57). The theological anthropology of *Gaudium et Spes* (Part I, Chapter 1) is the best example of this shift in the methodological framework, and it would be reflected in the social teaching of Paul VI. *Populorum Progressio* (especially ##15-16) and *Octogesima Adveniens* (##14, 26) employ an anthropology based on a theology of creation, which highlights the human being created in *imago Dei*, human dignity and rights, the social nature of the person in reflection of the Trinity, and the restoration of the temporal order as it was intended by God in creation. In *Justice in the World* creation theology is juxtaposed with a theology of salvation which emphasizes the presence of sin in the world and the need for temporal and spiritual liberation in the redemptive activity of Jesus Christ (##5-6, 31). The anthropology of *Evangelii Nuntiandi* shifts primarily to a theology of salvation (##9, 10, 12, 18, 27, 31, 34).

5. The world to which the various papal social documents were addressed changed considerably between 1891 and 1975. *Rerum Novarum* was promulgated in the midst of the bitter struggle in Europe between the capitalists and the working class for the rights of workers. *Quadragesimo Anno* called for the reconstruction of the social order in Europe in the midst of the Great Depression. The social teaching of Pius XII spanned a fateful nineteen years which included World War II, the reconstruction of Europe after the war, and the general worldwide economic prosperity of the 1950s. John XXIII's social encyclicals reflected his optimism about the possibilities of economic development and social progress in the late 1950s and early 1960s. The Second Vatican Council, in *Gaudium et Spes*, carried on the optimistic spirit of John XXIII.

   Although they were promulgated over a span of just eight years, the four major social documents of Paul VI were written in response to a rapidly evolving world situation. *Populorum Progressio* embodies the ongoing optimism of the 1960s about the possibilities for worldwide development and human solidarity. By 1971, as the limitations of purely economic advancement were becoming apparent, *Octogesima Adveniens* calls for political activity in the pursuit of economic and social advancement, and *Justice in the World* issues a call for greater justice in the world and within the Church. Paul VI's increasing wariness of the economic development effort, and of Church-inspired liberation movements in the developing world, inspired *Evangelii Nuntiandi's* advocacy of evangelization, and the assertion of the primacy of the spiritual dimension of human fulfillment over the economic and social dimensions.

6. At several points the social teaching of Paul VI reflects the thinking of Maritain, Lebret, Bigo, and others who interacted with him. For example, Maritain's vision of a "supranational community" is reflected in the pope's call for human solidarity on the international level. *Populorum Progressio* was inspired throughout by Lebret. Bigo's criticism of Marxism for its atheistic materialism was prominent in Paul VI's evaluation of Marxism. Yet because he was an intellectual in his own right, and because of his ability to synthesize the thoughts of others, Paul VI's social teaching always bears his own personal imprint.

7. The social teaching and the property teaching of Paul VI are entirely consistent with his lifelong personal concern for the poor and for social issues. His parents were models of social and political activism. Ministry to the poor was an important part of his work as a young priest. During his thirty years in the Vatican Secretariat of State he was constantly involved in the lives of the poor and dispossessed, both on the bureaucratic and personal levels. He took courageous stands on several controversial social and political issues, such as the priest-worker movement and the "opening to the left" in Italy. As Archbishop of Milan his commitment to the laboring class earned him the title "archbishop of the workers." And he was one of the guiding forces of the *aggiornamento* of John XXIII.

Pope Paul VI's property teaching illustrates more than anything else the profundity of the ancient teaching on the primacy of the social function of property. His consistent and faithful application of the teaching led him to some dramatic and far-reaching conclusions in the context of the complex world of the 1960s and 1970s. His placement of the property teaching within the framework of a biblically-based, theological anthropology situated the property teaching directly within the *kerygma*, giving it a power it would not have had if situated within the fundamentally philosophical framework of the natural law. The more pragmatic, more tentative, and less moralistic tone of his teaching means that, while it may not have made the claim of timelessness of the social teaching of his predecessors, it was certainly timely in the context of the world to which it was addressed. It is all the more valuable because of this.

BIBLIOGRAPHY

A. Primary Sources

1. Papal encyclicals and statements, conciliar and synodal statements

"Gaudium et Spes." *Acta Apostolicae Sedis* 58 (1966): 1025-1115. English text in *The Documents of Vatican II*. Edited by Walter M. Abbott. New York: America Press, 1966.

John XXIII, Pope. "Mater et Magistra." *Acta Apostolicae Sedis 53* (1961): 401-64. English text in *The Gospel of Peace and Justice*. Presented by Joseph Gremillion. Maryknoll, New York: Orbis, 1976.

________. "Pacem in Terris." *Acta Apostolicae Sedis 55* (1963): 257-304. English text in *The Gospel of Peace and Justice*. Presented by Joseph Gremillion. Maryknoll, New York: Orbis, 1976.

Leo XIII, Pope. "Rerum Novarum." *Acta Sanctae Sedis 23* (1890-91): 641-70. English text in *The Social Teachings of the Church*. Edited by Anne Freemantle. New York: Mentor-Omega, 1963.

Paul VI, Pope. "Address to the United Nations General Assembly." *The Pope Speaks*. Vol. 11 (1966): 47-57.

________. "Apostolic Exhortation 'Evangelii Nuntiandi.'" *Acta Apostolicae Sedis 68* (January 31, 1976): 5-76. English text in *Doctrine and Life* (March-April, 1977): 3-52.

________. "Ecclesiam Suam." *Acta Apostolicae Sedis 56* (August 20, 1964): 609-59. English text in *The Pope Speaks*. Vol. 10 (1965): 283-309.

________. "Humanae Vitae." *Acta Apostolicae Sedis 60* (September 30, 1969): 481-518. English text in *The Gospel of Peace and Justice*. Joseph Gremillion, presenter. Maryknoll, New York: Orbis, 1976.

________. "Octogesmia Adveniens" (Apostolic Letter on the Occasion of the Eightieth Anniversary of the Encyclical '*Rerum Novarum*'). *Acta Apostolicae Sedis 63* (May 14, 1971): 401-41. English text in *The Teachings of Pope Paul VI*, 1971. Washington, D.C.: United States Catholic Conference, 1972.

________. "Populorum Progressio." *Acta Apostolicae Sedis 58* (April 15, 1967): 257-99. English text in *The Gospel of Peace and Justice*. Presented by Joseph Gremillion. Maryknoll, New York: Orbis, 1976. French text in *Nouvelle Revue Thologique 89* (May 1967): 527-49.

Pius XI, Pope. "Divini Redemptoris." *Acta Apostolicae Sedis 29* (1937): 65-106. English text in *Twelve Encyclicals of Pius XI*. London: Catholic Truth Society, 1943.

________. "Quadragesimo Anno." *Acta Apostolicae Sedis 23* (1931): 177-228. English text in *Twelve Encyclicals of Pius XI*. London: Catholic Theological Society, 1943.

Pius XII, Pope. "Divino Afflante Spiritu." *Acta Apostolicae Sedis 35* (October 20, 1943): 297-326. English text in *Catholic Mind* 42 (May 1944): 257-83.

________. "Evangelii Praecones." *Acta Apostolicae Sedis 43* (1951): 497-528. English text in *Selected Documents of His Holiness Pope Pius XII - 1939-1958*. Washington, D.C.: National Catholic Welfare Conference, 1959.

________. "Summi Pontificatus." *Acta Apostolicae Sedis 31* (1939): 413-53. English text in *The Pope Speaks: The Words of Pius XII*. New York: Harcourt, Brace, and Company, 1940.

Synod of Bishops, Second General Assembly (1971). "De Iustitia in Mundo" (Justice in the World). *Acta Apostolicae Sedis 63* (December 23, 1971): 923-42. English text in *The Gospel of Peace and Justice*. Presented by Joseph Gremillion. Maryknoll, New York: Orbis, 1976.

2. Books

Administrative Committee of the National Catholic War Council. *Program of Social Reconstruction*. Washington, D.C.: National Catholic Welfare Council, 1919.

Basil the Great, Saint. "Homilia in Divitas." In Ryan, Rev. John A. *The Alleged Socialism of the Fathers*. New York: Harper, 1931.

________. "Homily 2 on Psalm 14." In *Exegetic Homilies*. Translated by Agnes C. Way, C.D.P. *Fathers of the Church*, vol. 46. Washington, D.C.: Catholic University Press, 1963.

Hobbes, Thomas. *Leviathon (or Matter, Form, and Power of a commonwealth, ecclesiastical and civil)* (1659). *Great Books of the Western World*, vol. 23. Encyclopedia Britannica, in cooperation with the University of Chicago. Founders' editor Robert Maynard Hutchins. Chicago: W. Benton, 1952.

Locke, John. *Treatise on Civil Government and a Letter Concerning Toleration* (1690). Edited by Charles A. Sherman. New York: D. Appleton Century, 1937.

Marx, Karl. *Capital.* 2 vols. Translated by E. Untermann. Chicago: G.H. Kerr, 1906.

Marx, Karl and Friedrich Engels. "Manifesto of the Communist Party." In *Marx and Engels: Basic Writings on Politics and Philosophy.* Edited by Lewis S. Feuer. Garden City, New York: Doubleday, 1959.

"Medellin Documents." *The Gospel of Peace and Justice.* Joseph Gremillion, presenter. Maryknoll, New York: Orbis, 1976.

Mill, John Stuart. *The Principles of Political Economy.* 5th ed. 2 vols. New York: D. Appleton, 1897.

Molina, Luis de, S.J. *De Iustitia de Jure.* Antwerp: Ioannem Kerrbergium, 1615.

Montini, Giovanni Battista, Cardinal. *The Christian in the Material World.* Baltimore: Helicon, 1964.

________. *The Church.* Baltimore: Helicon, 1964.

Patrologia Graeca. 161 volumes. Edited by Jacques Paul Migne. Paris: 1857-66.

Patrologia Latina. 221 volumes. Edited by Jacques Paul Migne. Paris: 1844-90.

Smith, Adam. *The Wealth of Nations* (1776). New York: Random House, 1937.

The Teachings of Pope Paul VI, December 29, 1967 - December 18, 1968. Vatican City: Libraria Editrice Vaticana, 1969.

The Teachings of Pope Paul VI (1970). Washington, D.C.: United States Catholic Conference, 1971.

Thomas Aquinas, Saint. *Summa Theologica II, II* (1266-73). English translation edited by Thomas Gilby, O.P. *St. Thomas Aquinas: Summa Theologiae.* New York: Mc Graw-Hill, 1963.

3. Articles

Montini, Giovanni Battista, Cardinal. "The Christian and the new society." *Jubilee 4* (March 1957): 32-35.

________. "Holy Year and world peace." *Catholic Action 31* (September 1949): 5-8.

________. "Housing Problems." *Catholic Mind 53* (April 1955): 254.

________. "The laity and the Church's mission." *Social Justice Review 50* (February 1958): 342-43.

________. "Letter addressed to Giorgio La Pira." *Labor Leader 17* (March 12, 1954): 3.

________. "Letter to the Italian Social Week." *Catholic Mind 51* (January 1953): 55.

________. "Preservation of human dignity in industry." *Catholic Action 34* (November 1952): 19-20.

Paul VI, Pope. "Address Delivered at the Opening of the Third International Synod of Bishops." *Catholic Mind 70* (January 1972): 2-4.

The Pope Speaks. Vols. 10-22 (1965-77). Edited by John O'Neil.

B. Secondary sources

1. Books

Aaron, R.I. *John Locke*. Oxford: Oxford University Press, 1937.

Abell, Aaron I. *American Catholicism and Social Action, 1865-1950.* Garden City, New York: Hanover House, 1960.

Adams, George J., Jr. *Competitive Economic Systems.* Crowell, New York: 1958.

Amato, Joseph. *Mounier and Maritain.* University, Alabama: University of Alabama Press, 1975.

Andrews, James F., ed. *Paul VI: Critical Appraisals.* New York: Bruce, 1970.

Avila, Charles. *Ownership: Early Christian Teaching.* Maryknoll, New York: Orbis, 1983.

Baraûna, Guilherme, ed. *L'Eglise dans le monde de ce temps.* Vol. 1. Bruges: Desclée de Brouwer, 1967.

Bardes, George F. *The Distribution of Profits in the Modern Corporation.* Washington, D.C.: Catholic University Press, 1951.

Barrett, William E. *Shepherd of Mankind: A Biography of Paul VI.* Garden City, New York: Doubleday, 1964.

Beaglehole, Ernest. *Property, A Study in Social Psychology.* London: G. Allen and Unwin, 1938.

Bell, Daniel. *The Cultural Contradictions of Capitalism.* New York: Basic Books, 1976.

Belloc, Hillaire. *The Catholic Church and the Principle of Property.* Dublin: Catholic Truth Society, 1937.

Berle, Adolph A., Jr. *Economic Power and the Free Society*. Santa Barbara, California: Center for the Study of Democratic Institutions, 1957.

________. *The Equitable Distribution of Ownership*. New York: Bureau of Personnel Administration, 1930.

________. *Power Without Property*. New York: Brace, 1959.

________. *The Twentieth Century Capitalist Revolution*. New York: Harcourt, Brace, 1954.

Berle, Adolph A., Jr., and Gardiner C. Means. *The Modern Corporation and Private Property*. New York: Macmillan, 1933.

Beutter, F. *Die Eigentumsbegründung in der Moraltheologie des 19. Jahrhunderts, 1850-1900*. Munich: Ferdinand Schöningh, 1971.

Biechler, James E., ed. *Law for Liberty: The Role of Law in the Church Today*. Baltimore: Helicon Press, 1967.

Bigo, Pierre, S.J. *The Church and Third World Revolution*. Translated by Sister Jeanne Marie Lyons. Maryknoll, New York: Orbis, 1977.

________. *La Doctrine Sociale de l'Eglise*. Paris: Presses Universitaires de France, 1966.

________. Letter to the author. August 27, 1990.

________. *Marxisme et Humanisme*. 3rd ed. Paris: Presses Universitaires de France, 1961.

Bolté, P.E. *Les droits des l'homme et la Papauté contemporaine*. Montreal: Fides, 1975.

Bopp, Jörg. *Populorum Progressio, Aufbruch der Kirche?* Stuttgart: Kohlhammer, 1968.

Boulding, Kenneth. *The Organizational Revolution*. New York: Harper, 1953.

Bouyer, Louis. *Christian Humanism*. Translated by A.V. Littledale. London: Geoffrey Chapman, 1958.

Bowe, Gabriel P. *The Third Horseman: A Study of World Poverty and Hunger*. Dayton, Ohio: Pflaum Press, 1967.

Brookings, Robert S. *Industrial Ownership, Its Economic and Sociological Significance*. New York: Macmillan, 1925.

Burns, Arthur R. *The Decline of Competition*. New York: McGraw-Hill, 1936.

Byers, David M., ed. *Justice in the Marketplace: Collected Statements of the Vatican and the U.S. Catholic Bishops on Economic Policy.* Washington, D.C.: U.S.C.C. Publications, 1985.

Cahill, E., S.J. *Capitalism and Its Alternatives.* Dublin: Catholic Truth Society, 1935.

________. *The Framework of a Christian State.* Dublin: M.H. Gill and Son, 1932.

Calvez, Jean-Yves, S.J. *The Social Thought of John XXIII.* Translated by George J.M. McKenzie. Chicago: Regnery, 1964.

Calvez, Jean-Yves, S.J., and Jacques Perrin, S.J. *The Church and Social Justice.* Chicago: Regnery, 1961.

________. *Eglise et société economique. L'enseignement social des Papes de Léon XIII à Pie XII (1878-1958).* Paris: Aubier, 1959.

Camp, Richard L. *The Papal Ideology of Social Reform.* Leiden: E.J. Brill, 1968.

Carlen, Sr. M. Claudia, I.H.M. *Guide to the Documents of Pius XII.* Westminster: Newman, 1951.

________. *The Papal Encyclicals.* 5 vols. Wilmington, North Carolina: McGrath Publishing Co., 1981.

Cayré, Fulbert. *Manual of Patrology and History of Theology.* Tournai: Desclee & Co., 1936.

CELAM, General Secretariat. *Cristianismo e ideologias en America Latina a la luz de la "Octogesima Adveniens."* Bogota: Secretariado General del CELAM, 1974.

Charles, Rodger, S.J., and Drostan Maclaren, O.P. *The Social Teaching of Vatican II: Its Origin and Development.* San Francisco: Ignatius, 1982.

Chenu, Marie-Dominique, O.P. *La dottrina della Chiesa: origine e sviluppo*, 1891-1971. Brescia: Editrice Queriniana, 1977.

________. *The Theology of Work.* Translated by Lilian Soirin. Chicago: Regnery, 1963.

Cirillo, Renato, ed. *Catholic Social Thought, An International Symposium.* Malta: Aqualina, 1956.

Clancy, John G. *Apostle for Our Time.* New York: Kennedy and Sons, 1963.

________, translater and arranger. *Dialogues by Paul VI*. New York: Trident, 1965.

Clark, Colin. *The Conditions of Economic Progress*. 3rd ed. London: Macmillan, 1960.

Clément, Marcel. *L'économie sociale selon Pie XII*. 2 vols. Paris: Nouvelles Editions Latines, 1953.

Coleman, John A., S.J. *An American Strategic Theology*. New York: Paulist Press, 1982.

Commons, John R. *The Distribution of Wealth*. New York: Macmillan, 1893.

________. *The Legal Foundations of Capitalism*. New York: Macmillan, 1924.

Congar, Yves. *L'Eglise dans le monde de ce temps: Constitution pastoral "Gaudium et Spes."* Tome III, *Reflections et perspectives*. Paris: Cerf, 1967.

Convegno di Studi sulla Civiltà contemporeana, 1st. *La pace e lo sviluppo dei populi nella Populorum Progressio*. Vicenza: Centro di studi N. Rezzara, 1968.

Crofts, A.M., O.P. *Property and Poverty*. Dublin: 1948.

Cronin, John F. *Catholic Social Principles*. Milwaukee: Bruce, 1950.

________. *Social Principles and Economic Life*. Revised ed. Milwaukee: Bruce, 1964.

________. *The Social Teaching of Pope John XXIII*. Milwaukee: Bruce, 1963.

Cunningham, Agnes, sscm, ed. *The Early Church and the State*. Sources of Early Christian Thought. Philadelphia: Fortress Press, 1982.

Cunningham, W. *An Essay on Western Civilization in Its Economic Aspects*. Cambridge: The University Press, 1900.

Curran, Charles E. *Catholic Moral Theology in Dialogue*. Notre Dame, Indiana: University of Notre Dame Press, 1976.

________. *Directions in Catholic Social Ethics*. Notre Dame, Indiana: University of Notre Dame Press, 1985.

Cusack, Sr. Mary Thomasine, O.P. *The Significance of a Changing Concept of Ownership in Social and Economic Planning*. Washington, D.C.: Catholic University Press, 1940.

Czajkowski, Casimir J. *The Theory of Private Property in John Locke's Political Philosophy*. Ann Arbor, Michigan: Edwards Brothers, 1941.

Dahrendorf, Ralf. *Class and Class Conflicts in Industrial Society*. Palo Alto, California: Stanford University Press, 1959.

D'Arcy, Martin C. *Communism and Christianity*. Baltimore: Penguin, 1956.

Dawson, Christopher. *Religion and the Modern State*. London: Sheed and Ward, 1938.

DeAdder, James W. *The Meaning of the Theological Principle "In Extreme Necessity All Things Are Common."* Rome: Catholic Book Agency, 1968.

Decloux, Simon and others. *"Evangelii Nuntiandi" e la Compagnia di Gesù*. Rome: Centrum Ignatianum Spiritualitatis, 1978.

Dictionnaire de Théologie Catholique. Paris: Librairie Letouzey et Ané, 1946.

Dietze, Gottfried. *In Defense of Property*. Chicago: Regnery, 1963.

Dirksen, Cletus, C.PP.S. *Catholic Social Principles*. St. Louis: B. Herder, 1961.

Doering, Bernard E. *Jacques Maritain and the French Catholic Intellectuals*. Notre Dame, Indiana: University of Notre Dame Press, 1983.

Dondeyne, Albert. *Contemporary European Thought and Christian Faith*. Translated by Ernan McMullin and John Burnheim. Pittsburgh: Duquesne University Press, 1962.

Dorr, Donal. *Option for the Poor*. Maryknoll, New York: Orbis, 1983.

Drucker, Peter F. *Concept of the Corporation*. New York: John Day, 1946.

Dunaway, John. *Jacques Maritain*. Boston: Twayne, 1978.

Editors of Herder Correspondence. *John XXIII: Pope Paul on His Predecessor and a Documentation*. New York: Herder and Herder, 1965.

Elbow, Matthew H. *French Corporative Theory, 1789-1948*. New York: Columbia University Press, 1953.

Eldridge, J.E.T. *Max Weber: Interpretation of Social Reality*. New York: Scribner, 1975.

Ellis, John Tracy. *Perspectives in American Catholicism*. Baltimore: Helicon, 1963.

Ely, Richard T. *Property and Contract in Their Relations to the Distribution of Wealth.* 2 vols. New York: Macmillan, 1914.

The Encyclopedia of Philosophy. 8 vols. Paul Edwards, editor in chief. New York: Macmillan, 1967.

Fanfani, Amintore. *Catholicism, Protestantism, and Capitalism.* London: Sheed and Ward, 1938.

Farrell, Walter, O.P. *Companion to the Summa.* 4 vols. London: Sheed and Ward, 1938.

Fesquet, Henri. *Le Synode et l'avenir de l'Eglise.* Paris: Le Centurion, 1972.

Flannery, Austin, O.P., ed. *Evangelization Today.* Northport, New York: Costello, 1977.

Fliche, Augustin and Victor Martin, eds. *Histoire de l'église.* Paris: Blaid and Gay, 1951.

Freemantle, Anne, ed. *The Papal Encyclicals in Their Historical Context.* New York: Mentor, 1956.

________. *The Social Teachings of the Church.* New York: Mentor, 1963.

Friedman, Milton. *Capitalism and Freedom.* Chicago: University of Chicago Press, 1962.

Friedmann, G. *Ou va le travail humain?* Paris: Gallimard, 1950.

Fuchs, Joseph. *Natural Law: A Theological Investigation.* New York: Sheed and Ward, 1965.

Furubotn, Eirik and Svetozar Pejovich. *The Economics of Property Rights.* Cambridge, Massachusetts: Ballinger, 1974.

Galbraith, John Kenneth. *The Affluent Society.* Boston: Houghton Mifflin, 1958.

________. *American Capitalism: The Concept of Countervailing Power.* Boston: Houghton-Mifflin, 1952.

Gauthier, Paul. *Christ, the Church, and the Poor.* Westminster, Maryland: Newman, 1965.

Geffré, Claude and Gustavo Guttierez, eds. *The Mystical and Political Dimension of the Christian Faith.* Concilium series, vol. 6, no. 10. New York: Herder and Herder, 1974.

George, Henry. *Progress and Poverty.* New York: Schalkenbach Foundation, 1954.

Gestel, C. van. *La doctrina social de la Iglesia*. Translated by Gabriel Ferrer. Barcelona: Herder, 1952.

Giardani, Idino. *The Social Message of the Early Church Fathers*. Patterson, New Jersey: St. Anthony, 1957.

Gierke, O. *Natural Law and the Theory of Society*. Cambridge: Cambridge University Press, 1934.

Gilbert, Neal. *Capitalism and the Welfare State: Dilemnas of Benevolence*. New Haven: Yale University Press, 1983.

Gilson, Etienne, ed. *The Church Speaks to the Modern World: The Social Teachings of Leo XIII*. New York: Image Books, 1954.

Girvetz, Harry K. *The Evolution of Liberalism*. New York: Collier, 1963.

Gonzalez, J.L. and T. Perez. *Paul VI*. English version by Edward L. Heston, C.S.C. Boston: Daughters of St. Paul, 1964.

Gordon, Marshall. *In Search of the Spirit of Capitalism*. New York: Columbia University Press, 1982.

Grace, Frank. *The Concept of Property in Modern Christian Thought*. *Illinois Studies in the Social Sciences*, vol. XXXL, nos. 1-2. Urbana, Illinois: University of Illinois Press, 1953.

Greeley, Andrew M. *Crisis in the Church: A Study of Religion in America*. Chicago: Thomas More Press, 1979.

Gremillion, Joseph, presenter. *The Gospel of Peace and Justice*. Maryknoll, New York: Orbis, 1976.

Gudorf, Christine E. *Catholic Social Teaching on Liberation Themes*. Lanham, Maryland: University Press of America, 1980.

Guerry, Most Rev. Emile. *The Social Doctrine of the Catholic Church*. Boston: St. Paul, 1961.

Guitton, Jean. *The Pope Speaks*. New York: Meredith, 1968.

Habiger, Matthew, O.S.B. *Papal Teaching on Private Property: 1891-1981*. Lanham, Maryland: University Press of America, 1990.

Hagen, Everett. *The Economics of Development*. Homewood, Illinois: R.D. Irwin, 1968.

Hales, E.E.Y. *The Catholic Church in the Modern World*. Garden City, New York: Hanover House, 1958.

________. *Pope John and His Revolution*. Garden City, New York: Doubleday, 1965.

Häring, Bernard. *The Law of Christ*. vol. 2. Westminster: Newman, 1964.

Harrelson, Walter. *The Ten Commandments and Human Rights*. Philadelphia: Fortress Press, 1980.

Harte, Thomas J. *Papal Social Principles*. Milwaukee: Bruce, 1956.

Haughey, John C., ed. *The Faith That Does Justice*. New York: Paulist Press, 1977.

Hengel, M. *Property and Riches in the Early Church*. Philadelphia: Fortress Press, 1974.

Hennelly, Alfred, S.J. and John Langan, S.J. *Human Rights in the Americas: The Struggle for Consensus*. Washington, D.C.: Georgetown University Press, 1982.

Hoffman, Paul. *World Without Want*. New York: Harper and Row, 1962.

Holland, Joe and Peter Henriot. *Social Analysis: Linking Faith and Justice*. Washington, D.C.: Center of Concern, 1980.

Hollenbach, David. *Claims in Conflict*. New York: Paulist Press, 1979.

Hollis, Christopher. *The Achievement of Vatican II*. New York: Hawthorne Books, 1967.

Houtart, Abbé Francois. *The Challenge to Change: The Church Faces the Future*. New York: Sheed and Ward, 1964.

Huber, Georges. *Paul VI, Esquisse biographique et psychologique*. Paris: Editions du Centurion, 1963.

Hughes, Emmet John. *The Church and the Liberal Society*. South Bend, Indiana: Notre Dame Press, 1961.

Husslein, Joseph, S.J., ed. *Social Wellsprings*. 2 vols. Milwaukee: Bruce, 1940, 1942.

Johnson, L. *Sharing Possessions: Mandate and Symbol of Faith*. Philadelphia: Fortress Press, 1981.

Johnston, Herbert. *Business Ethics*. 2nd ed. New York: Pitman, 1962.

Juffe, Madeleine. *Paul VI*. Paris: Editions Fleurus, 1963.

Kelso, Louis O. and Mortimer J. Adler. *The Capitalist Manifesto*. New York: Random House, 1958.

Kernan, Julie. *Our Friend Jacques Maritain*. Garden City, New York: Doubleday, 1975.

Keynes, John Maynard. *The General Theory of Employment, Interest, and Money*. New York: Harcourt, Brace, 1936.

Kirwan, J.R. *Christianizing the Social Order*. 2nd ed. Oxford: Catholic Social Guild, 1963.

Klüber, F. *Eigentumstheorie und Eigentumspolitik*. Osnabrüch: Fromm, 1963.

Lamprecht, S. *The Moral and Political Philosophy of John Locke*. New York: Columbia University Press, 1918.

Landauer, Carl. *European Socialism*. Berkeley: University of California, Press, 1959.

Larkin, P. *Property in the Eighteenth Century With Special Reference to England and Locke*. Dublin: Cork University Press, 1930.

Laski, Harold J. *English Democratic Ideas in the Seventeenth Century*. Cambridge: Cambridge University Press, 1927.

________. *The Rise of Liberalism*. New York: Harper and Brothers, 1936.

Laurentin, René. *L'Evangélisation aprés le quatrième Synode*. Paris: Editions du Seuil, 1975.

________. *Nouveaux Ministères en Fin du Clergé Devant Le Troisième Synode*. Paris: Editions du Seuil, 1971.

________. *Réorientation de l'église après le Troisième Synode*. Paris: Seuil, 1972.

Laveleye, E. de. *De la propriété et de ses formes primitives*. Paris: Felix Alcan, 1891.

Lebret, Louis-Joseph, O.P. *Dynamique concrète du développement*. Paris: Economie et Humanisme, Les Editions Ouvrières, 1961.

________. *Human Ascent*. Translated by Robert and Martha Faulhaber. Chicago: Fides Publishers, 1955.

________. *The Last Revolution*. Translated by John Horgan. New York: Sheed and Ward, 1965.

________. *Pour Une Civilisation Solidaire*. Paris: Éditions ouvrières, 1963.

LeClerc, Jacques. *Christ in the Modern Conscience*. New York: Sheed and Ward, 1963.

Leclerq, Jean. *The Love of Learning and the Desire for God*. New York: Fordham University Press, 1961.

Lessourd, Paul. *Qui est le pape Paul VI?* Paris: Editions de Paris, 1963.

Letourneau, C.J.M. *Property: Its Origin and Development.* New York: Scribner's Sons, 1907.

Lio E. *Morale e beni terreni: la destinazione universale dei beni terreni nella Gaudium et Spes.* Rome: Città Nuova, 1976.

Lubac, Henri de, S.J. *The Drama of Atheistic Humanism.* New York: Sheed and Ward, 1950.

Maclaren, Drostan. *Private Property and the Natural Law.* Aquinas Papers 8. Oxford: Oxford University Press, 1948.

Malherbe, Abraham J. *The Social and Economic History of the Roman Empire.* Baton Rouge, Louisiana: L.S.U. Press, 1977.

Malley, François, O.P. *Esquisse pour un portrait du Père Lebret.* Études religeuses, vol 785. Brussels: La Pénsée Catholique, 1969.

________. *Le Père Lebret: L'Économie Au Service des Hommes.* Paris: Les Éditions du Cerf, 1968.

Maritain, Jacques. *Christianisme et Démocratie.* Paris: Hartmann, 1947.

________. *The Rights of Man and the Natural Law.* Translated by Doris C. Anson. New York: C. Scribner's Sons, 1943.

________. *Freedom in the Modern World.* London: Sheed and Ward, 1935.

________. *Scholasticism and Politics.* New York: Macmillan, 1960.

________. *Three Reformers: Luther - Descartes - Rousseau.* New York: C. Scribner's Sons, 1936.

________. *True Humanism.* 4th ed. Translated by M.R. Adamson. London: The Centenary Press, 1946.

Masse, Benjamin L., S.J. *Justice for All.* Milwaukee: Bruce, 1964.

McDonald, William J. *The Social Value of Property According to St. Thomas Aquinas.* Washington, D.C.: Catholic University Press, 1939.

McLaughlin, Terrence P., ed. *The Church and the Reconstruction of the Modern World: The Social Encyclicals of Pope Pius XI.* Garden City, New York: Doubleday Image Books, 1957.

Mealand, D.L. *Poverty and Expectations in the Gospel.* London: S.P.C.K., 1980.

Michel, Virgil, O.S.B. *Christian Social Reconstruction.* Milwaukee: Bruce, 1937.

Mitchell, W.C., ed. *What Veblen Thought: Selected Writings of Thorstein Veblen.* New York: Viking, 1936.

Monsen, Joseph R., Jr. *Modern American Capitalism.* Boston: Houghton-Mifflin, 1963.

Moody, Joseph N. *Church and Society: Catholic Social and Political Thought and Movements, 1789-1950.* New York: Arts, 1953.

Moody, Joseph N. and Justus George Lawler. *The Challenge of Mater et Magistra.* New York: Herder and Herder, 1963.

Myrdal, Gunnar. *Challenge to Affluence.* New York: Knopf, 1962.

Neil, Thomas P. *The Rise and Decline of Liberalism.* Milwaukee: Bruce, 1953.

Nell-Breuning, Oswald von, S.J. *Reorganization of Social Economy.* Milwaukee: Bruce, 1936.

________. *Soziallehre der Kirche.* Vienna: Europaverlag, 1983.

________. *Wirtschaft und Gesellschaft.* Freiberg: Herder, 1956.

The New Catholic Encyclopedia. 15 vols. Prepared by an Editorial Staff at the Catholic University of America. New York: McGraw-Hill, 1967.

Noyes, Charles Reinold. *The Institution of Property; A Study of the Development, Substance, and Arrangement of the System of Property in Modern Anglo-American Law.* New York: Longmans, Green, 1936.

Nurnberger, Klaus. *Socio-Economic Ideologies in A Christian Perspective.* Durban, South Africa: Lutheran Publishing House, 1979.

O'Brien, David J. and Thomas A. Shannon. *Renewing the Face of the Earth.* New York: Doubleday, 1977.

Padellaro, Nazareno. *Portrait of Pius XII.* Translated by Michael Derrich. New York: E.P. Dutton, 1957.

Pallenberg, Corrado. *Pope Paul VI.* New York: G.P. Putnam's Sons, 1968.

Pearson, Lester. *The Crisis of Development.* New York: Praeger, 1970.

Phan, Peter C., ed. *Social Thought.* Message of the Fathers of the Church, vol. 20. Thomas Halton, general ed. Wilmington, Delaware: Michael Glazier, 1984.

Proudhon, Pierre-Joseph. *What is Property?* Translated by Benjamin R. Tucker. Princeton, Massachusetts: B.R. Tucker, 1876.

Quasten, Johannes. *Patrology.* Westminster, Maryland: Newman, 1950.

Quill, James E. *Restitution to the Poor: Its Origin, Nature, and Extent.* Milwaukee: Bruce, 1961.

Rauscher, Anton, ed. *Ist die Katholische Soziallehre antikapitalistisch?* Cologne: Bachem, 1968.

Riga, Peter. *Catholic Thought in Crisis.* Milwaukee: Bruce, 1963.

________. *The Church Made Relevant.* Notre Dame, Indiana: Fides Publishers, 1967.

________. *The Church of the Poor.* Techny, Illinois: Divine Word Publications, 1968.

________. *Peace on Earth: Commentary on Pope John's "Pacem in Terris."* New York: Herder and Herder, 1964.

Rubio, Andrés. *III Sínodo.* 3rd ed. Madrid: Edicions Palabra, 1972.

Ryan, John A., Msgr. *The Alleged Socialism of the Fathers.* St. Louis: Herder, 1913.

________. *The Christian Doctrine of Property.* New York: Paulist Press, 1923.

________. *A Better Economic Order.* New York: Harper, 1935.

________. *Distributive Justice.* 3rd ed. New York: Macmillan, 1942.

________. *A Living Wage.* New York: Macmillan, 1912.

Samuelson, Paul. *Economics.* 4th ed. New York: McGraw-Hill, 1958.

Schall, James V., S.J. *The Sixth Paul.* Canfield, Ohio: Alba Books, 1977.

Schlatter, Richard. *Private Property: The History of an Idea.* London: George Allen and Unwin, Ltd., 1951.

Schumacher, L.S. *The Philosophy of the Equitable Distribution of Wealth.* Washington, D.C.: Catholic University Press, 1949.

Schumpeter, Joseph A. *History of Economic Analysis.* London: Oxford University Press, 1954.

Sheuring, Walter. *Rich and Poor in Christian Tradition.* London: Burns, Oates, and Washbourne, 1948.

The Social Teachings of Wilhelm Emmanuel von Ketteler. Washington, D.C.: University Press of America, 1981.

Stegemann, W. *The Gospel and the Poor.* Philadelphia: Fortress Press, 1984.

Sterpa, Egidio. *Paolo VI, un Papa diverso.* Milan: A.M.Z., 1963.

Suenens, Leo Cardinal. *The Gospel to Every Creature*. Preface by Cardinal Giovanni Montini. Westminster: Newman Press, 1965.

Synod of Bishops 1974. Washington, D.C.: United States Catholic Conference, 1975.

Tawney, R.H. *Religion and the Rise of Capitalism*. London: John Murray, 1926.

Troeltsch, Ernst. *The Social Teaching of the Christian Churches*. Vol. 1. New York: Macmillan, 1931.

Veblen, Thorstein. *Absentee Ownership*. New York: B.W. Heubsch, 1923.

________. *The Theory of the Leisure Class*. New York: Penguin, 1967.

Vernon, Raymond. *The Economic and Political Consequences of Multinational Enterprise*. Cambridge, Massachusetts: Harvard University Press, 1972.

Vidler, Alec R. *A Century of Social Catholicism: 1820-1920*. London: S.P.C.K. 1964.

Vorgrimler, Herbert, ed. *Commentary on the Documents of Vatican II*. 5 vols. New York: Herder and Herder, 1967-69.

Ward, Barbara. *The Rich Nations and the Poor Nations*. New York: Norton, 1962.

Walsh, James, S.J. *The Mind of Paul VI*. Milwaukee: Bruce, 1964.

Walsh, Michael and Brian Davies. *Proclaiming Justice and Peace*. Mystic, Connecticut: Twenty-third Publications, 1984.

Watson, Alan. *The Law of the Ancient Romans*. Dallas: S.M.U. Press, 1970.

Watt, Lewis, S.J. *Pope Pius XI and Social Reconstruction*. Oxford: Catholic Social Guild, 1938.

Weber, Max. *Economy and Society*. 3 vols. Edited by Guenther Ross and Claus Wittich. New York: Bedminster, 1968.

________. *The Protestant Ethic and the Spirit of Capitalism*. New York: Scribner's, 1956.

Wilson, William J. *Paul: The Missionary Pope*. Maryknoll, New York: Maryknoll Publications, 1968.

________. *The Third World: A Christian View*. Maryknoll, New York: Maryknoll Publications, 1969.

Zizola, Giancarlo. *The Utopia of Pope John XXIII*. Translated by Helen Barolini. Maryknoll, New York: Orbis, 1978.

2. Articles

Alves, Rubem A. "The Case Against the New Roman Catholic Spirituality." In *Paul VI: Critical Appraisals.* Edited by James F. Andrews. New York: Bruce, 1970, 41-60.

Aubry, R. "Evangelii Nuntiandi y misión." *Catequesis Latinoamericana* 9 (1977): 9-16.

"A Blessing for Secular Error." *Wall Street Journal*, 30 March 1967, 14.

Baum, Gregory, O.S.A. "Commentary." In *Pastoral Constitution on the Church in the Modern World.* New York: Paulist Press, 1967, 3-18.

Belloc, Hiliare. "Land Tenure in the Christian Era." In *The Catholic Encyclopedia.* Vol. 8. New York: Universal Knowledge Foundation: 775.

Bentley, J. and Tom Oberhofer. "Property Rights and Economic Development." *Review of Social Economy* 39 (April 1981): 51-65.

Bigo, Pierre, S.J. "Análisis Marxista y Materialismo Dialéctico." *Medellin 12* (March 1986): 96-102.

________. "Meditacion Sacerdotal Sobre El Marxismo." *Christus* (Mexico) 36 (November 1971): 36-41.

Brown, Robert McAfee. "Paul VI's Secular Ecumenism." *Commonweal* 86 (May 19, 1967): 262-64.

Bruce, Francis. "The Archbishop of the Workers." *The Sign* 34 (May 1955): 15.

Burnham, Philip. "The encyclical's challenge." *Triumph* 2 (May 1967): 10-12.

Cahill, Edward, S.J. "The Catholic Social Movement: Historical Aspects." In *Readings in Moral Theology No. 5.* New York: Paulist Press, 1986, 3-31.

Calvez, Jean-Yves, S.J. "The Social Thought of Paul VI: From Development to Liberation." *Month 11* (September 1978): 297-300.

Camp, Richard L. "The Rights and Duties of Labor and Capital." In *Readings in Moral Theology No. 5.* New York: Paulist Press, 1986, 32-50.

Campion, Donald, S.J. "Commentary." In *Pastoral Constitution on the Church in the Modern World.* New York: Paulist Press, 1967, 54-67.

________. "The World-Wide Response." In *The Challenge of Mater et Magistra.* Joseph N. Moody, ed. New York: Herder and Herder, 1963.

Catao, F. "Justice in the World." *IDOC International* 28 (June 26, 1971): 51-61.

Cirillo, Renato. "Capitalism, Private Property, and Freedom." *Review of Social Economy* 24 (September 1966): 157-66.

Clark, Colin. "The development of peoples; some implications of the papal encyclical." *Tablet* 221 (April 15, 1967): 400-401.

Cochran, Kendall P. "Why a Social Economics?" *Review of Social Economy* 37 (April 1979): 121-32.

Coleman, John, S.J. "Development of Church Social Teaching." In *Readings in Moral Theology No. 5.* New York: Paulist Press, 1986, 169-87.

Comblin, Jose. "Evangelização e libertação." *Revista Ecclesiastica Brasileira* 37 (September 1977): 569-97.

"Contribution de la Commission pontificale Justice et Paix à la reflexion du Synode sur la justice dans le monde." *La Documentation Catholique* 68 (November 21, 1971): 1018-23.

Cosmao, Vincent, O.P. "Louis-Joseph Lebret, 1897-1966." *New Blackfriars* 51 (February 1970): 62.

Cronin, John F., S.J. "Forty Years Later: Reflections and Reminiscences." In *Readings in Moral Theology No. 5.* New York: Paulist Press, 1986, 69-76.

Cunningham, T. "The Pope's Easter Message: A Plea for the Needy." *Irish Ecclesiastical Record* 107 (May 1967): 334-38.

Curran, Charles E. "The Changing Anthropological Bases of Catholic Social Ethics." In *Readings in Moral Theology No. 5.* New York: Paulist Press, 1986, 188-218.

Davis, T. "Pope John's Letter; Interpretation of 'Pacem in Terris.'" *America* 108 (May 18, 1963): 707-10.

Demsetz, Harold. "The Exchange and Enforcement of Property Rights." *Journal of Law and Economics* 13 (April 1970): 49-70.

________. "Toward a Theory of Property Rights." *American Economic Review* 57 (May 1967): 347-59.

Dorr, Donal. "Evangelization in the Modern World: Reflections on Pope Paul's document." *Furrow* 27 (October 1976): 531-39.

Dugger, William M. "Property Rights, Law, and John R. Commons." *Review of Social Economy* 38 (April 1980): 41-53.

________. "Social Economics: One Perspective." *Review of Social Economy* 35 (December 1977): 229-310.

Elsbernd, Mary. "Rights Statements: A Hermeneutical Key to Continuing Development in Magisterial Teaching." *Ephemerides Theologicae Louvaniensis* (December 1986): 308-32.

"Encyclical on the Development of Peoples and the Intellectual Apostolate." *Christian World* 12 (May-June 1967): 199-204.

"'Estudios'; commentaries on 'Evangelii Nuntiandi'; symposium." *Catequesis Latinoamericana* 8 (1976): 9-23.

Ferkiss, V. "Pacem in Terris: An Opening to the Left?" *Catholic World* 198 (November 1963): 100-108.

Flick, Maurizio, S.J. "Riflessioni Metodologiche per una Teleogia del Progresso." *Civilta Cattolica* (1969): 119-28.

Furubotn, Eirik and Svetozar Pejovich. "Property Rights and Economic Theory: A Survey of the Recent Literature." *Journal of Economic Literature* (December 1972): 1137-62.

Gordon, Robert A. "Ownership by Management and Control Groups." *Quarterly Journal of Economics* 52 (May 1938): 367-400.

Grima, G. "Method in the Social Teaching of the Church." *Melita Theologica* 33 (1982): 11-33.

Hamel, Edouard, S.J. "L'Eglise et les droits de l'homme: Jalons d'histoire." *Gregorianum* 65 (1984): 271-99.

Higgins, George G. "A Commentary on the Apostolic Letter." *Catholic Mind* 69 (November 1971): 58-64.

Hobhouse, Leonard T. "The Historical Evolution of Property, in Fact and Idea." In *Property, Its Duties and Rights*. London: Macmillan, 1914, 3-26.

Horchler, Richard. "The Church's 'Yes' and 'No' to the World." In *Eyes on the Modern World.* New York: P.J. Kennedy, 1965, 19-42.

Jarlot, Georges, S.J. "L'Eglise et le développement, l'encyclique Populorum Progressio." *Etudes* 326 (May 1967): 674-88.

________. "Lo Sviluppo Economico e la Pace nel Mundo Nell'Enciclica 'Populorum Progressio.'" *Civilta Cattolica* (1967): 3-10.

Joblin, Joseph, S.J. "Chiesa e Sviluppo nella 'Populorum Progressio.'" *Civilta Cattolica* (1968): 437-49.

________. "Papal Encyclical Pacem in Terris." *International Labor Review* 88 (July 1963): 1-14.

"Justice in the World; working paper prepared by Secretariat of the Synod of Bishops." *Catholic Mind* 69 (September 1971): 29-42.

Kerber, Walter, S.J. "Octogesima Adveniens." *Stimmen der Zeit* 188 (September 1971): 168-78.

Land, Philip, S.J. "The Social Theology of Pope Paul VI." *America* 140 (May 12, 1979): 392-94.

Leaper, R.A.B. "The World is My Neighbor: The Message of Mater et Magistra." *Wiseman Review* 237 (Autumn 1963): 289-95.

Lindsay, Samuel. "The Economic Revolution in the Ownership of Property in the U.S." *Proceedings of the Academy of Political Sciences* 11 (April 1925): 1-6.

Mac Chesney, Nathan W. "Changing Concept of Property." *Trust Companies* 65 (November 1937): 584-86.

Maritain, Jacques. "Les conditions spirituelles du progrèss et de la paix." In *Rencontre des cultures a l'UNESCO sous le signe du Concile oecumenique Vatican II*. Paris: Meme, 1966, 127-38.

________. "Personality, Property, and Communism." *University of Toronto Quarterly* 3 (1934): 167-84.

Masse, Benjamin L. "The Pope's Plea for Poor Nations." *America* 117 (August 5, 1967): 129-32.

McKeon, Richard. "The Development of the Concept of Property in Political Philosophy." *Ethics* 48 (1938): 297-366.

McMahon, Thomas F., C.S.V. "Moral Responsibility and Business Management." *Social Order* 13 (December 1963): 5-17.

Messineo, Antonio, S.J. "L'umanesimo plenario e lo sviluppo integrale dei populi." *Civilta Cattolica* (1968): 213-26.

Moody, Joseph N. "Leo XIII and the Social Crisis." In *Leo XIII and the Modern World*. Edited by Edward T. Gargan. New York: Sheed and Ward, 1961, 65-88.

Murphy, Charles M. "Action for Justice as Constitutive of the Preaching of the Gospel: What Did the 1971 Synod Mean?" In *Readings in Moral Theology No. 5*. Charles E. Curran and Richard A. McCormick, eds. New York: Paulist Press, 1986, 150-168.

Murphy, Francis X. "A Brief Biography of Paul VI." In *Paul VI: Critical Appraisals.* Edited by James F. Andrews. New York: Bruce, 1972, 131-42.

Nell-Breuning, Otto von, S.J. "Octogesimo Anno." *Stimmen der Zeit* 187 (May 1971): 289-96.

Newman, J. "The Encyclical Pacem in Terris." *Irish Ecclesiastical Record* 99 (May 1963): 308-22.

Noyes, Charles Reinold. "Property: The Crucial Issue." *Journal of Social Philosophy* 4 (1938): 45-56.

O'Donnell, Charles. "Jacques Maritain: Political Philosopher." In *Jacques Maritain: The Man and His Achievement.* Edited by Joseph W. Evans. New York: Sheed and Ward, 1963, 161-79.

Overstreet, Henry Allen. "The Changing Concept of Property." *International Journal of Ethics* 25 (January 1915): 165-78.

Parsons, Kenneth H. "The Basis of Commons' Progressive Approach to Public Policy." In *Labor, Management, and Social Policy.* Edited by Gerald G. Somers. Madison: University of Wisconsin Press, 1963, 3-22.

Pessoa, Camara H., Most Reverend, and others. "A Message to the People of the Third World." *Catholic Mind* 66 (January 1968): 37-46.

Pinto de Oliveira, C.J. "Image de Dieu et dignité humaine." *FZFPT* 27 (1980): 401-36.

"Populorum Progressio a l'heuere du novel ordre international." *Le Documentation Catholique* 74 (May 15, 1977): 473-75.

Poupard, P. "Populorum Progressio, 10 ans. après." *Le Documentation Catholique* 74 (May 15, 1977): 463-72.

"Private property." Symposium. *Studies* 72 (Fall 1983): 209-363.

Prondzynski, Ferdinand von. "The Nature of Private Property in Modern Society." *Studies* 72 (Autumn 1983): 210-12.

Quinn, Donald. "Man's Social Relationships to a Changing World." In *Eyes on the Modern World.* New York: P.J. Kennedy, 1965, 58-78.

Refoule, F. "L'Église et les libertes, de Leon XIII a Jean XXIII." *Le Supplement* 125 (1978): 243-59.

Riga, Peter J. "Humanae Vitae." *Catholic World* 208 (December 1968): 107-11.

Rouquette, Robert, S.J. "Pope of Reform." *Catholic Mind* 62 (April 1964): 4-12.

Ryan, Leo V., C.S.V. "The Natural Objectives of the Business Enterprise." *Journal of Catholic Business Education* 15 (Summer 1964): 5-15.

________. "World Justice: Call to Education and Action." *American Ecclesiastical Review* 165 (October 1971): 93-104.

Salvadori, Massimo. "Capitalism in Postwar Europe." In *Europe's Needs and Resources.* Edited by J. Frederic Dewhurst, John O. Coppock, and P. Lamartine Yates. New York: Twentieth Century Fund, 1961, 734-58.

Schönborn, Christoph, O.P. "L'homme créé par Dieu: le fondement de la dignité de l'homme." *Gregorianum* 65 (1984): 337-63.

Schweitzer, Arthur. "Property and Economic Power." *Review of Social Economy* 38 (April 1980): 21-40.

Simon, Yves R. "Jacques Maritain: The Growth of a Christian Philosopher." In *Jacques Maritain: The Man and His Achievement.* Edited by Joseph W. Evans. New York: Sheed and Ward, 1963, 3-24.

Simons, F. "Is Property Theft?" *IDOC* 28 (June 26, 1971): 69-71.

Sorge, Bartolomeo, S.J. "L'apporto dottrinale della Lettera Apostolica 'Octogesima Adveniens.'" *Civilta Cattolica* (1971): 428.

________. "Teleogia e Storia nell'enciclica 'Populorum Progressio.'" *Civilta Cattolica* (1968): 8-22.

Sousberghe, Leon de. "Propriété 'de Droit Naturel.'" *Nouvelle Revue Theologique* 72 (1950): 580-607.

Sturm, D. "Naturalism, Historicism, and Christian Ethics: Toward A Christian Doctrine of Natural Law." *Journal of Religion 44* (January 1964): 40-51.

Suenens, Leo, Cardinal. "The Meaning of Pacem in Terris." *Catholic Mind* 61 (September 1963): 4-14.

Thils, G. "Droits de l'homme et théologique catholique." *Revue Theologique Louvaniensis* 11 (1980): 352-61.

Valadier, P. "L'evangélisation dans le monde moderne." *Etudes* 344 (April 1976): 605-10.

Valesquez, H. "Vision Papal de la sociedad." *Christus* 36 (August 1971): 14-17.

Vergara, Aceves J. "La carta Apostólica Octogesima Adveniens." *Christus* 36 (October 1971): 13-19.

Vermeire, Rik. "Reflections on Development." *World Justice* 8 (June 1967): 479-94.

Villain, J. "L'encyclique Mater et Magistra: son apport doctrinal." *Revue de l'Action Populaire* (September-October 1961): 898+.

Ward, Barbara. "Looking Back at Populorum Progressio." *Catholic Mind* 76 (November 1978): 9-25.

Waterman, Anthony M.C. "John Locke's Theory of Property and Christian Social Thought." *Review of Social Economy* 40 (October 1982): 97-115.

Watt, Lewis, S.J. "The Right to Private Property." In *Moral Principles and Practice*. Edited by George John MacGillivray. New York: Sheed and Ward, 1932, 173-93.

Wilensky, Harold L. "Leftism, Catholicism, and Democratic Corporatism." In *The Development of Welfare States in Europe and America*. Edited by Peter Flora and Arnold J. Heidenheimer. New Brunswick, New Jersey: Transaction Books, 1981, 126-54.

Wolf, Charles. "Beyond Populorum Progressio." *National Catholic Reporter* 3 (May 10, 1967): 8.

C. Dissertations

Bender, Reginald. "The Doctrine of Private Property in the Writings of Monsignor John A. Ryan." S.T.D. dissertation, The Catholic University of America, 1973.

Bergen, William J. "The Evolution of the Pastoral Constitution on the Church in the Modern World. A Study in Moral Methodology." S.T.D. dissertation, The Catholic University of America, 1971.

Christman, John P. "Property Rights and Economic Justice: Toward a Theory of Egalitarian Property Rights." Ph.D. dissertation, University of Illinois-Chicago, 1985.

Danielson, Peter Andrew. "The Justification of Property Rights." Ph.D. dissertation, University of Toronto, 1975.

Dering, Judy. "Labor, Liberty, and Property: A Critique of the Liberal Theory of Locke, Nozick, and Rawls." Ph.D. dissertation, University of Rochester, 1983.

Elsbernd, Mary. "Papal Statements on Rights." Ph.D. dissertation, Catholic University of Louvain, 1979.

O'Neill, David P. "Sociology of Knowledge and the Development of the Ethic of Property in the Social Encyclicals." Ph.D. dissertation, Boston University Graduate School, 1970.

Paterson, Gene Paul. "Private Property in Marxian and Catholic Social Thought." Ph.D. dissertation, Colorado State University, 1979.

Raridan, Robert Lee. "The Right to Property: Its Sources and Limits." Ph.D. dissertation, University of Miami, 1983.

Sessions, Robert Paul. "Ethical Criteria for the Use of Income and Property." Ph.D. dissertation, Boston University Graduate School, 1968.

Sullivan, Maureen Eileen. "The Christian Humanism of Paul VI: Its Christological Foundations." Ph.D. dissertation, Fordham University, 1985.

D. Bibliographies

Paul VI Institute of Brescia, eds. *Paulus PP. VI 1963-1978, Elenchus Bibliographicus*. Brescia: Vatican Polyglot Press, 1981.

Vian, Nello, ed. *Anni e Opere di Paolo VI*. Rome: Istituto dell' Enciclopedia Italiana XLII, 1979.

Index

DDS